GARFIELD *VERSUS* MARSHALL

Also by Eddie Nickels

MARINE CORPS DRAFTEE:
A Vietnam Era Draftee's Personal Experiences of Parris Island and Infantry Training Regiment

SIX YEARS TO LIVE:
An Odyssey of Life, Death, and Adversity

GARFIELD *VERSUS* MARSHALL

THE CIVIL WAR BATTLES and SKIRMISHES in the MOUNTAINS of SOUTHEASTERN KENTUCKY and SOUTHWESTERN VIRGINIA

Eddie Nickels

GARFIELD *VERSUS* MARSHALL

EDDIE NICKELS

ISBN   978-0-9886933-4-0

Printing information for this book may be found on the last page of book.

Contents

ACKNOWLEDGEMENTS xv

Introduction xi

Chapter One 1

   War Clouds 1

Chapter Two 10

   Early Actions.................................10

Chapter Three..................................19

   Engagement at Ivy Mountain.....................19

Chapter Four 28

   Retreat 28

Chapter Five 39

   Marshall at the Gap 39

Chapter Six 51

   Return to the Big Sandy 51

Chapter Seven..................................64

   Action at Middle Creek........................64

Chapter Eight 80

   Withdrawal 80

Chapter Nine 91

   Retreat to Letcher County 91

Chapter Ten 104

   Marshall at Gladesville 104

Chapter Eleven 116

   Skirmish at Pound Gap.........................116

Chapter Twelve.................................139

   A Call for Militia 139

Chapter Thirteen 152

   On to Princeton 152

Chapter Fourteen 163

   On to Kentucky 163

Chapter Fifteen...176

   Carter Comes Calling..........................176

Chapter Sixteen 191

   Marshall Exits the Scene 191

Chapter Seventeen 203

   Federals Raid East Tennessee 203

Chapter Eighteen......................................214

   Second Gladesville Raid 214

Chapter Nineteen 230

   Morgan's 1864 Raid...............................230

Chapter Twenty 241

   The Burbridge Raid 241

Chapter Twenty One 251

   Mountain Rebels Surrender 251

      Epilogue 263

      Appendix B..............................285

      BIBLIOGRAPHY...................290

      Index 292

ACKNOWLEDGEMENTS

Civil War history has been a passion of mine ever since the fourth grade, when I first saw the illustration of a Union soldier at the top of the flagpole during the bombardment of Fort Sumter with a hammer in his hand, nailing the broken pole together with "Old Glory" still waving from the pole. Something about that scene managed to bring together all the things that combine to make a nation and its people strong and proud, especially in the eyes and mind of a nine year old boy. Patriotism, bravery, country, pride, the flag still flying even though it had been temporarily broken, the look of pride in the Union soldier's eyes; it all came together to make it an unforgettable moment in time for me.

I haven't been the same since that long ago incident in class, and I can vouch for the importance of studying history beginning at a young age. Almost all my vacations and spare time through the years have been spent on battlefields, in book stores, and in libraries, researching and daydreaming about those days long ago. I'm fortunate that my extended family has been very helpful in supplying me with both ideas and oftentimes with books and mementoes of the Civil War they would find when out shopping or when just browsing at a yard sale somewhere. I owe them all a huge debt for their kindness. To acknowledge them all would fill up several pages, so I'll just say that I have a very special family and I appreciate them very much.

Even with my interest of the Civil War at such a young age, it took several years of research to discover that my own great-grandfather was a Confederate soldier, although I suspected that I must surely have at least one ancestor that was a participant in that war, due to the fact that both of my g-great grandfathers were of that generation. I never gave up and was rewarded when I discovered my great grandmother, Nellie Taylor Sexton, had applied for, and received, a Confederate pension from the State of Kentucky in 1912, at the rate of $12.00 per month. From there it was easy to research Nathaniel Sexton's records at the National Archives and get copies of his Civil War service. He served as 1st Corporal in the Tenth Kentucky Mounted Rifles, in Company H, joining at Whitesburg, Kentucky, September 13, 1862, and serving until April, 1865, when he surrendered and gave his parole at Louisa, Ky.

My paternal g-g-grandfather, William Nickels, was a private in the 26th Virginia Cavalry, but only served a few months, making any of his service difficult to prove, with no record other than a mention in the 1890 special census. Even so, I am glad that now I know of the service of both grandfathers.

Thanks to the Harry M. Caudill Whitesburg library staff, who have been very helpful with copying, research, and information I have requested while writing this book.

Introduction

When the Civil War began on April 12, 1861, Governor Beriah Magoffin of Kentucky and the state legislature issued a proclamation of neutrality which forbid troop movements of both United States troops and the forces of the newly formed Confederacy from the soil of the state. This was a short-lived proclamation, as the Confederates soon moved to occupy the western Kentucky town of Columbus which bordered the Mississippi River. This move opened the floodgates to increased violations of Kentucky's sovereignty by both sides and before long each side was openly vying for control of the state. General Leonidas Pope of the Confederate Army and General Ulysses S. Grant soon dropped all pretentions of neutrality and moved troops freely around the western portions of Kentucky.

The people of Eastern Kentucky knew little of the Governor's proclamation due to the dearth of newspapers in their portion of the state and the miserable condition of the few roads leading into and out of the area. Most travelers had to rely on horses and farm wagons for transportation on roads so miserably bad that they hardly deserved the name of roads. Even what few trails they managed to carve out of the hillsides and mountains were very seldom wide enough to allow more that three of four horses and riders to travel abreast. Meeting another wagon on roads such as these was interesting to say the least.

Despite the bad roads which predominated the Kentucky River Basin, the Big Sandy River Valley, and the western counties of Virginia, Mountaineers began to choose sides and enlist in the armies of both sides. They traveled to the county seats of their respective counties and began to sign their name or make their x on the dotted line of the enlistment papers. Many families had members who enlisted in the Southern Army at one county seat, either Prestonsburg, Piketon, (today known as Pikeville), or Whitesburg, while their brother, father, or son traveled a little further up the river to Louisa, Kentucky to enlist in the federal army.

The volunteers in the early part of the war were prone to enlist into infantry or cavalry units indiscriminately but as the war fever quieted down and the hardships of marching over rocky, muddy, and torturous roads of the region became too much for the tired infantrymen they began favoring reorganizing as cavalry outfits. This was a problem for both sides as the war progressed, with several units requesting and receiving permission to switch from infantry to cavalry.

The Big Sandy counties of Johnson and Floyd, and the Kentucky River county of Letcher were predominately southern sympathizers, while Perry, Pike, and Harlan Counties were mostly aligned with the northern forces. A fair number of volunteers of both persuasions joined one side only to desert to the other side as the war progressed.

While no major battles were fought over these grounds there were more than a few skirmishes and minor actions which left a bitter taste in the mouths of participants of both sides to hash over even when the war was long over. The many feuds which flared up over several decades after the war lasted well into the 20th century and caused many deaths and injuries to the feudists.

The Hatfield and McCoy feud was partially caused by those two families being on opposite sides during the war, as was the Clabe Jones and "Bad" John Wright difficulties. It's true that the war wasn't the only cause of so many feuds but the seeds were sown at that time. The wounds caused by the war festered after the guns were silenced and many old scores were settled for years afterwards.

The mountain people of Kentucky and Virginia were in a war of sorts even before the fighting flared up in the region. Their war was one of survival. With no industry to speak of, citizens of the region lived by the sweat of their brow, eking out a hardscrabble living from small plots of land that were tilled by horses and mules attached to an old worn plow with tattered tack linking them to the animal. With their husbands, sons, and fathers likely serving in one of the local regiments, the one doing the plowing was probable the wife or very young son doing the plowing. There was no money to hire anyone even if anyone was available. Almost all needed items were acquired by barter alone and almost all food eaten was raised by each family.

As if the mountain people didn't have it hard enough in life, try interjecting thousands of starving troops of both sides tramping through rural areas, scrounging for a mouthful of food wherever they can find it and you can imagine the difficulties the war brought to this depressed area. The wonder is that any one survived these conditions.

As the armies contended with man and nature to hold their little pieces of territory and mountain passes, they would pass over the same area sometimes advancing, sometimes retreating, and sometimes just trying to out-maneuver their adversary. This back and forth maneuvering in the mountains, hills, and valleys of Eastern Kentucky made for several minor skirmishes, incidents, and actions during the early days of the war for control of these vital mountain passes through which armies of both sides would pass through repeatedly during the war years.

Two people that would play an important role during the early war years in the mountains of Kentucky were, in 1861, gathering their forces and gearing up for the right to control this barren land. One of these very important people was Confederate Brigadier General Humphrey Marshall. The other was Colonel, (soon to be Brigadier General), James A. Garfield, United States Army.

The winner of these skirmishes would someday become president of the United States, no doubt because of a boost in prestige in winning several battles in Eastern Kentucky. The loser would manage to become a productive lawyer and citizen after the guns of war were silenced despite his military failures. Their story of adversarial maneuver in the mountains and valleys of Southeastern Kentucky and Southwestern Virginia is one of hardship, triumph, and often failure in the Cumberland Mountains Plateau.

The struggles to control the gaps through these mountains often turned into nothing more than "bushwhacking on a grand scale," especially when mountain fighting offered so much concealment from one's enemy. Because of the few openings in the high walls of Pine Mountain, which formed an almost impenetrable barrier between Eastern Kentucky and Western Virginia, the poor roads of Pound Gap, Cranks, Gap, Scuttle Hole Gap, and Cumberland Gap became vital military objectives that each belligerent strived to control.

This struggle pitting mountain rebels against the forces of the United States would continue throughout the war, with first one side, then the other, in control of the mountain gaps. Rebels to the end, some of the mountain men were among the last to lay down their arms after General Lee surrendered.

The Cumberland Mountains of Eastern Kentucky and Western Virginia also gave many of her sons to the Union cause, with recruiters of both sides of the conflict sometimes vying for men even in the same neighborhoods. It was inevitable that the civilian population would be caught up in the war eventually. The following letters from some concerned citizens of Wise and Russell Counties, Virginia will show war's contentious nature when war is fought in guerrilla style. The letters are addressed to Colonel Giltner, a brigade commander in the Confederate Army and Col Benjamin E. Caudill, Commander of the Tenth Kentucky Mounted Infantry, of Giltner's brigade.

Col. H. Giltner,
Commanding, etc.:
The undersigned citizens of Russell County, protesting that they are good, loyal, and peaceable citizens of the Confederacy, would most respectfully represent that a few men professing to belong to the command of Col. C. J. Prentice have congregated together in the lower end of Castlewoods, in Russell County, a number of bad women, where they stay together for unlawful purposes and keep a most disorderly house or houses; that they have gone through the neighborhood of Copper Ridge and other places and wantonly robbed various good and lawful citizens of their provisions, clothing, bed clothing, stock, etc., and carried them to those women for their support. To such an extent has this thing been carried on that the whole neighborhood was in continual dread and alarm for their lives and property, as some of the same company have, or are believed to have, committed sundry murders in the country, In view of this state of things, and to try to put a stop to its continuance, a few of the citizens a few nights ago assembled together and went for the purpose of trying to break up the bad houses

above named and to secure back some of the stolen property in their possession, and they burned up one of the houses in which they were congregated and recovered back some of the stolen property, and in the encounter a man by the name of Fletcher, a ringleader of the band, was killed by a soldier that had gone along with the citizens. Your petitioners now understand that, instead of desisting from their unlawful practices, the said party are now making arrangements to take revenge upon the citizens by killing, and burning their houses-ten for one, as they allege. Your petitioners do not wish to engage in anything unlawful or without proper authority, or having the semblance of disloyalty. They therefore pray that such steps may be taken by the military authorities as will effectually put a stop to such unlawful proceedings or to further bloodshed; and, as in duty bound, they will ever pray,

John P. Carty, R.P. Vicary, James Hartsock, James Baker, L.D. Vaughan, James B. Monk, [And 67 others.]

[Inclosure]
Wise County, Va. January___,1865

Col. B. E. Caudill:
Dear Sir: I drop you a line, informing you that my house has been pillaged and my family abused by Lieut. A.J. Ciphers, James C. Talbert, William D. Horn, and S. P. Porter of (Col.) Prentice's command. (7th Battalion Confederate Cavalry.) They, in open daylight,

came to my house, there being no person but my wife at the house; endeavored to take some of my bed clothes; my wife caught hold of them; they jerked her down and around, abusing her person, and in spite of her succeeded in taking off some few articles of my own manufacture. I therefore pray you that such men may be apprehended and held accountable for their conduct. This is the second time some of the same party have pillaged my house. You will please, if in your power, have something done with the party, or forward for me to the proper authorities. If we can get no protection from some source, we will be ruined by those thieves of Prentice's.

Yours, truly, John Burton.

(From *War of the Rebellion*, Official Records, Series 1, Vol. 45, part 2, pgs. 798, 799.)

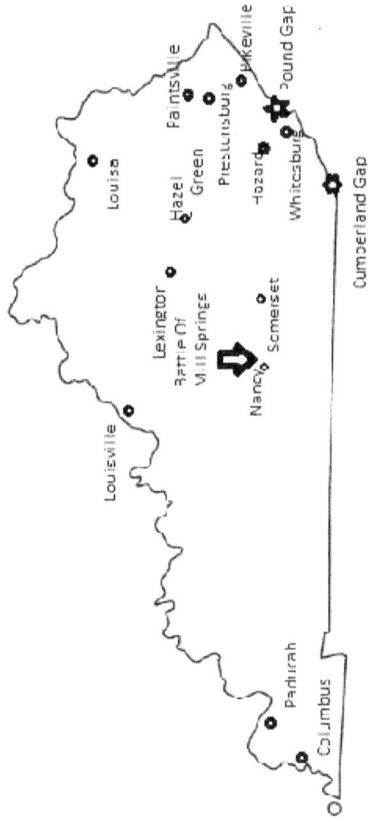

Map by Jeffrey Nickels

General Humphrey Marshall
Confederate Army

General James A. Garfield
United States Army

Chapter One

War Clouds

It's not especially surprising that so many Kentuckians, especially those that hailed from the eastern, southern, and central part of the state, decided to cast their lot with the Southern Confederacy. Blood is thicker than water as the old adage goes, and the fact that most immigrants to Eastern Kentucky came from the states of Virginia, Tennessee, and North Carolina, leads one to understand why so many fought under the Stars and Bars of the Confederate flag.

Conversely, most of those residing in the northern part of the state were the descendents of those pioneers that had immigrated to the state via the Ohio River from Pennsylvania, Maryland, and other northern states. Geography had as much to do with their choices as any other reason, although a large percentage chose sides due to their political beliefs.

The opening in the Pine Mountain Range of the Cumberland Plateau on the border between Kentucky and Virginia known variously as the Pound, Sounding, or Horse Gap, acted as a funnel to those settlers coming from the southern states to start new lives and acquire new lands. A few of those who braved the bad roads, the long rides by horseback, and the jolting of the wagons, decided to settle in the lee of Pine Mountain in Letcher County when they crossed through the Gap to the northern side.

These hardy souls, few as they were in those days, were to experience the disruption of their lives in ways few others have known in this area. Both Northern and Southern troops would pass through the Gap many times during the war, with hunger and destitution as their constant companion. They would naturally fan out as foragers and sometimes act as marauders out of desperation. If one gets hungry enough, he is capable of literally taking food out of the mouths of women and children in order to survive.

When hundreds and maybe even thousands of tired and hungry soldiers came down the northern side of the Gap they turned to the north and traveled down, (yes, down) the head waters of Elkhorn Creek which had its source just below the gap, towards Piketon, Prestonsburg, Paintsville, Louisa, or the Ohio River country. If their intention was to travel to the Bluegrass section of the state or the southern section, they turned left, (south) from the Gap and went down the head waters of the North Fork of the Kentucky River.

Those few family farms unlucky enough to be in the path of these hoards of troops usually had to bear the burden of trying to provide food and shelter for them. Sometimes a local farmer agreed to provide overnight

2

accommodations for some few officers and other distinguished travelers who might be traveling with the army for safety.

One of those hungry young men who was a very frequent traveler to and from Whitesburg, Kentucky during the war was Captain Edward O. Guerrant, of Flatwood in Montgomery County, Kentucky. He was adjutant on General Humphrey Marshall's staff and had traveled alone from Virginia, then through Pound Gap to visit the camp of Colonel Hawkins 5th Kentucky Infantry on Rock House Creek as he headed for his home on leave.

He traveled down the North Fork of the Kentucky River and turned up Millstone to Jesse Bate's home where he says he "talked Mrs. Bates out of a dinner for us,"(his horse and himself.) He considered the meal a great favor, as there was hardly enough food for the inhabitants and almost none for the horses. This was in May, 1863, when most families were running out of foodstuffs that their small garden plots had yielded the year before.[1] Multiply this one incident by hundreds or thousands of soldiers as they passed through the area and the picture becomes clearer as to what the local people living near the gap experienced.

Those hungry soldiers who were headed down Elkhorn Creek had the same intentions as did Captain Guerrant when he turned in the opposite direction towards the Bluegrass section of the state. Many of the soldiers were

---

[1] BlueGrass Confederate,diary entry, page 273, Edited by William C. Davis and Meredith L. Swentor, Louisiana State University Press, 1999.

from the Big Sandy Valley and they were anxious to go home even if they only managed to wave as they passed by. Many units made the trip several times through the Gap as they chased after the enemy or ran from the rumor of an invasion force headed for the Gap.

Although the soldiers in blue suffered from some of the same difficulties of supply that the boys in gray contended with, the Big Sandy River made life somewhat easier for those U.S. forces operating around and along the Big Sandy River Valley. Much of their subsistence and ammunition needs were supplied by flatboats plying up the river bringing supplies for men and horses from the mouth of the Big Sandy where they were transferred from bigger vessels, usually steamboats, which carried the supplies from Cincinnati and other points on the river.

The only difficulty of supply for the Federals occurred when seasonal floods affected the rivers. In case of emergency the Union forces always had access to using the poor roads towards West Liberty and Mount Sterling, but had to contend with the Confederate troops which often passed through that area. Many deserters and rogue bands from both sides roamed throughout the state from time to time and robbed and stole from anyone and everyone they might encounter. This problem persisted throughout the war and was a plague to both sides.

As the troops from either side moved from place to place, they often picked up new recruits to replace their sick, lame, and lazy, who often outnumbered the troops available for duty. When word reached a section of the area that soldiers from one side or the other were coming or moving through, the few men still left at home literally headed for the hills and the caves. Those that were unable to run or hide because of age or illness were liable to be, and most often were, recruited into the army at the point of a gun, if necessary.

While both sides were guilty of these tactics, one usually never knew which side they were being forced into. Full uniforms were almost unattainable for the impoverished rebel soldiers who seldom had enough to fill their bellies, much less to wear on their backs. The Confederate soldiers recruited locally often had only pieces of uniforms and most had only their clothing brought from home.

No one can accuse these young men of fighting for the pay either. While local recruits were often promised $100.00 bounty and $11.00 per month pay, they seldom received any, and many received none throughout their enlistment. The ugly truth is that the Confederate Government could hardly even pay their soldiers in the Richmond environs, despite their presence near government paymasters and the seat of government.

While several regiments of Confederate cavalry were recruited from the mountains of Kentucky, most of them never actually fought as cavalry, but rather as mounted infantry. Very few cavalry swords could be found among these mounted soldiers who used their horses to ride into battle, but fought on foot. Even their weapons were often shotguns brought from home instead of government issued rifles or carbines. Because of the many kinds of ammunition required to make their weapons useful, supply was often unattainable until or unless a comrade similarly armed became sick or was wounded in battle.

One of these locally recruited cavalry units was the 10th Kentucky Mounted Rifles, which was recruited in Whitesburg in Sept. and Oct., 1862. Most of the recruits were from Letcher County, with a sprinkling of volunteers from surrounding counties. This included recruits from Wise County, Virginia, and the Kentucky counties of Johnson, Pike, Floyd, Lawrence, Perry, and Wolfe, in addition to those from Letcher County.

The 10th Kentucky Mounted Rifles was often confused with the 10th Kentucky Cavalry. As a result, the 10th Mounted Rifles became the 11th Mounted Rifles for a short period of time. In March, 1865 the regiment became the 13th Kentucky Cavalry, too late to make much difference since the war had only a month to go at that point in time.[2]

Several soldiers from the divided counties of Eastern Kentucky fought for the Union forces in the 39th Kentucky Infantry Regiment, Colonel Dils commanding, which was recruited mostly from the Big Sandy River area. This regiment played a pivotal role in the capture of the larger part of the 10th Ky. Mounted Rifles at Gladesville (now Wise) Virginia, in July, 1863. Col. Benjamin F. Caudill of the 10th was among the captured and was sent to the federal prison camp in Fort

---

[2] The author's g-grandfather, Nathanial Sexton, was a member of company H of this regiment.

Delaware, an island prison located in the Delaware River on Pea Patch Island which was, and is located across from Wilmington, Delaware. Colonel Caudill was later transferred to Camp Chase, where most of the enlisted men from his regiment who were captured at the same time were sent. He was eventually sent to Morris Island in South Carolina as one of the hostages who were confined there in Charleston Harbor by the Federals who had been undergoing some destructive shelling of Fort Sumter from the rebel batteries surrounding the fort.

Pound Gap straddled the boundary line between Kentucky and Virginia. The Virginia side was in the county of Wise and the county seat was located in the town of Gladesville, or Wise Courthouse as it was known at the time. The Kentucky side of the Gap was in Letcher County and the county seat was the small hillside town of Whitesburg.

This town would be a hotbed of activity for the southern soldiers, not only because of its proximity to Pound Gap, but also because of the large Confederate hospital located at the western edge of the city. Today the large cemetery located in the Westwood section of Whitesburg contains a section where several Confederate soldiers are buried. Most of them were the victims of various illnesses and diseases which have been the frequent demise of soldiers in all wars since the beginning of time. The lack of proper food, clothing, and shelter, combined with homesickness, were all contributing factors in the demise of these poor soldiers.

The Letcher County Sons of Confederate Veterans (Colonel Ben E. Caudill Camp) has in the past several years been engaged in a nothing but Herculean effort to set headstones for all Civil War veterans of local units. They were also instrumental in discovering and clearing the brush and debris from the heretofore unknown section where these hallowed veterans rest. The Confederates also have new headstones thanks to the Ben E. Caudill Camp.

While passing through Whitesburg in 1862, General Marshall's future adjutant wrote in his diary that, "Whitesburg was the poorest excuse for a town I ever saw. It was one great hospital for the sick and wounded. It made me heartily desire that the war was ended."[3]

With the Confederates controlling the Pound Gap for most of the Civil war period, except for brief periods of occupation by Union raiders, the importance of Letcher County as a food source for the soldiers cannot be overstated. As mentioned previously, both sides came down or up the headwaters of the Kentucky and Big Sandy Rivers, either crossing over for a raid in Eastern Kentucky or on their way through the Gap heading south on a raid to the salt-works in Saltville, Virginia or to destroy the railroad in Wytheville, Bristol, or Abingdon, Virginia.

The poor dirt farms of Letcher and surrounding counties could barely support their owners and their own families, not

---

[3] BlueGrass Confederate, diary entry, page 23,edited by William C. Davis and Meredith L. Swentor, Louisiana State University Press,1999

8

counting the thousands of extra souls the war brought to the region. Most farms consisted of very few acres of arable land that had been hacked out of the wilderness only five or so decades before and were incapable of large production of almost anything other than for their own use.

One exception to the small farms was the Letcher County farm of Stephen Caudill, who in 1850 farmed 30 acres on which he grew wheat, corn, potatoes, sweet potatoes, oats, tobacco, peas, beans, wool, flax, beeswax and honey, maple sugar, and butter. He also had 3 horses, 5 milk cows, 6 other cattle, 28 sheep, and 15 swine. His livestock was valued at $125.00.[4] This was an exceptionally large farm for Letcher County, modest as it was in total acres.

It's not difficult to imagine how a farm of this size must have suffered with the coming of the war to Eastern Kentucky and the people of the region. Although all counties in the region of the Gap suffered because of all the marches and counter marches of the soldiers of both armies, the counties of Letcher in Kentucky and Wise in Virginia paid the price of having a common border which included such a vital pathway between two warring factions.

_____

[4] Appalachian Frontiers, Robert D. Mitchell, Editor, The University Press of Kentucky, 1991, page 226

Chapter Two

Early Actions

At the beginning of the Civil War in 1861, President Jefferson Davis, the newly installed leader of the fledging eleven states of the Confederacy, appointed Gen. Albert Sidney Johnston, a native Kentuckian, as the commander of Department No. 2 , with his headquarters at Bowling Green, Kentucky. Gen. Johnston was charged with holding the border state of Kentucky for the Confederacy and was given just over 20,000 troops to accomplish his mission.

From the storied Cumberland Gap to the Mississippi River there were few troops and fewer forts and strong points with which Gen. Johnston could stop an invasion of the south if the northern forces chose to invade. Gen. Johnston had no illusions as to the difficulty of the task at hand.

The only two forts the Confederates controlled on the southern border of Kentucky were the closely sited forts of Fort Henry on the Tennessee River and Fort Donelson on the Cumberland. These two forts were just a few miles apart, as both rivers flowed very close together in this area as they meandered their way to flow into the Ohio River.

With the capture of these two forts by Gen. Grant's Federal forces in Feb. 1862, and the defeat of the rebel army under Gen. Felix Kirk Zollicoffer at the Battle of Fishing Creek, Mill Springs, or Logan's Crossroads near Somerset, Kentucky in Jan. 1862, the whole southern border from eastern to western Kentucky was open to invasion. This increased the importance of the Pound Gap in Eastern Kentucky which provided an egress and ingress for the invasion of Kentucky from the south, or likewise an invasion of the north by southern forces. This fact would lead to many minor clashes involving both organized and guerilla forces through the war.

The clashes in the Big Sandy Valley and the Kentucky River Basin were nearly all small affairs due to the Cumberland Mountain Range which dominated the border area. Pound Gap is located on Pine Mountain, which is a spur of the Cumberland Mountains. Pine Mountain stretches all the way from the Breaks of the Big Sandy River on the Virginia line for over 130 miles to Northern Tennessee. Pine Mountain contains the headwaters of three major rivers of Kentucky, the Kentucky, Cumberland, and Big Sandy Rivers. Thus the importance of Pound Gap may be easily discerned.

It was inevitable that Pound Gap and the counties surrounding the gap on both sides of the Kentucky - Virginia border would be an area heavily traveled and contested by both antagonists in this war which would come to pit brother against brother, neighbor against neighbor, with no holds barred. This is the way of civil war and ours was no different from any other nation in which factions of that nation found themselves in disagreement.

Threats of Invasion

On Oct. 1, 1861 Gen. Zollicoffer reported in a letter to Adjutant-General Cooper in Richmond, Va. that he had received word from some reliable sources that a "Lincoln" force numbering 2,500 was assembled near Louisa, in Lawrence County Kentucky , on the Lower Sandy River, for a raid into Russell, Wise, Buchanan, Lee, and Scott counties in Virginia. He was unable himself to " give any attention to the companies he was authorized to organize" in Lee and Scott, and suggested that an officer of military experience be appointed there instead. [5]

Gen. Zollicoffer had his hands full in his own command around Somerset, Kentucky and his sensible recommendation for a commander to organize the southern forces near Pound Gap was eventually acceded to by the appointment of recently promoted General Humphrey Marshall to the command of all the troops assembled at Prestonsburg for the defense of that frontier. He was ordered to report to Gen. Johnston at Bowling Green by letter for orders and instructions. He was also

---

[5] War of the Rebellion: Official Records of the Union and Confederate Armies , (Washington, 1884) Series 1, Vol. 4, pg. 434

fully authorized to take into service "as many men as you may be enabled to raise," and to organize them into companies, battalions, or regiments, as he thought might be required. He also placed seven companies at Abingdon, Va. at his disposal, as well as the three companies already guarding Pound Gap.[6]

The Confederate War Department at Richmond, Va. sent Gen. Johnston a letter on Nov. 3rd to inform him that President Davis had appointed Gen. Marshall to take command of the forces at Prestonsburg, Ky., and that he was taking with him enough arms enough for a regiment, with a regiment of Virginians that was to join him at Christiansburg, Va., and still another regiment would join him in a few days. With these regiments and forces then gathered at Prestonsburg, Colonel (John S.) Williams would be enabled to succeed in uniting two or three regiments more with them. These forces would then form sufficient force to prevent the enemy from passing into Southwestern Virginia by Pound Gap. He was also informed that Gen. Marshall would have a battery of six field pieces with him. [7]

On the same date, Wm. Gribboney, who was the Assistant Quartermaster to Major Hawes, who was the quartermaster for John S. William's 5th Kentucky Infantry Regiment of the Confederate States Army, notified the Hon. J.P. Benjamin, Acting Sec. of War, that he was forwarding a letter from Major Hawes concerning his requisition for ammunition etc. The original letter from Major Hawes was

---

[6] ibid, page 495.
[7] ibid, page 502, 503, 504

13

written on Oct. 28, 1861, stating that he had reached Piketon the night before where Colonel William's Regiment was camped, 25 miles above Prestonsburg. His regiment consisted of about 1,000 men who were deficient in ammunition. Major Hawes explained that he had sent down (to Prestonsburg) 4 kegs of powder, 16 bags buck shot, and 200 lbs lead. He expected to have an abundance of fixed ammunition, which was sent to him by Capt. Gibboney at Wytheville, Virginia. (In addition, Capt. Gibboney sent Major Hawes 1,000 lbs of buck shot and 3,000 bars of lead for smelting into ammunition.)

Major Hawes remarked that the whole Sandy River upriver for a considerable distance was alarmed about Colonel William's safety. (Many of the recruits in Col. William's regiment were from the Big Sandy River area.)The federal forces were reported to be at West Liberty and Hazel Green, which is less than 50 miles from Prestonsburg. The enemy were reported to have 4,000 men, fully armed, with four pieces of artillery with them.

On Oct. 22nd an advanced guard consisting of 60 men of Colonel William's regiment had attacked a large Federal force from the bushes and hillsides in which the Federals suffered the loss of 30 killed and a number wounded. William's regiment suffered no losses in this ambush.

Major Hawes went on to express his opinion that if Col. William's regiment was able to sustain their position in the Big Sandy Valley it would be only at the cost of great peril, although he expected that Col. Williams would hold on until the last extremity. He reminded the Secretary that their base of operations was then at Wytheville, Virginia which is 150 miles in distance, and on a tolerable mountain road. [8]

The Federal version of the Oct. 22nd skirmish mentioned above had a different outcome of the skirmish as did Major Hawes. In the Federal version, two companies of the 33rd Ohio under Major Joshua V. Robison reached Hazel Green at 4: a.m. and completely surprised a detachment of 1,550 rebels under the command of Captain Andrew Jackson May, a native of Prestonsburg, Kentucky. The Federals captured several Confederate leaders in the fighting. The next day William O. Nelson, who was still an official Navy Lieutenant but soon to be a Brigadier General, arrived on the scene at Hazel Green, accompanied by the 21st Ohio, part of the 33rd Ohio, and four guns. A wagon train was also part of the new arrivals.[9]

Capt. Andrew May retreated first to Prestonsburg, then Piketon, where he found Col. Williams and his regiment had already withdrawn to that town. Col. Williams had between 1,000 and 1,200 men which he was engaged in trying to muster and organize. He complained in a report to Gen. John B. Floyd that with so much scouting and picket duty to perform it had been impossible to compile muster rolls for his command. He reported the number of Federals in Hazel Green and West

---

[8] ibid, pages 507, 508

[9] The Civil War in the Big Sandy Valley of Kentucky, John David Preston, Gateway Press, Inc, Baltimore, 1984

15

Liberty as 5,000 under the command of Gen. Nelson. With his disorganized command, all he hoped to accomplish if that force moved up the Sandy Valley was to fight a guerrilla fight, fall back and kill as many Federals as possible.[10]

In the wake of Capt. May and Gen. Williams, Federal Gen. William O. Nelson arrived in Prestonsburg, Ky. on Nov. 5, 1861 and published this proclamation to the people of the area,

Proclamation
Headquarters at Prestonsburg
November 5, 1861.
Having this day occupied the town of Prestonsburg with the force under my command, I declare to all whom it may concern that the jurisdiction of the state of Kentucky is restored in this section of the state, and that the regular fall terms of the courts will be held in those counties in which the time for holding the same has not passed; and all civil officers are ordered to attend at the regular times and places of holding said courts and attend to the duties of their respective offices.

Given under my hand this 5th day of November, 1861. W. Nelson [11]

On the same day, and possibly at the same time Wm. Nelson was writing his proclamation to the concerned citizens of Eastern Kentucky, Gen. Humphrey Marshall had arrived in Wytheville, Va. on his journey to

---

[10] <u>War of the Rebellion</u>, Series 1, Vol. 51, part 2, page 362.

[11] ibid Series 1, Vol. 4, page 345.

16

Prestonsburg to "assume command of the forces at that point and in its vicinity, for the protection and defense of that frontier. I should have obeyed my orders literally by delaying this report, (to Gen. Johnston in Bowling Green,) until I arrived at Prestonsburg, but the distance hence is so great (170 miles) and the means of communication so precarious, I consider it best to address you from this point."

He went on to inform Gen. Johnston that Gen. Williams had succeeded in mustering 600 or 700 men into the Confederate service and that there were around 2,000 Kentuckians in all collected at that place. (Gen. Marshall had not yet learned that Gen. Williams had retreated further up the Big Sandy to Piketon.) He stated that his orders contemplated the immediate use of two Virginia regiments, (John H. Trigg's 54th Va. and A. C. Moore's regiment, the 29th Va. regiment,) and one battery of four pieces, commanded by Capt. Jeffress, of Virginia. [12]

On the very day that Gen. Marshall arrived in Wytheville where seven companies of Moore's regiment awaited him, the Adjutant and Insp. General's Office published Special Order No. 206, which combined the three companies of Volunteers who were guarding the mountain top at Pound Gap into the 29th Va. Volunteers mentioned above. The orders also called for them to proceed immediately to Prestonsburg, Ky., and report to Gen. Humphrey Marshall (who of course was still in Wytheville,Va.) who will organize them into a regiment, (the 29th) the field officers of which,

---

[12] ibid, pages 518, 519.

Col. A. C. Moore, Lieut. Col. William Leigh, and Major James Giles, "will immediately join the command." [13]

A few days before, Gen. Williams had received a letter from Gen S. Cooper, the Adjutant and Inspector General, to "detach an armed company (cavalry preferred) and direct it to proceed to Jeffersonville, (Va.), there to unite with the battery company of Captain Jeffress whence they will together proceed to Prestonsburg." General Marshall's command was slowly coming together to try to protect the Pound Gap from invasion by the Federals.

The Federal commander, Wm. Nelson, was now poised to rid the Kentucky mountains of the rebels in Prestonsburg and beyond. He had after all been able to chase hundreds of them away from Hazel Green and West Liberty with the Oct. 22nd skirmish and had even been able to release some Union men from the jail in West Liberty. Now all that remained to secure the Big Sandy Valley was to chase the rebels through the Pound Gap and out of the state. [14]

[13] ibid, Series 1, Vol.52, part 2, page 196.
[14] ibid, Series 1, Vol. 4, page 214.

Chapter Three

Engagement at Ivy Mountain

Brig. Gen. William O. Nelson was still a Naval Lieutenant when he was assigned to special duty by the Adjutant General's office on July 1, 1861. He was charged with mustering into service five regiments of infantry and one regiment of cavalry in East Tennessee and one regiment in West Tennessee for service in West and East Tennessee and in East Kentucky. To enable him to do so he was supplied with 10,000 stands of arms and accouterments, six pieces of field artillery, two smooth bore and two rifled cannon, and two mountain howitzers with ample supplies of ammunition.

He was authorized to use these men and war materials anywhere and in any such matter as he might direct. He was also to raise and muster into service three regiments of infantry in Southeast Kentucky for service there and in adjacent counties. [15]

After the actions at West Liberty and Hazel Green on Oct. 22 with the forces under Capt. Andrew Jackson May, the now Brig. Gen.

---

[15] War of the Rebellion, Series 1, Vol. 4, pages 251, 252.

Nelson had issued his Proclamation which had again established the courts in Floyd County, and he no doubt hoped that the other area counties would soon follow suit. He meant to encourage the population of Eastern Kentucky to get back to business as usual, even if he had to use a little force against those pesky rebels that were trying to secure Pound Gap, the Big Sandy Valley, the Kentucky River Basin, and all Eastern Kentucky for the Confederacy.

Gen. Nelson allowed his tired command to rest at Prestonsburg for a couple of days, allowing his wagon train to catch up with him and giving his men time to rest, write letters, and getting their weapons ready for action in the coming days. Like soldiers from all wars, Civil War soldiers were either motivated or deeply depressed by the simple act of writing letters to, or receiving mail from, their loved ones at home. No self-respecting military commander would ever deprive their soldiers of the simple courtesy of contacting those whom they might never see again after the battle or battles which surely must come at any time during war, even during a guerrilla war that their Confederate foe had been busily waging in the Eastern Kentucky Mountains of late.

On November 7th, 1861, Gen Nelson dispatched Colonel Joshua Sill, with his own regiment, the Thirty-third Ohio, and a light battalion under Major Hurt, Kentucky Volunteers, composed of a flank company from each of the regiments –- the Second, Thirty-third, and Fifty-Ninth Ohio Volunteers, and two Kentucky companies, together with 142 mounted men, under command of Colonel Metcalf, Kentucky Volunteers, (made up of men mounted from the wagon train teams), plus 36 gentlemen volunteers under Colonel Apperson, and a section of artillery, all to march by way of John's Creek and pass to the left (east) of Piketon where the Confederates had taken post.

Colonel Sill started his march at 11 a.m. that morning. Their designated route would take them a distance of forty miles from their starting point in Prestonsburg and would, if successful, turn or cut off the rebel force that had retreated to Piketon.[16]

At 5 a.m. the next day, Nov. 8th, Gen. Nelson marched from Prestonsburg with his remaining command, the Second Regiment Ohio Volunteers, Colonel Harris; Twenty first Ohio Volunteers, Colonel Norton; Fifty ninth Regiment Ohio Volunteers , Colonel Fyffe; the battalion of Kentucky volunteers under Colonel Chas. A. Marshall, and two sections of artillery, Captain Konkle, and took the direct State road towards Piketon, which was some 28 miles away.

Around eight miles into their march, Nelson's column ran into the advanced guard of mounted pickets numbering 40 men that Gen. John S. Williams had sent from Piketon under the command of Captains Clay and Thomas to observe the movements of the enemy. The Federals fired at the pickets but the fact that they had no cavalry with them allowed the rebels to get away and send word back to Piketon where Colonel Williams was waiting

---

[16] ibid, page 226

for word of the enemy. Williams had also sent another small mounted party, Captain Holliday commanding, on the John's Creek road to watch for the enemy in that direction.[17]

After receiving word of the attack on the mounted picket he had sent out, Gen. Williams immediately ordered Captains May and Hawkins, with their companies of infantry, and Lieutenant Van Hook, with 20 mounted men, to the position of Captain Thomas, near Ivy Creek, which was located between Piketon and Prestonsburg.[18]

Gen. Williams decided to accompany the force he was sending to Ivy Creek. When they arrived there they found the bridge spanning Ivy Creek had been burned by Captain Thomas. Since the enemy hadn't as yet made his appearance at Ivy Creek, Williams allowed his men to refresh themselves and ordered the horses to be hid in a deep mountain cave nearby. The whole rebel force moved on foot to a strong position half a mile in front of the burned bridge to await what they thought was the advanced guard of the enemy's force.[19]

In the early morning hours of Nov. 8th, Gen. Williams left for his camp in Piketon and at daylight met the report of Captain Holliday, who while picketing the John's Creek road had been fired upon by the advanced guard of the enemy of about 150 men. (This was of course Col. Sill's force which had been sent by Gen. Nelson to turn the Confederates out of Piketon.)

---

[17] ibid, pages 228,229.
[18] ibid, page 229
[19] ibid

Captain Holliday reported that he had killed eight of the enemy, losing only one of his own men wounded and one horse killed in the affair. Williams then dispatched Captain Shawn, with his own company together with Captain Cameron's companies to observe the movements of the enemy on John's Creek and instructed him to engage any party of the enemy not more than twice his number. He also instructed Shawn to not attack the enemy's full force.[20]

On Nov. 8th, at 1 p. m., Gen. Nelson's column of about 1,600 troops had advanced along the narrow defile of the mountain that ends at Ivy Creek which, as Nelson reported, is at its highest along the river and very precipitous and thickly covered with timber and undergrowth. He goes on to say that; "The road which is but 7 feet wide, is cut along the side of it about 25 feet above the river, which is close under the road. The ridge descends in a rapid curve and very sharp to the creek, or rather gorge, where it makes a complete elbow"[21].

As the head of Colonel Chas. Marshall's battalion of Kentucky Volunteers, who had the lead, reached the elbow in the road, a sudden rapid fire of rifles and shotguns blasted the head of the column. Colonel Marshall himself was leading the column but somehow escaped injury. The opening salvo of gunfire was very sharp and accurate and Colonel Marshall's men paid the price of at least 4 men killed and 13

---

[20] ibid, 229
[21] ibid, pages 225, 226.

23

wounded. Nelson passed the order for Colonel Marshall to charge the hill.

The whole side of the steep mountain was blue with puffs of smoke but not an enemy was to be seen. The 250 rebels had waited quietly and unseen in ambush for the expected arrival of the Federal column and they were busily pouring the lead at the Yankee invaders.

After the first volley by the rebels, Colonel Harris led his 2nd Ohio Regiment up the mountain-side and deployed them along the face of the mountain. Not much could be done but Harris' men began popping away at the puffs of visible smoke.

The main column of Federals, having initially fallen back from the ambush, were halted just beyond the defile and anticipating an order from Nelson, led his 21st Ohio up the northern ridge of the mountain and deployed along the ridge face and crest and began firing furiously at the enemy. Meanwhile Captain Konkle had managed to get one section, (two guns), in position in the narrow road, and opened on them. Due to the steepness of the mountain it took much time to get these troops into position to effectually fight back.

Meanwhile, some here-to- fore unseen rebel skirmishers were also now making their presence known by taking pot-shots at the nearly trapped Federal column. The river here was narrow, but deep and swift, which kept the rebels deployed there reasonably safe from a counter attack by the federals.

After at least an hour and 20 minutes of killing and being killed, the Rebel Mountaineers fell back behind the burned bridge where they made another stand but the Federals were satisfied to let the Confederates go. Gen. Williams, from Piketon, ordered three companies of infantry to advance towards Captain May's little band near Ivy Creek to either help repel the enemy or to cover May's retreat.

After the battle Gen. Nelson bivouacked his command 4 miles beyond Ivy Creek, where it was raining a heavy rain which made the march heavy and slow. The Confederates had cut trees across the roads which necessitated removing them and repairing the numerous bridges also destroyed by the rebels.[22]

The battle of Ivy Mountain wasn't a battle of the scope of most of those taking place in other areas of the country but the importance of protecting the Sandy Valley and the Pine Mountain gaps and passes cannot be overestimated and was worth fighting for by both sides. The Federals wanted to bring the people of Eastern Kentucky back into the fold, and to open Pound Gap and other areas for a invasion pathway to the southern railroads, and especially to stop the salt-making capability of the south at Saltville, Virginia, which was the primary source of salt in the south. The Southern forces wanted to hold Eastern Kentucky for recruiting and to stop any invasion of the south through the mountains.

Both sides were now aware that neither side was ready to give up without a fight for their right to stay in Eastern Kentucky. All doubt of the determination of both sides was

---

[22] ibid, 225, 226, 227, 228, 229.

25

removed by their first major fight in the Big Sandy area.

After the battle General Nelson reported his casualties as totaling 6 killed and 24 wounded. He also reported that 32 dead rebels were found killed on the ground, and a number of their wounded were scattered on the mountain side. Among the killed reported was H.M. Rust, late State Senator from Greenup County, Kentucky. Gen. Nelson remarked that he would have taken or slain the whole of them if he had had any cavalry with him. He mentioned in his report that Captain Berryhill, Second Ohio Infantry, was severely wounded while leading the attack on the mountain side.

Gen. Williams reported his loss in the Ivy Mountain fight as 10 killed, including Lieutenant Rust, (former State senator), 15 wounded, and 40 missing. He also doubtless exaggerated the number of Federal casualties by reporting "300 killed with the usual proportion of wounded," as Gen. Williams put it. It's possible that both sides under reported their wounded, mortally wounded, and killed in the clash of arms. The reports of both Generals are gruesome enough, with the total reported list of casualties adding up to 16 killed, 39 wounded, and 40 missing for the battle. [23]

Gen. Nelson made no commendations but Gen. Williams commended the gallantry of Captains May, Thomas, Hawkins, and Clay, also Lieutenants Van Hook and Sam Clay. He mentioned all his officers and men as "deserving of commendation for their courage

---

[23] ibid

26

and coolness in the battle."[24] Without a doubt the Confederates had managed to put up a good fight against their Northern foe and had shown a good deal of courage against their better armed and equipped enemy.

---

[24] ibid, page 229.

Chapter Four

Retreat

As the night settled over the scene of the action at Ivy Mountain, General Nelson's men were trying to recover from the trial they had gone through that afternoon. The 24 wounded the Union forces suffered were being treated as well as possible on this Civil War battle ground with no medical facility within miles. The mixed lot of flintlock rifles, smoothbores, and shotguns the Confederates were using could still do a lot of damage to the human body. The shotguns were deadly at close range and could inflict ugly wounds even if just a few pellets from those shotguns struck a body. The slightly better arms of the Union forces could do their own amount of carnage also and the rebels were badly outgunned. The Federals had rebel wounded to contend with too, as most of the enemy wounded were left in their hands.[25]

Most of the rebels of Captains Thomas, and Clay's commands, along with Lieutenant Van Hook's twenty mounted men , were able to

---

[25] War of the Rebellion, Series 1, Vol. 4, page 226.

retreat in comparative ease back along the poor road to Piketon, but the two companies of infantry commanded by Captains May and Hawkins, and the three companies of infantry sent by Gen Williams to cover the retreat, had a much more difficult time of it as they hurried back towards their campgrounds.

At 12 o'clock the night of the battle, Captain Shawn, who had been sent to scout on the John's Creek road, came rushing back into Piketon to report to General Williams that the enemy were advancing in full force and with great rapidity towards the town. Williams then ordered Captains May, Shawn and all the other outposts in, including those in retreat from Ivy Mountain, and sent his exhausted infantry in the direction of their retreat along the road to Pound Gap.[26]

Williams made a pretense of his intension to hold the town by displaying his men throughout the town to give his infantry a head start in their retreat. With the balance of his forces he awaited the enemy's arrival. They came slowly and cautiously, but were detained for an hour by Captain Thomas' company of sharpshooters who were stationed near the ford of the Sandy River leading into town. This stand by the small detachment of rebel marksmen prevented the Federal artillery from being able to rake the town with shot and shell.[27]

Eventually, the small rebel force of sharpshooters began a slow retreat from the ford and allowed the enemy to cross and enter

---

[26] ibid, page 229.
[27] ibid

29

the town. Williams then began retreating with the rearguard of 400 men that had been defending the town. The Federals opened on the retreating forces with a tremendous fire of artillery and musketry, and were replied to by the company of sharpshooters, who were protecting the rear. The killed and wounded in the defense of the ford and the beginning of the retreat from the town totaled one man killed and 3 wounded among the Confederate forces. Gen. Williams also reported that 6 Federals had been killed in the affair.[28]

General William's opponent during the defense and retreat from Piketon was the Union force under Colonel Sill which left on the 7th from Prestonsburg under Gen. Nelson's orders to approach Piketon by way of the John's Creek road. As his men approached the ford into town, Colonel Metcalf's mounted men were in advance and exchanged fire with Captain's sharpshooters, who had crossed the river at the ford. After a few shots from both sides the Southern skirmishers retreated back across the river.[29]

As the Confederates hastily retreated on their horses across the river, Colonel Sill deployed Colonel Metcalf's regiment, the 33rd Ohio, and Major Hurt's company of Kentucky volunteers, as skirmishers on the hillside flanking the road as the road debouched at the ford. Entering the village, they found the enemy's camp deserted and the main street of town occupied by mounted men who were

---

[28] ibid.

[29] ibid, page 227.

30

making haste as they retreated by way of the Shelby- Pound Gap road.

A few rounds of shell were sent after the retreating rebel force as Metcalf's force mounted their horses and took possession of the town. The Federal infantry waiting at the ford crossed the river on a raft bridge. [30]

In his report on Nov. 10th of the action between his forces and the command of General Williams as they retreated from the town, Colonel Sill wrote that he had discovered that the enemy were occupied all day before (the 9th) in leaving the town. General Williams himself was also in town when the skirmishers opened fire, Metcalf reported. As a matter of fact, Colonel Metcalf was occupying Gen. William's old headquarters even as he wrote his report to Gen. Nelson.

Colonel Sill's report differed from that of Gen. William's report of the action, in that Sill reported his loss as one man killed and none wounded. He wrote General Nelson that there were many other particulars that he would speak of when they met up.

His men were very hungry after their labors and all they could get was beef, but a nearby mill would provide plenty of corn meal as soon as he could set it in motion today.[31]

While General Williams was preparing to withdraw from Piketon he had written a report to General Humphrey Marshall in Wytheville, Virginia detailing his clash with General Nelson's forces at Ivy Mountain. In the report he said he was occupied in preparing to

---

[30] ibid.
[31] ibid.

fall back in the direction of Pound Gap but his transportation was so limited that he would be compelled to abandon some amount of public property. "The enemy is so perfectly equipped, he said, with plenty of artillery, are well instructed, and fight with courage. *We have nothing in the world on our side*, he lamented, *but courage.* The disparity in the loss was due alone to our position, he continued. Infantry armed with rifles are the men for this country. Cavalry is almost useless except for picket duty."

He went on in his report to Gen. Marshall to inform him that he would continue to fall back until he was either able to make a stand, or until he was re- enforced. He reported his command on the retreat as nine companies of infantry, four of them not yet full, and five companies of mounted men, and two of these not yet full, making an aggregate of 1,100 poorly armed and badly clothed men, with scarcely any discipline.[32]

By the 11th of Nov., General Marshall at Wytheville, Va. had received General William's report of the defeat at Ivy Mountain, the loss of Piketon, and the retreat to Pound Gap. Marshall wrote a report to Adjutant-General Cooper at Richmond to inform him of the setback. He informed Gen. Cooper that the road to Wytheville was now open to the enemy because of the defeat. Marshall had also ordered Colonel Moore and his 29th Virginia Regiment to head to Pound Gap to re-enforce Gen. Williams at the Gap. He also stated to Gen. Cooper that the force of the enemy at

---

[32] ibid, page 228.

Piketon was numbered at 3,000 to 3,500 men. If General Cooper would only give him two regiments at once and another battery (besides the six pieces of Captain Jeffries command) "I will succeed quickly, and return what may be left, (after the expected clash with the enemy.) If this cannot be done, I will do all I can," he wrote.[33]

On Nov. 12th Gen. Cooper replied to Gen. Marshall's letter of the 11th and told him to act on the best information he had, concerning William's retreat from Piketon. In a note of the same date he told Marshall to hold Col. Trigg's 54th Virginia Regiment in Wytheville until Gen. William's intentions were better known.[34]

Gen. Marshall wrote a lengthy letter on the 12th while at Jeffersonville, Va., which informed Cooper that he had ordered Col. Trigg on the road to Pound Gap as soon as Jeffress' battery's transportation had arrived at Wytheville. It had so arrived on Sunday, the 10th, and Trigg and Jeffries had already left that town. Jeffress had had to leave one caisson behind but had brought the gun and ammunition along after leaving a squad to bring the caisson along later.[35]

Marshall enclosed the report of Gen. Williams to him of the fights he had at Ivy Mountain and Piketon on the 9th of Nov. with his letter, and commented that he couldn't tell if Gen. Williams had abandoned either point to the enemy or not, because he (Marshall) had no means of forming a military judgment on

---

[33] bid, page 538.
[34] ibid, 538, 540.
[35] ibid, page 541.

33

these points. He also said that he appreciated the sense of responsibility under which an officer acts who has responsibility of an undisciplined and badly armed force; yet he could see no reason for alarm.

Marshall went on to say that 300 cavalry would now be perfectly unobstructed if he should choose to come through Pound Gap, pass down the Wytheville road, pass through Buchanan County, descend upon Richland, destroy the salt-works and the railroad between Wytheville and Abingdon, and hold a position until re-enforced. "They could ravage the whole country and the loss of the salt-works would be irreparable, for the whole Confederacy depends on these salt- works greatly."[36]

General Williams and his battered force reached Pound Gap on the 12th of Nov, after a forty mile retreat over some of the most miserable roads in the Cumberland Plateau. His route up Elkhorn Creek took him and his tired troops to the very head of the source of that creek which eventually empties into the Big Sandy River. On the south side of that same ridge of Pine Mountain is the head of the North Fork of the Kentucky River which flows over 255 miles northwesterly until it empties into the Ohio River at Carrollton, Kentucky, Along the way, it merges with the South Fork and the Middle Fork of the river at Beattyville. Each of these forks has their beginning on or near the Pine Mountain Range which traverses from north to south down the Eastern Kentucky area. Pound Gap is located just above the

---

[36] ibid, page 541.

beginning of the Sandy River which begins as a trickle on the northwest side of this mountain, while the beginning trickle of the Kentucky River flows down the southwest side of the mountain. This is not all. On the southern side of this same mountain the mighty Cumberland River also has it's beginning on the rocky, wooded slopes of Pine Mountain. Thus this area of the Pine Mountain Range was a historic one even before the Civil War came along to make it even more so.

On the 13th of Nov. General Williams had settled in well enough in Pound Gap to write the following further report to General Marshall, with more information of his fight at Ivy Mountain and his retreat from Piketon; I have omitted the part of the report which repeats some details already mentioned above:

Camp near Pound Gap, Nov. 13, 1861

General: Since my last report to you I have been compelled to abandon Piketon by an overwhelming force that advanced upon me in two columns, one directly up the river from Prestonsburg, 1,600 strong, with a battery of six pieces, and the other from Louisa up John's Creek, a branch of the Sandy, numbering 1,800 men, with a battery of field pieces. Both of these columns converged upon Piketon.

My whole force consisted of 1,010 men, including sick, teamsters, and men on extra duty. I did not believe that the advance of the enemy would be so rapid, and hoped that the artillery and re-enforcements promised would arrive before they could disturb me at Piketon. Upon this confident hope I commenced gathering supplies, explored the leather

35

resources of the country, found them abundant, and organized a corps of shoemakers, and had them at work. Major Hawes had purchased 1,000 fat hogs and a number of beef cattle, and was making preparations to salt them. My men were badly clad and badly armed, with not a knapsack, haversack, or canteen. They carried their power in horns, gourds, and bottles. This was our condition when the enemy commenced the advance upon us. Retreat was inevitable, but there was too much public property to be abandoned without an effort to save it. I at once ordered all the transportation possible to be collected, and sent the wounded , and the livestock to the rear on the Pound Gap road for the Tazewell route was no longer safe................ If we had had 1,000 more men and a battery of six pieces we could have whipped and destroyed both columns; but with the small force I had it was impossible to fight both at once, and to have exposed my whole force to one would have exposed my rear to the other. Our cartridge boxes arrived the other day after the fight. We had powder and lead, and made our own cartridges and molded our own bullets.

The enemy have 6,000 troops near Piketon; 1,000 of them advanced 10 miles this side of that place. They have not more than 1,500 at Prestonsburg. What they have below as reserves I know but little of, for all communication is cut off and the whole country is frightened out of its wits, and but few men will act as scouts or guides. I am satisfied that this large force was not moved up the Sandy merely for the purpose of intending to move upon the Virginia and dispersing the unorganized and half-armed, barefooted squad under my command. They intended to move upon the Virginia and Tennessee Railroad, I think, by way of the Tazewell Court-House. They fortify their positions, and have a large number of wagons. The Sandy is now navigable for steamboats to a point above Piketon.

We want good rifles, clothes, great-coats, knapsacks, haversacks, and canteens-indeed, everything, almost, except a willingness to fight. Many of our men are barefooted, and I have seen the blood in their tracks as they marched from Ivy to this place. You know what we want, general. Send such articles as we need to Abingdon. There is but little subsistence here, and I fear I shall be compelled to fall back to a point where I can subsist until our organization is perfected. We have been so constantly fighting that we have not had time to complete our muster rolls. I have now over 1,200 men. If I could make a forward movement the effect would be good upon the country.

Mr. Thomas has just received from the governor of Florida a commission as aide-de-camp, with rank of colonel. I cannot insist on retaining him from such increased rank. Send somebody else.

If the enemy should move by way of the Pound I have not a sufficient force to resist them—no artillery, no intrenching tools, nor axes, spades, or picks. If they come we will give them a fight, but this will do us no good but to destroy a few of them.

I have just learned from a spy that a steamboat arrived at Piketon yesterday with supplies to the enemy.

Major Hawes wants more money. He has bought hogs, horses, wagons, etc.

Your obedient servant,

John S. Williams, Colonel, C.S.A.[37]

Thus Colonel Williams had managed to transfer his whole command from their mustering in location at Prestonsburg on the Big Sandy to the comparatively safety of Pound Gap on the Kentucky-Virginia border, bloody feet and all.

---

[37] ibid, pages 228, 229, 230.

38

Chapter Five

Marshall at the Gap

When General William's Fifth Kentucky Infantry and a few dozen mounted men, totaling 1,010 in all, reached Pound Gap on Tuesday, the 12th of November, 1861, they found Major John B. Thompson's 21st Virginia Battalion of 350 men already camped in and around the Gap and engaged in guarding against invasion by Federal forces through that passage and other mountain passes.

On August 14, 1861, Brigadier General Felix Kirk Zollicoffer, who was a former newspaper man and Tennessee congressman, had, as the Confederate commander of the Eastern Kentucky District, authorized Major Thompson to raise a battalion of six companies of troops from Wise, Scott and Lee counties in Virginia for "special service." They were to furnish their own rifles and their service was limited to guarding the mountain passes in those three counties , including Pound Gap on the Kentucky- Virginia border.

The battalion was collected and had some brief period of drilling at Camp Lane, near Jonesville, Va., in Lee County. Major Thompson, who had spent some time in the mounted forces of the United States Army previously, served as the battalion's drillmaster while they were training at Camp Lane. [38]

Since Major Thompson's men had, as part of their enlistment contract, had to furnish their own weapons, it's likely that they were poorly armed with flintlocks and shotguns much like Colonel William's 5th Kentucky were armed. It's also not beyond reason to think that they also had no cartridge boxes or canteens and were reduced to carrying their powder like Col. William's men, in horns, gourds, and bottles.

In the few weeks the 21st had been at Pound Gap they had managed to build a few rudimentary breastworks on the Kentucky side of the Gap and had been engaged in cutting logs to build a few log huts for shelter in the coming winter months. By the time all the huts were finished there were 60 log huts capable of holding 15 to 20 men each and 2 larger huts that held what few quartermaster and commissary stores they might accumulate over the treacherous roads leading to Gladesville, Abingdon, and Wytheville, Virginia.

The 21st Va. Battalion was in reality little more than home guards, since they had been organized strictly for guarding the mountain

---

[38] War of the Rebellion, Series 1, Vol. 4, page 388.

passes. This being the case, Major Thompson refused to budge from the Gap except when the enemy forced him from the mountain a few months later.

The 5th Kentucky Infantry was right at home in Pound Gap, as the regiment had been largely recruited in the Big Sandy Valley and the Kentucky River area. Their initial gathering in Prestonsburg had been for the purpose of mustering in as a regiment there. Their Ivy Mountain fight and retreat from Piketon had put a stop to the official mustering in process and Gen. Williams had reported that not more than 600 men had officially been mustered in when they were forced to retreat from Prestonsburg.

The fact that some had not yet been mustered as soldiers when they reached Pound Gap makes it easy to imagine that several men had deserted as they retreated from Piketon. No one could expect men that had little to eat, were marching over miserable roads, were wet and cold, had little winter clothing, and whose weapons were barely serviceable, to camp in the open on top of a miserable ridge where the cold winter winds would 'cut you in-two.' The right to secede from the Union and to fight for what you think is right means little when the human constitution is stressed out, miserable, and depressed.

Company F of the 5th Ky. had in fact been recruited in Whitesburg and the Letcher County area just a few weeks before their return to Pound Gap. The company had been recruited and assembled in Whitesburg in October before proceeding to Prestonsburg to

41

be sworn in by General Williams there. Their first action, like the rest of the 5th, had been at Ivy Mountain and Piketon.

Major General McClellan published on Nov. 14th, Congratulatory General Orders No. 99, that was in part, an announcement that *"announces to the Army with sincere pleasure the victory achieved by Brig. Gen. William Nelson at Pikeville, Ky., in which, after two days hard fighting, the rebels were completely defeated and put to flight. ....He commends them to the imitation of the whole army."*[39]

On Nov. 24th Gen. Marshall finally arrived in Pound Gap. He had been ordered to Prestonsburg the 1st of Nov, but had run into so much difficulty in organizing his command that only the defeat of General Williams had spurred him to hurry on to take command at Pound Gap at last.

In a Nov. 25th report to Adjutant General Cooper at Richmond, Va., Marshall announced his arrival at Gen. William's camp at the Gap. He informed Cooper that the enemy had fallen back to probably occupy the area from the mouth of Sandy to the county seat of Bath, (Owingsville.) He stated he had ordered his cavalry up from Clinch River in Virginia, and would start them to the front immediately to "ascertain the where-abouts of the enemy and to inspire our friends." He went on to say that he would press forward cautiously, but sufficiently, to address himself successfully to the mountain people.

I find that some misinformation has been given to you about the companies at

---

[39] ibid, Series 1, vol. 6, page 66.

Pound Gap destined to form a regiment for Colonel Moore. They were raised by order of General Zollicoffer, with a condition that they were to be kept in Scott and Wise counties only to defend the mountain passes, and not to leave this state. They are under the command of Major Ward, who raised them at the instance of general Zollicoffer. They (the 21st Battalion) are unwilling to be placed in a regiment under Colonel Moore in any event, but especially refuse to be taken from their own officer or to change the term of their service from one special in its character to one which will be general. Colonel Moore has not moved any of his five companies from Abingdon yet. I think it highly probable he never will, and if he is not capable of responding more rapidly than he has done to my orders, it makes little difference if he never does. I have received your order to organize this battalion into a regiment, under Colonel Moore, but under the circumstances I deem it prudent to delay the execution of that order until you are possessed fully of all the facts of the case. Meanwhile the battalion will remain on duty subject to Major Ward. In any event, there will be required a reserve at this point to guard the pass and the line of supply, and these men will do very well for such service. I will cause them to build cabins and so arrange them as to fortify the gap, and it can be made a depot for supply to an army in front.

Marshall went on in his report to ask for another battery to be sent forward to him at the Gap. He would then have "8 pieces of artillery with the additional battery," he stated. He said that one could not expect men without blankets or overcoats or shoes in the snow and ice of a mountain range to be contented. He nominated Dr. Basil C. Duke as chief of the medical staff of the brigade and requested his commission for such. "This completes my staff,"he continued.[40]

Since the 21st battalion refused to even talk about serving in another regiment or under another officer, General Marshall decided to accept the inevitable and ordered the battalion to finish building the log huts and to fortify the road leading from Kentucky through the Gap. He also made it clear in his report that Colonel Moore's 29th Va. Regiment might never come forward, and if he did, he would only have an undrilled battalion with him which wouldn't be much help.[41]

In the conditions in which he found upon arriving at the Gap, Gen. Marshall decided not to attempt the organization of Colonel Moore's 29th Va. with the battalion of Major Thompson's 21st Virginia. Marshall had given orders to Moore to move his command to the Gap as early as the 6th of Nov. and repeated them in writing on the 9th of the same month, but Moore had yet to move up. He used as an excuse the want of arms, clothing, rations, and transportation. If all the other Confederate regiments wanted, they could sit still by making this same argument. The rebel army was one vast body of men without a sufficiency of all war making material at this point in their organizations, and there would be little improvement throughout the war.

---

[40] ibid, Series 1, vol. 7, pages 702,703.
[41] ibid, page 716

Colonel Moore only had 350 to 400 men in his few organized companies of the 29th Va., so it could hardly be called a regiment without the addition of a few more companies. The loss of being able to add Major Thompson's little command to those totals would have helped to augment Marshall's command, but Thompson's refusal made that question mute now.

General Marshall reported Gen. William's total infantry force at the Gap as between 799 to 835 men, enlisted and officers. He reported his total mounted force as being 400, and a battery of four pieces with 65 artillerymen. The total of his command at Pound Gap and in Virginia, he reported to Gen. Sidney Johnston, who was at Bowling Green Kentucky, as 2,100 infantry, 400 mounted men, and a battery of four pieces and 65 men, for a grand total under his command of 2,500 troops. He had thought and hoped for at least 5,000 men with which to protect the Sandy and Kentucky River area, but it was not to be.

The men of Gen. William's regiment of Kentuckians were still in their summer clothing, even though requisition after requisition had been made. They had had no drill at all and were as unskilled as the common militia of the country. The officers were very capable though, including Captain Benjamin E. Caudill of Company F, of the 5th Reg.

Trigg's regiment was still in Virginia at this point but was ordered in the direction of Piketon and Moore's orders were to move towards Pound Gap to offer re-enforcements to Col. Williams no matter where he might be found. Trigg's regiment would enter Kentucky via Jefferson ,Va., which town covers the road from Saltville to the Sandy Valley.

After accessing the situation, Gen. Marshall voiced that his purpose was to move his mounted force into Kentucky immediately, and to send it as far as West Liberty, and if possible, as far as the line from Louisa to Olympian Springs, while his infantry would be located on a line from Whitesburg, in Letcher County, to the Sandy. He knew there was a passable road from the one point to another.

The way Marshall saw it, if his plan worked, Trigg's 54th Virginia Regiment would, with Jeffress' four pieces of artillery, occupy the right flank from Prestonsburg, William's 5th Kentucky would be on the head of Beaver Creek, and Moore's 29th Virginia would anchor the line by posting his regiment in Whitesburg, and the special service men (the 21st Va. Battalion,) would protect the Pound Gap.

General Marshall was still convinced that the enemy had suffered a severe set-back , especially at Ivy Mountain, when he was led to believe that the Federals had lost 300 killed and many wounded in that battle. He still believed that the report of 396 of Union soldier's graves was a fact without dispute. He considered the whole affair a success, brilliant in its execution.

On November 21st, 1861, the Adjutant and Inspector General's office in Richmond, Virginia, in Special Orders No. 232, assigned to Gen. Humphrey Marshall's command the 56th Va. Regiment, Colonel William D. Stuart commanding. The Lieutenant Colonel of the

Regiment was Philips Peyton Slaughter; the Major was William E. Green. The orders required the 56th to proceed without delay via Wytheville, to Jeffersonville, Va., and report for duty to Brigadier- General Marshall.[42]

This regiment didn't remain under Gen. Marshall's command very long, as Special Orders No. 111, May 14, 1862, ordered the 56th to proceed immediately to Drewry's Bluff, near Richmond, Va., for duty there. After much anticipation and many plans for Stuart's Regiment to augment Marshall's meager command, Marshall received word on the 28th of Dec. that the 56th Va. would not be coming to him after all. The regiment had been very adverse to this service (in the mountains) and Marshall wrote to Adj. Gen. Cooper in Richmond that such a regiment would be of very little service to him with that mood.[43]

The expected re-enforcements would likely have made a huge difference in the actions to come in Eastern Kentucky and the mountains of Western Virginia. Marshall would have to make do with the few forces he had when he met the enemy.

In a lengthy letter to General Albert Johnston at Bowling Green, Kentucky, on Nov. 28, 1861, Marshall reported that Colonel Moore still had not moved his troops from Abingdon for reason of want of arms, clothing, rations, and transportation. Marshall guessed that Moore's Regiment would number from 350 to 400 men, closer to a battalion than a regiment. The whole Virginia force in the Gap would then

---

[42] ibid, Series 1, Vol.51, pt2, pages 308, 386.
[43] ibid, pg.555 , also Ser. 1, Vol. 10, pt.2, pg. 346.

number 1,200 to 1,300 men, or just a little more than a regiment. John S. William's force would number 835 infantry, with a mounted force of 400 men, and a battery of four cannon (Jeffries) with 65 men, making a rough total of all arms of 2,500 men to take the field with.[44]

General Marshall outlined his itinerary when coming from Virginia to Pound Gap to Gen. Cooper thus: *I traveled by Lebanon to this place – distant from Col. Trigg's to wit: From Trigg's camp to Lebanon road, 5 miles, thence to Lebanon, 22 miles; Lebanon to Castlewood (Clinch River) 20 miles; Castlewood to Gladesville, 23 miles; Gladesville to Pound, 12 miles; Pound to Pound Gap, 5 miles; total, 87 miles- intending to see to the defenses proper for Pound Gap and to ascertain the exact condition of organization in this force.* Marshall found the mounted force of William's command at Pound Gap had fallen back to Castlewood, behind Clinch River, to recruit and forage, there being no forage nearer to Pound Gap. He organized the mounted force into a battalion while at Castlewood, and asked their preference as to who should command them. The troops asked for Hon. W.E. Simms and Marshall concurred. He asked President Davis to issue the commission to Simms.[45]

Marshall reported to Gen. Cooper that he had found a total of 800 men at the Gap upon arrival and that all were badly clothed-indeed miserably clad—very inexpert in the use of the gun, but brave and good looking. He

---

[44] ibid, Ser. 1, Vol. 7, pgs. 715, 716, 717,718.
[45] ibid, pg. 722, 723.

described Major Thompson's battalion as being very excellent in appearance though the battalion had just gone through a bout with measles. He recommended that the battalion had best be kept where it would be more within the conditions of its enlistment. "It's officer (s) I cannot commend as very attentive, energetic, or efficient."[46]

Marshall ended his report by stating that he intended moving his whole command into Kentucky within a day or two and would occupy the line from Prestonsburg to Whitesburg.

From his camp at Pound Gap Marshall wrote to Major General Crittenden that he intended moving his command that day, Dec. 1st, for Prestonsburg, Ky., To which place his original orders had directed him, "to protect and defend that frontier." It was impossible to occupy his camp at Pound Gap any longer because forage for the horses cannot be procured and "the country is absolutely stripped to its ruin of all provisions." They were relying for flour and meal to be hauled 55 miles through the deepest and worst sort of roads, and "corn is just not to be had for the horses engaged in transportation."[47]

Marshall's main object in passing through the mountains was first, to obtain food and forage, which he had learned could be had within a line drawn from Pound Gap to Prestonsburg; second, "to inspire our friends in Kentucky."[48]

---

[46] ibid, pgs. 722, 723.
[47] ibid, 729, 730.
[48] ibid

49

Marshall had already dispatched a column on the Louisa Fork of the Big Sandy to move upon Pikeville, which had been on the move for several days. He reported that because of these moves he would not send Colonel William's Regiment to Abingdon (as called for by a request from General Albert Sydney Johnston.) [49]

He reported the number of his troops as follows: William's Reg. 800
Trigg's Reg. 560
Mounted battalion..400
Jeffress' battery 60
Moore's Reg. (in Va.)... 400
Stuart's Reg. (in Va.)... 600

Total force in Va. & Ky. 2,820[50]

General Marshall didn't yet know that Stuart's Regiment would be taken away from him and sent to Eastern Virginia.

[49] ibid.
[50] ibid.

Chapter Six

Return to the Big Sandy

General Marshall's command left Pound Gap and traveled down the North Fork of the Kentucky River to Whitesburg, in Letcher County, then through the corner of Perry County, and then through Floyd County. This route was through some of the roughest country in Eastern Kentucky at that time and was likely chosen by Marshall in order to by-pass Piketon and surprise the Federals to the degree possible. By Dec. 10th he had reached Prestonsburg, in Floyd Co, Ky., and was encamped at Camp Recovery, located one mile from Prestonsburg.

He commented in a letter to General Cooper from Camp Recovery that, *"I think I have established friends for the Confederate States on a sound basis wherever I have been. My effort has been to conciliate the people, and to teach them by example that the Army of the Confederate States comes not to maraud*

(*maraud*) *and oppress, but to respect the constitutional rights of the people."* [51]

He related that, in contrast, "*the Army of the United States, invited here to defend this people, halted at no excess. They burned and ravaged the towns, insulted females and violated their persons, stole wearing apparel, and killed stock, and frequently deprived poor people of the means of subsistence."* [52]

He informed Cooper that he had found prisoners at Pound Gap that had been arrested for their political beliefs but that he had released them after explaining to them the principles he himself advocated. Upon release the prisoners had told Marshall that the veil had been removed from their eyes and they afterward were involved in getting recruits for his command.[53]

Marshall advanced his cavalry to West Liberty in Morgan County, not to station it, but to inspire potential friends and to prevent the enemy from stripping the country of stock. He also had heard a rumor that Colonel Moore, with his long awaited Abingdon battalion, had actually started to him but was making only 5 to 6 miles a day on their journey. The rumor also brought word that six field pieces was waiting at Abingdon for transportation. He hoped that this battery might be manned and equipped and moved towards him at once,

---

[51] <u>War of the Rebellion</u>, Series 1, Vol. 7, pgs. 755, 756.

[52] ibid, 756.

[53] ibid.

before the ice gathers, so as to make the mountains impassible.[54]

Gen. Marshall also had a detachment of troops making salt for the use of his command at the Salt Works at Brashearsville, on the North Fork of the Kentucky River, 20 miles below the town of Whitesburg. He hoped to make 35 or 40 bushels of salt per week, which would not only supply his current demand, but would enable him to pack and preserve as much meat ration as will serve his army for future purposes.[55]

The process of manufacturing salt from brine involved boiling the water in large iron kettles or pans until it evaporated, leaving the salt residue in the bottom of the pan or kettle. Large amounts of coal or wood were required in this process, and there was an abundant supply of both around the salt-works in Brashearsville.

When Marshall wrote his letter of the 10th, to Gen. Cooper, he had already been in camp at Prestonsburg for several days and was waiting for the arrival of Trigg's Regiment and Jeffress' battery, which had advanced from Richlands, Virginia, by the Louisa Fork of the Big Sandy River by the way of Piketon.[56]

With the arrival of Trigg and Jeffress, and the fact that Marshall's command was gradually being filled by a few recruits and some few parts of his scattered force, he felt that he would be guarded from surprise. He heard that young men in the interior of the

---

[54] ibid.
[55] ibid.
[56] ibid, pg. 755.

53

state were beginning to hear of his whereabouts and were moving. With an auspicious start, he had high hopes that the future may realize Confederate hopes for the Big Sandy Valley and for Kentucky.

On Dec. 13, Marshall and his command were still encamped at Prestonsburg. From here he wrote a letter to General A. Sidney Johnston at Bowling Green, Kentucky. In it he acknowledged a telegram he had received from Johnston, through Gen. Crittenden, asking for all the men that Marshall could spare without stripping his command to its ruin. Marshall said he had placed the absent Fifty-Sixth Va. at the discretion of Gen. Crittenden, though it was at the extreme risk of ruining the command. He had only 1,250 men with him, he said. Col. Moore's regiment still hadn't passed the Clinch River, and it "will not unless the men are first paid." It was a great pity, he said, that he didn't have men enough to penetrate to Mount Sterling (in Montgomery County, Ky.) and hold it. Marshall then asked for Stuart's regiment's return to him, and would be much obliged if Johnston could spare some other regiments to aid him in developing this column.[57]

The Federal forces in Kentucky had either anticipated or been informed of Marshall's intentions and had on Dec. 2nd. ordered Col. L.T. Moore in Catlettsburg, Ky., to establish his Fourteenth Reg. Ky. Volunteers at or near the town of Prestonsburg, with a view of giving security to the inhabitants of the region of the Big Sandy and of punishing the

---

[57] ibid, pgs. 767,768.

marauding bands of the enemy who annoy that part of the state. [58]

On Dec. 9th, Col. Moore notified Gen. Buell in Louisville that the secessionists were 4,000 strong in Prestonsburg, with a reinforcement at hand of 2,000, and six pieces of artillery; Jenkins cavalry composing a part.[59]

This report of the forces available to the rebels was a far cry from Marshall's report of his forces on Dec. 13th, when he reported 1,250 men as his available force. Of course, nearly all commanders either habitually over reported or under reported their forces, depending on which was to their advantage. This is as true today as it was during the Civil War.

ON Dec. 17th, 1861, in Special Orders No. 35, a Federal brigade was formed for duty in Eastern Kentucky, to be constituted as follows:

Eighteenth Brigade
Colonel Garfield, commanding,

42d Regiment Ohio Volunteers, Colonel Garfield,
40th Regiment Ohio Volunteers, Colonel Cranor,
14th Regiment Kentucky Volunteers, Col. L.T. Moore,
.... Regiment Kentucky Volunteers, Colonel Lindscy.[60]

---

[58] ibid, pg. 466, 467.
[59] ibid, pg. 485.
[60] ibid, pg. 503.

Colonel McLaughlin's squadron of Ohio cavalry and three squadrons (six companies) of the First Kentucky Cavalry (Colonel Wolford's) are attached to the brigade.

By command of Brigadier-General Buell, James B. Fry, Asst. Adj. General.

Brig. Gen. Buell wrote Col. Garfield on Dec. 17th that the brigade organized under his command is intended to operate against the rebel force (Marshall's) that was threatening, and indeed actually committing depredations in Kentucky, through the valley of the Big Sandy. Buell then said that the actual forces of the enemy probably does not exceed 2,000 or 2,500, (which was closer to the truth), but that some rumors put his force as high as 7,000. He ordered Garfield to first go to Lexington and Paris, and place the 40th Ohio Regiment on the route to Prestonsburg in such position to oppose any advance of the enemy by that route.

He should then proceed without delay to the mouth of the Sandy, and move with the force in that vicinity up the river, and drive the enemy back or cut him off. Having done that, he should occupy Piketon as the best position to prevent further incursion by the enemy.

He cautioned Garfield that his supplies must necessarily be taken up the river, and it ought to be done as soon as possible, while the navigation is open. He added that Garfield should report frequently and fully all matters concerning his command.[61]

On Dec. 26, Col. Garfield arrived at George's Creek with 900 men. He reported

---

[61] ibid, pg. 22.

2,500 rebels at Paintsville, 18 miles distant, with four guns, who were preparing for battle by fortifying there. He expected the 14th Kentucky with its 500 men to be with him soon. He reported Colonel Lindsey's regiment of Kentuckians also would soon join him at Paintsville, but the regiment had only 600 men and no equipments. Garfield requested that four small howitzers, with shell and shrapnel, be sent him if possible. He would use boats and mule teams to haul the cannon to his command.[62]

Col. Garfield reported the roads along the Sandy valley as being almost impassable. It required four days hard labor to bring his train of 25 wagons, nearly empty, a distance of 28 miles. Therefore he decided to bring his supply stores to George's Creek by river.[63]

After comparing statements from citizens, scouts, and prisoners, Garfield learned that Col. Williams (and Marshall) had returned about three weeks ago with the force that had retreated from before Gen. Nelson; and that ten days ago (Dec. 16th) a regiment of troops from some neighboring state, probably Virginia, passed to Prestonsburg, via Piketon, with a train of 55 wagons and four iron guns, one of large caliber, the others probably 6-pounders. (This was Colonel Trigg's Regiment and Jeffress' battery that had been sent by way of Richlands, Virginia, then through Piketon.)[64]

By the 22nd of Dec., Gen. Marshall had moved down the Big Sandy valley to

---

[62] ibid, pg. 25.
[63] ibid.
[64] ibid, pg. 26.

Paintsville, Ky. From there he wrote a report to Gen. A. Sydney Johnston explaining some of his actions since taking command of his troops. He informed Johnston he had been compelled to arrest Colonel Moore of the Twenty-eighth (29th Va. Reg. and had directed him to remain at his home in Abingdon until Johnston could order a court to try his case. Marshall outlined the charges against Moore and remarked that he would send the formal charges and specifications forward if he (Marshall) shall consider it absolutely essential to press the matter to a hearing. He related how he had been trying to get Moore to move his command forward to Prestonsburg since Nov. 9th, and had explained to him the apprehension he had felt for Gen. William's safety since the 6th day of November, He had first urged him to move, then gave him written orders to move immediately on receiving arms and ammunition. From Pound Gap he urged Col. Moore to move forward with his command and demanded an explanation for his conduct. He rendered an explanation and set a start date for his command but did not start on the appointed day. When he did start, he only moved four or five miles per day. When Moore's command reached the Clinch River, they refused to move across the Clinch until they had been paid. Finally on the 14th of Dec., they reached the other (west) side of Cumberland Mountain but there halted again. From there Moore sent Marshall a message that he was doing all he could to get his men forward, but his men would not come, and besides, he had to go back after some that he had permitted to go home to prepare wood for the winter for their families, etc., and expected to be detained for some seven or eight days. This was the point at which Gen. Marshall had ordered Col. Moore's arrest and directed him to return to his home "until you (Johnston) could order an investigation of his case." [65]

Marshall informed Johnston that his position at Paintsville was 33 miles above Louisa and about 60 miles from the Ohio River. Below him were several large towns: Louisa, 900 population; Catlettsburg, 1,000, at the mouth of the Sandy; four miles below Catlettsburg is Ashland, 1,200 population; 20 miles below is Greenupsburg; at 7 miles below, on the Ohio side, is Ironton, with 4,500 population, and this is the terminus of a railroad running to the interior of Ohio.[66]

Marshall reported that the whole population there is against the south. He arrested one man within 10 miles of Louisa, the only arrest he had sanctioned to this point. He sent the man to the post at Pound Gap, to be detained there until further orders. "He ought to have been shot; he is a native of Tennessee and I found him with an Enfield rifle in hand, a Lincoln uniform on his back, orders in his pockets, and the proof was positive that he was in company when two Southern rights men were killed by Lincoln bands, and when a store was robbed. He was here (at Paintsville) with Nelson's command, vapering through these streets, conducting himself towards old, respectable, and defenseless females in the

---

[65] ibid, pg. 40.
[66] Ibid, pg. 41.

59

most brutal and insolent manner; in one instance making an old lady named Preston (the wife of a very respectable old man whom they bailed at $25,000) cook for a mess of Irish and Dutch soldiers for a whole week in her own house. I felt like having him shot but thought imprisonment was probably the best course to take with him."[67]

While at Paintsville on the 22nd of Dec., Gen. Marshall reported his strength as only about 1,100 men and four field pieces of Jeffress' battery, with another 400 mounted men then at Licking Station, 16 miles from Paintsville. His scouts reported the enemy's strength as 1,200 men at Catlettsburg, and 400 cavalry at Louisa. He also sent forward a mounted detachment from Paintsville as far as West Liberty, in Morgan County, and covered the march of 50 unarmed recruits to camp, collecting at the same time a drove of about 130 hogs, and making contracts for about 30,000 weight of bacon for the rebel command.[68]

Around this same time period, a man by the name of John Hagins, of Magoffin County, Kentucky was arrested in Montgomery County and charged with furnishing supplies of stock to the rebel army under General Williams. Hagins was taken by Federal authorities "while in transit with cattle for the rebels," and also that they have "plenty of evidence to hang him." He was taken to Fort Lafayette (in New York harbor) on the 20th of Dec., 1861.[69]

---

[67]ibid, pg. 41.

[68] ibid, pg. 42

[69]Ibid, Series 2, Vol. 2, pg.327. Hagins was released on parole Feb., 22, 1862.

No enemy troops had yet appeared to the rebels encamped in Paintsville by the 30th of Dec. when Gen. Marshall sent his last letter of the year to Adj. Gen. Cooper in Richmond. A false rumor of the enemy firing on Gen. William's pickets was the extent of the action as of that date. Since Gen. Marshall's letter outlining his charges against Col. Moore, the Colonel had actually arrived in camp with 450 men, passing the courier that was carrying Gen. Marshall's letter with the order of arrest to Gen. Cooper. Because Moore had shown up at last Marshall determined not to press the issue of his disobedience upon him; "better to make out with what I have than to commence with a court-martial." [70]

The last three or four days of December had seen recruits come in for the rebel army at the rate of 60 per day. The only problem was that there were no extra arms for the new recruits. With the addition of the new recruits, Gen. Williams command had now (Dec. 30th) increased to 1,000 men in the field. The formation of a new regiment had also begun. A new regiment could be formed in a short time unless it appeared there were no arms and ammunition to distribute. A few Belgian rifles, (caliber .69) had been sent from Governor Letcher of Virginia and issued to the men who were the best drilled, and who had old flint-lock muskets to place in other hands, but these were soon exhausted.[71]

A well-informed person had brought some information that three regiments from

---

[70] ibid, Series 1, Vol.7, pg. 42.
[71] ibid, pgs. 42, 43.

Ohio were seen passing Maysville, Ky. On the Ohio River, headed for the mouth of the Sandy, and three others were said to be coming from Wheeling or Pittsburg.

On this date Marshall estimated his forces as equal to 3,000 men. Say, Williams 1,000, Trigg, 550; Moore, 450; mounted battalion, 400; battery of four pieces, equal 600 men—total, 3,000.[72]

In his report of Dec. 30th Gen. Marshall identifies the man arrested near Louisa as a Dr. Chilton, whom he then had in custody in Pound Gap. He again alleges that the prisoner should have been shot instead of arrested, "for he is one of the worst men in the country and has been a scourge to our friends." He proposed to send all his prisoners to Pound Gap where the battalion stationed there can easily guard them, and the winds of the Cumberland Heights can properly ventilate them. He stated that he had a log house erected there for their especial accommodation. "Mr. Chilton is the only tenant as yet, although Mr. Diltz[73] would have been better there, I fear, than at large. One Mr. Filson (a deputy United States Marshal) ventured to Paintsville yesterday and I had him arrested last night but I have not seen him yet."[74]

The forces of General Marshall and Colonel Garfield were now in position to wage a battle for the right to control the destiny of the Big Sandy River valley and the road to the

---

[72] ibid, 42, 43.
[73] Marshall could have had Col. Dills of the U. S. 39th Ky. Volunteers in mind here.
[74] ibid, pg. 44.

mountain pass at Pound Gap. Both armies now had reasonably competent generals and near equal numbers of troops to allow either side the victory; with bravery, determination, audacity, and leadership abilities being the remaining unknown factors in the coming clash between the two untried and poorly trained armies. The skirmishes and battles still remaining to be fought in the mountains of Eastern Kentucky would be fought mostly between those men born and raised in those mountains. The fighting would sometimes invariably be between those friends and neighbors from the same or adjoining counties who held different political beliefs. After all, a lead bullet doesn't have eyes, and a soldier fighting for his life isn't bashful about killing someone who's trying to kill him. The coming battle, although not of the scale of many battles yet to be fought, would sorely test the resolve of both the Northern and Southern mountain bred soldiers to endure the trials of a soldier fighting for his beliefs and his home.

Chapter Seven

Action at Middle Creek

Being ever more an optimist, General Marshall, on Jan. 3rd, 1862, requested of Gen. Johnston to send him some blank commissions for magistrates, sheriffs, clerks, and county judges so that civic order could be reinstituted in the Johnson County town of Paintsville. Marshall also wanted a commission of circuit judge sent to Harvey Burns so that courts could be held at proper times. Marshall wanted the people to know that "they belong to the Southern Confederacy, and the State provisional government by its operations should be seen and not merely heard of."[75]

Gen. Marshall doubtless felt confident of his ability to hold the Big Sandy valley and the Pound Gap area at this stage in his plans. He had thus far successfully managed to assemble his troops in the very area from which the troops under General Williams had suffered a couple of setbacks in the skirmishes of Piketon

---

[75] ibid, Series 2, Vol. 2, pgs. 1410, 1411.

and Ivy Creek in early November past. The fact that his command had marched all the way to Paintsville without meeting the enemy was a good omen to this point, but the enemy wasn't about to give up Eastern Kentucky without a fight. Union forces were on the move and the next few days of the new year of 1862 would be critical for both antagonists.

In a letter to General A.S. Johnston on Jan. 3rd, 1862, General Marshall reported that the Federal force in front of him numbered 4,000 as nearly as he could ascertain it, and that he had had their encampments inspected. He stated that Garfield and Laban T. Moore's Kentucky Regiment had advanced to Sycamore Creek , which is only 7 miles from Paintsville. Having intrenched himself, Marshall decided not to await them in position because he had a heavy force approaching him on his eastern flank, consisting of Cranor's regiment, with 500 cavalry and a battery. Marshall gave his total strength on that date as:

Trigg's Reg., Fifty fourth Va., ...	669
Moore's Reg., Twenty-ninth Va.	330
William's Reg., Sixth (Fifth) Ky., ...	756
Simms mounted battalion	375
Worsham's co., (William's Reg.)......	50
Jeffress' battery	60

Total	2,240

Not all the men in the total number of troops were fit for duty; measles and mumps had played sad work among the men. The field report of yesterday, (January 2nd, 1862,) had shown non- commissioned officers and men present and fit for duty:

Trigg's Regiment..................578
William's Regiment.............594
Mounted battalion...............360
Jeffress' battery.....................58
Moore's Regiment.................327

                                  1,917
Add Worsham's co.   ------------
(at Prestonsburg)   50

                  Total   1,907

Marshall commented in his report of the 3rd of Jan. that this return was accurate as exhibiting the actual strength, but many of William's men were undrilled; some of the companies have been in camp for only a week.

The rebel pickets had already had a brush with McLaughlin's squadron of Ohio cavalry, Marshall reported. The skirmish had resulted in 5 horses, a sergeant, and three men being captured by the rebel pickets. "The Federals were well mounted and finely armed," said Marshall. They carried sabers and navy revolvers in their sword belts, and Sharp's breech-loading carbines, rifled. The arms and horses were given to some of the dismounted rebels of his cavalry battalion. The picket (of the Federals) consisted of about 30 men and the rebel party consisted of 25 men under Captain Thomas. Thomas cut off the pickets of the Federals and returned to camp for more force to take the whole party, but when he returned they were gone, leaving behind one or two dragoon hats and the horse of their guide. Marshall said that he had the prisoners in hand, and would send them to Pound Gap by the first opportunity.[76]

On Dec. 28th, Colonel Garfield had sent Col. Jonathan Cranor an order to advance his 40th Ohio Volunteers "with the greatest dispatch" toward Prestonsburg by the way of Hazel Green and Burning Spring, which was in the interior of the state. Garfield also ordered him to send a sufficiently strong force to protect his flank as his infantry marched toward Prestonsburg. If Marshall should hold his position near Paintsville, Col. Cranor's attack would come in on the rear of the rebels from the direction of Prestonsburg, while Garfield and his own command attacked the enemy from the Paintsville road. He hoped that Cranor could manage to reach Prestonsburg by Wednesday or Thursday, as he hoped to offer the rebel army battle by Thursday or Friday.[77]

On Friday, Jan. 3rd, the day Garfield had initially set for the attack on Marshall, a note from Garfield to Cranor assured him that from what he had learned about the condition of the country through Craner would have to pass, that he was quite sure that he couldn't be

---

[76] ibid, Series 1, Vol. 7, pgs. 45, 46.
[77] ibid, pg. 35.

more than half or two- thirds the distance of Prestonsburg.[78]

Garfield informed Cranor that the main body of the enemy was still camped on Hagar's farm, about three miles from Paintsville on the road leading to Prestonsburg. He also had a force of 300 to 400 cavalry encamped at the mouth of Jennie's Creek, two miles above Paintsville, on Paint Creek. He informed Cranor of a rumor of re-enforcements coming in from Virginia by way of Piketon for the rebels. He expected to be at the mouth of Jennie's Creek by Monday night. (Jan. 6th) [79]

On Sunday, Jan. 5th, Garfield reported to Brig. Gen. Cox, Commanding Division of Kanawha, that he was now within 5 miles of Paintsville. The main force of the enemy was entrenched on two hills, 3 miles back of the town, on the road to Prestonsburg. Five hundred of the enemy's cavalry were encamped at the mouth of Jennie's Creek, (where Garfield had hoped to be by this time), 2 miles west of Paintsville. The scouts of both sides were engaged in skirmishing daily. Garfield had but 1,300 men with him but expected 500 of the Twenty- second Kentucky to reach him in a few days. Colonel Bolles, of Gen. Cox's department, with 500 cavalry, was also expected to join him. [80]

It had taken Colonel Garfield nearly two days to get his train 3 miles over the mountains to Camp Pardee, which was within 5 miles of Paintsville. He reported his command as

---

[78] ibid, pg. 36
[79] ibid.
[80] ibid, pg. 37

having two slight skirmishes with the enemy within the last twenty four hours. He had some reason to believe that (Col. A.G.) Jenkins had now joined the rebel force with 400 of his men.[81]

Gen. Garfield was exceedingly anxious to reach the river where he could receive his stores by boat. He also wanted to occupy the mouth of Jennie's Creek. He planned to move forward on the 6th, and if Colonel Bolles cavalry should reach him he expected to accomplish both these goals soon.[82]

On Monday, Jan, 6th, Gen. Garfield moved his command to the mouth of Muddy Branch. That same evening the rebel forces came down off his entrenched hill, with one 12 pounder and two regiments of infantry, and occupied the southern bank of Paint Creek. As Garfield advanced his whole column, Marshall immediately broke up his camp, burned many of his wagons, and a large amount of corn, oats, meal, sugar, rice, and other provisions, and during the night of January 5 and all of the following day he was hurrying his trains and infantry away in retreat. His cavalry covered the retreat and put up a show of resistance while the rest of his forces pulled back. Colonel Bolles and 300 of his Second Virginia (U.S.) Cavalry having joined Garfield that same day at noon, moved forward along with the Forty-second Ohio and the Fourteenth Kentucky Inf., and occupied the town of Paintsville.[83]

---

[81] ibid.
[82] ibid.
[83] ibid, pgs. 27, 28.

69

Garfield then on the 7th sent Bolles and his 300 cavalry to attack and drive back the rebels at Jennie's Creek while Garfield himself advanced with 1,000 men to attack General Marshall's position. The Federals were slowed by the fact that they had to build a pontoon bridge across Paint Creek; therefore it was sunset before they were in motion. They found the rebel campfires still burning and the whole camp showed signs of panic and disorderly retreat. The Federals then marched down to Jennie's Creek to aid Bolles in his attack, but he had already attacked and routed the enemy. Bolles' advance of 60 men had attacked 200 rebel cavalry, killed 6, wounded several, and scattered them among the hills. Col. Bolles had 2 killed and I wounded. [84]

The 15 rebel prisoners captured in the fight at Jennie's Creek were sent to Newport Barracks in Northern Kentucky. The vicinity of the rebel camps presented a scene of utter desolation after the battle. An immense amount of property was also destroyed before their retreat. The fear of the Federal commander was that they would not be able to catch the enemy in a "stern chase". Garfield decided to fore-go taking artillery on the chase, since the enemy had left his stronghold.[85]

The report of General Marshall on the collision with Garfield's forces was more subdued than that of the Federal commander. He described how the force in his front (Garfield) advanced to his front and upon his left flank, at Paintsville, in Johnson County.

---

[84] ibid, pg. 28.
[85] ibid.

The Federals had advanced to the mouth of Sycamore Creek, five miles from the rebel position at Paintsville, and remained in camp there several days. Marshall reported their force as 4,000 men strong. He said that the Cincinnati Enquirer of Dec. 28 had reported the Union forces as five full regiments of infantry, 200 cavalry, and two batteries of field artillery, the whole under command of Colonel Garfield of Ohio, acting as chief of brigade. [86]

It was his purpose, Marshall said, to wait the attack of his force at Hager's farm, near Paintsville, but he had intercepted a letter from Colonel Garfield addressed to Col. Cranor, that the latter, with a cavalry force of 400 to 500 was advancing from West Liberty upon Prestonsburg. His scouts having reported this force as 1,300 at Salyersville, upon his left, he presumed that the enemy was to mass in his rear while attacking with superior force in his front. He had hoped to intercept Col. Cranor and fight him before his arrival at the post he hoped to occupy, but he had found the roads impassable. On Jan 9th he had sent a detachment to the mill, one mile below Prestonsburg, to which he was compelled to withdraw, (to make bread for his men,) but the enemy drove them away during the night.[87]

On Jan. 8th, Colonel Garfield began his preparations to pursue the rebel force. The transportation of his stores from George's Creek had been met with so much difficulty that not enough provisions were available to supply his command with three days rations

---

[86] ibid pg. 46.
[87] ibid pgs. 46, 47.

before starting after the enemy. Finally one small boat had arrived from below but it carried only enough rations of hard bread for three days for 1,500 men. He issued that amount, then sent 450 of Colonel Wolford's and Major McLaughlin's cavalry, under command of Lieutenant-Colonel Letcher, to advance up Jennie's Creek, and harass the enemy's rear. At the same time he took 1,100 of the best men from the Fortieth and Forty-second Ohio and the Fourteenth and Twenty-second Kentucky, and at noon started up the Big Sandy towards Prestonsburg. After ten miles the rebel pickets fired on the head of the column, then retreated.[88]

At 8 o'clock on the 9th of Jan., the Federal column reached the mouth of Abbott's Creek, one mile below Prestonsburg. Garfield found that the enemy was encamped only three miles above, on Middle Creek. He sent back to Paintsville an order to move up his whole force to Prestonsburg. His troops camped that evening on the crest of a wooded hill where they had to sleep in the rain under arms, until 4 o'clock in the morning, when the whole force moved up Abbott's Creek one mile and crossed over to the mouth of Middle Creek, which empties into the Big Sandy opposite Prestonsburg. Garfield supposed that the rebels were encamped on Abbott's Creek and his intension was to advance up Middle Creek and cut off their retreat. [89]

Advancing slowly, and throwing out flankers, they reached the mouth of Middle

---

[88] ibid, pg. 30
[89] ibid

72

Creek at 8 o'clock in the morning, where they found the rebel cavalry waiting for them. A brisk skirmishing between the two parties began and continued as they advanced up the creek for 2½ miles up the stream, to within 1,000 yards of where the rebel troops were then occupying.[90]

Marshall had posted Captain Jeffress' battery of two pieces, a smoothbore six pounder and a 12 pounder howitzer, in the gorge at the mouth of the Left Fork of Middle Creek. William's Fifth Kentucky, Col. Moore's Twenty-ninth Virginia, and part of Simm's mounted battalion, fighting on foot, occupied the spurs and heights of the surrounding hills on the rebel right; Trigg's Fifty-fourth Virginia Regiment occupied the height covering the battery of two guns; Witcher's and Holliday's companies were in reserve covering the batteries; Thomas and Clay's companies were dismounted and armed with Belgian rifles; and thrown forward on the opposite side of Middle Creek to the heights commanding the main plain of Middle Creek. These last companies were also to resist any advance of skirmishers from the opposite heights.[91]

As the Federal forces advanced up Middle Creek, Garfield sent forward 20 mounted men to dash across the plain to make a demonstration so as to disclose the position of the rebels. This ruse succeeded when a few shots from the surrounding hills disclosed the rebel positions behind the farther point of the

---

[90] ibid.
[91] ibid, pg.47

very ridge the Federals had occupied that morning.

Colonel Trigg's 54th Va. Reg. occupied the ridge where the fire had come from, along with the dismounted companies of Captains Clay and Thomas, who were aligned where they could observe the plain of main Middle Creek. This position would also allow those companies to resist the advance of Federal skirmishers from the opposite heights. [92]

With part of the rebel position now exposed, Garfield immediately sent forward two Kentucky companies to pass along the crest of the ridge to their right where Trigg's force and the two dismounted companies were positioned. At the same time, one company of the Forty-second Ohio, under command of Capt. F. A. Williams, together with one under Capt. Jones, Fortieth Ohio, was ordered to cross the creek, which was nearly waist deep here, and occupy a spur of the high rocky ridge in front and to the left (east) of the Federals. As these companies advanced, the two cannon of Captain Jeffress' opened fire on them with their aim being so accurate that one shell dropped right into the midst of the Federal skirmishers who were advancing on the right. Unfortunately, for the Confederates, that shell failed to explode, as did most, if not all of the shots from the rebel battery.[93] (The fuses were most likely the cause of the failures, as the rebel artillery had major problems with non-exploding missiles throughout the early years of the war.)

---

[92] ibid, pg. 30, 47.
[93] ibid, 30.

74

Soon after the opening of the rebel battery, the U.S. detachments sent to the left engaged the rebels lying in wait on the rocky ridge. These were the forces of Col. William's 5th Kentucky Reg., Moore's 29th Va., and some dismounted cavalry, who were fighting on foot.

As the volleys rolled throughout the surrounding hills, and the fighting intensified, Garfield sent forward a re-enforcement of two companies to the right, under Major Burke, of the Fourteenth Kentucky, and 90 men, under Major Pardee, of the Forty- second Ohio, to support Capt. William's Ohio troopers.[94]

At this point in the fighting the regiments of Williams and Moore were being pressed by the Federals, causing Gen. Marshall to send the 54th Va. across as re-enforcements to Williams and Moore. The fighting became general all along the line with neither side able to gain the upper hand.

The fighting had been raging for two hours, when at 2 o'clock Garfield ordered Col. Cranor, with 150 men from the Fortieth and Forty-second Ohio and Twenty-second Ky., to advance and re-enforce Major Pardee on the right. While all this was happening, a very heavy fire was coming from the ridge where Col. William's and Col. Moore's regiments were posted, and who were engaged in firing on Garfield's reserve, causing some alarm. [95]

Fearing the rebels would outflank him, Garfield sent Lieutenant-Colonel Monroe, of the Twenty-second Kentucky, with 120 of his own and the Fourteenth Regiment, to cross the

[94] ibid
[95] ibid.

75

creek below the point Garfield then occupied, and drive back the enemy from his position. This he did, with Garfield reporting afterwards that 15 or 20 rebels were killed by Monroe's attack.[96]

Gen. Marshall asserted that the cavalry of the Federal forces advanced only at the beginning of the battle and did not make its appearance again. He said he plainly heard the command to "force the cavalry forward," but no cavalry appeared again during the battle. The Federals charged up the points above the mouth of Spurlock's Branch three times but were repulsed with great loss. [97]

Several hours into the fight, Marshall shifted his smoothbore 6-pounder to the summit of the hill first occupied by Trigg's regiment, and obtained a flank fire on the enemy, while occupying a piney point in front of Moore's 29th Virginia. The fire of this gun, whether that fire was effective or not, soon attracted a hot fire directed at the gun but caused no damage except the killing of one artillery horse, shot through the head. [98]

At 4 o'clock in the evening the battle had been raging for four hours when the re-enforcements called for by Col. Garfield came in sight. These re-enforcements were under the command of Lieutenant Sheldon of the Forty-second Ohio. This enabled Garfield to send the remainder of his reserve, under Lieutenant-Colonel Brown, to pass around the right and attempt to capture the rebel battery, which

---

[96] ibid, pg. 31
[97] ibid, pg. 47.
[98] ibid.

Garfield asserted had been firing against the Federal forces for three hours, but without effect. During the fight the rebel battery had fired 30 rounds from his cannon, but they were badly served, as only one of his shells exploded, and none of his shot, and none of his canister rounds taking effect.

At 4:30 Marshall began withdrawing from the battleground. Garfield contended that he had actually driven the rebels from every point by 5 o'clock that evening. Many of the Federals had fired 30 rounds during the fight. As the fighting ceased and as the rebels withdrew, the Federals noticed a "brilliant light" which streamed up from the valley to which the rebels had retreated. He (Marshall) was burning his stores and "fleeing in great disorder." [99]

Garfield reported that twenty five of the enemy dead were left on the field, and 60 more were found the next day thrown into a gorge in the hills. A field officer and 2 captains were found among the dead. Garfield reported his own loss at one killed and 20 wounded, 2 of which were mortally wounded. He claimed 25 prisoners, among whom was a rebel captain. No more than 900 Federals were engaged while he asserted the enemy had not less than 3,500 men. Garfield now conceded that a few howitzers would have made a difference in the battle if he hadn't left them behind. [100]

General Marshall contended that Garfield had withdrawn his force at dark and retired down Middle Creek, on the route to

---

[99] ibid, pg. 31.
[100] ibid.

Prestonsburg, whence, the next day, he retraced his steps to Paintsville. Marshall listed his own loss as 11 killed and 15 wounded. He supposed the enemy loss to be 250 killed and about 300 wounded! He stated that the rebels had seen his dead borne in numbers from the field. "The field itself bears unerring testimony to his severe loss."[101]

The battle of Middle Creek was over. Both sides had stood the test of mortal combat and had come through it still determined to hold to their beliefs. If anything, this action stiffened the resolve of most of the combatants that they could stand up to an enemy and not lose face. They had proved that mountain boys of both armies, from Kentucky, Virginia and Ohio, could fight as well as any other American soldier. There were still more than three years of fighting awaiting them and more killing and dying to do, but for now each side had met the enemy in something more than a skirmish and had fought them to a draw.

---

[101] ibid, pgs. 49,50

[Inclosures.]

Sketch of Battle of Middle Creek
Official Records, Series 1, Vol.7, Pg.51

Chapter Eight

Withdrawal

The Federal forces entered and occupied Prestonsburg on Jan. 11th, the day after the fight at Middle Creek. They found the town almost deserted. They took several horses, some 18 boxes of quartermaster's stores, and 25 flint-lock muskets. The whole community in the vicinity of Prestonsburg had been stripped of everything in the way of supplies for an army. Finding that there was not enough forage for their horses for more than one day, the cavalry and their horses were sent back to Paintsville. Having ordered the first boat to reach Paintsville to hurry on up the river to Prestonsburg, Garfield found that it would be impossible to bring up his tents and supplies until more provisions could be brought up the river. Therefore he abandoned Prestonsburg and retreated to Paintsville; taking the better part of the 12th and 13th in taking his sick, injured, and foot-sore men back on boats.

The tired soldiers were greatly in need of rest and good care after their engagement of the 10th.[102]

At best, both sides had battled to a draw at Middle Creek, but Garfield felt emboldened enough to issue the following proclamation to the population of the Sandy Valley:

Headquarters Eighteenth Brigade
Paintsville, Ky. January 16, 1862

Citizens of the Sandy Valley:
I have come among you to restore the honor of the Union, and to bring back the old banner which you all once loved, but which by the machinations of evil men and by mutual misunderstandings has been dishonored among you. To those who are in arms against the Federal Government I offer only the alternative of battle or unconditional surrender. But to those who have taken no part in this war, who are in no way aiding or abetting the enemies of the Union- even to those who hold sentiments averse to the Union, but yet give no aid and comfort to its enemies-I offer the full protection of the Government, both in their persons and property.

Let those who have been seduced away from the love of their country to follow after and aid the destroyers of our peace lay down their arms, return to their homes, bear true allegiance to the Federal Government, and they shall also enjoy like protection. The Army of the Union wages no war of plunder, but comes to bring back the prosperity of peace. Let all

---

[102] <u>War of the Rebellion</u>, Series 1, Vol. 7, pg. 31.

peace- loving citizens who have fled from their homes return and resume again the pursuits of peace and industry. If citizens have suffered from any outrages by the soldiers under my command I invite them to make known their complaints to me, and their wrongs shall be redressed and the offenders punished. I expect the friends of the Union in this valley to banish from among them all private feuds, and let a liberal-minded love of country direct their conduct towards those who have been so sadly estranged and misguided. Hoping that these days of turbulence may soon be ended and the better days of the Republic soon return, I am, very respectfully,

J.A. Garfield

Colonel, Commanding Brigade[103]

In a report to Brig. Gen. Buell on Jan. 17, Col. Garfield reported the Fortieth and Forty-second Ohio to be in good condition after the battle, "considering the hard service they have rendered", although the Fourteenth Kentucky was "in a wretched state of discipline, but composed of excellent material. Very few of its members have been drilled in the school of the soldier and the regiment can be considered little better than a well-disposed Union-loving mob which, if its scattered fragments can be gathered up, may well be converted into a serviceable regiment." [104]

Garfield reported that three companies (200 men) of the Twenty-second Kentucky had arrived just in time to aid him at the late

---

[103] ibid, pg. 33.
[104] ibid, pg. 32

battle, with the remnant, about the same number, having been left at Louisa to guard stores. They seemed to be in a tolerably good state of condition. The six companies, (300) of the First Kentucky Cavalry, under Lieutenant-Colonel Letcher, had been hard worked, and had reported 207 men as sick. [105]

The upper part of the Sandy Valley was reported as almost deserted, as the expedition of General Nelson, followed by Marshall's intrusion, had swept away everything on which an army could subsist. Indeed, Marshall's army had come from Pound Gap to the Sandy Valley by way of the Kentucky River, because they could find neither food nor forage between Piketon and Prestonsburg. [106]

Garfield learned from prisoners that Marshall had retreated to the Forks of Beaver Creek (Martin's Mill, today known as Martin) and seemed to be on his way towards the valley of the Kentucky River, either to winter or to join Confederate forces at Cumberland Gap. The prisoners informed the Federals that Marshall definitely intended to winter at Whitesburg, in Letcher County.[107]

General Marshall had in fact retreated to Martin's Mill, arriving there the day after the Mill Creek fight. He headed there, he said, in order to get bread for his men, " some of whom had had nothing to eat for thirty hours."He felt that the Confederate government ought to either provide him with a much greater force or

---

[105] ibid, pg. 32.
[106] ibid.
[107] ibid, pg. 33.

that it should be withdrawn from the Sandy River Valley altogether.

He called attention to the fact that the Sandy River traverses from Piketon to its mouth at Catlettsburg, Ky., about 100 miles, all of which is navigable by small steamers at high stages of water, and is navigable to Louisa at nearly all stages of water, and nearly at all seasons of the water. This long line of sandy required a corps d'armée, simply because you must have a force sufficient to hold the point of the Sandy's confluence with the Ohio or the enemy could use the water transportation for his troops to land them (with) in a few miles of your position fresh and ready for action. [108]

General Marshall was bitter about the lack of cooperation and help he had received thus far from the local citizens of Eastern Kentucky and he had no hesitation in expressing his disappointment in a letter to an unnamed general while at Martin's Mill on Jan. 14,1862. In his letter he said that his troops had been subsisting by going to the fields, shucking the corn, shelling it, taking it to the mill, grinding the meal, and then taking it to camp. "The people of the country will consent to do nothing, he complained. They will not assist to gather the corn nor to shell it, nor will they let us have the use of their horses, or anything that is theirs---nothing, either for love or money. They will not enter the army on either side, and seem to be actually terror-stricken. I have tried to shame them into a sense of what was due to

---

[108] ibid, pg. 48.

84

themselves and their families, but it is of no use."[109]

Not only was Gen. Marshall having difficulty recruiting in Kentucky, but one of the regiments he already had in his brigade was trying to get away from Marshall's command. On Jan. 9th, just before meeting the Federals in battle at Middle Creek, the following letter was written to Marshall by some of the officers of Col. Trigg's 54th Virginia Infantry Regiment.

Camp at Middle Creek, Ky., Jan., 1862:

As officers of your brigade, who have willingly rendered the promptest obedience to your orders, in no manner desiring to dictate to you as our superior officer, but feeling, with you, the deepest interest in the success of your command, we nevertheless feel constrained to make known to you, in the most respectful manner, our views and wishes, and solicit your earnest attention to them. We started from Virginia with but part of our men, leaving more than 200 sick, and since the first day's march we have left all along the way our sick and disabled soldiers. The men now doing duty-- and doing it without a murmur—have been necessarily subjected to hardships, exposure, and the deprivation of regular and adequate supplies of food, which are every day exhausting their energies and breaking down their health. Besides the ordinary inflammatory diseases incident to a winter campaign, fully one-half our men have been for more than a week suffering from dysentery and diarrhea.

---

[109] ibid, pgs. 48, 49.

These men are first-rate soldiers, whose term of enlistment does not expire until next fall, and whose strength and energies should be preserved for the more active and efficient duties of the coming summer and fall; but we feel much more interested in the preservation of their health as our neighbors and friends who have at our solicitation entered into the service, and whose friends and families look to us for their safety and preservation. While we would be willing to make any sacrifice to advance our cause, we feel satisfied that we can accomplish no good result this winter. The people among whom we have come have not appreciated our cause to the extent of quitting their homes to unite with us., and we are now in midwinter, in a country poorly provided with the means of subsistence, exposed to an enemy more than double or treble our number, with roads which, if not now entirely impassible, must shortly become blocked up with snow and ice. This condition of things must necessarily increase the exposure of our men and render their supplies of food more uncertain, and thus every day aggravate the causes which are now wasting their energies and strength.

We do therefore most earnestly and respectfully solicit you to order our regiment to such point that we can go into winter quarters without the apprehension of being harassed by our enemies; where supplies can be procured and conveyed without the chance of failure, and the health and lives of our men can be preserved and protected.

With due deference to your judgment, we suggest some point in Virginia or

Tennessee, contiguous to a line of railroad, where we can, during the winter, be subject to your orders, and from which we can move out in the spring strong, healthy, and able to do efficient service in the cause we all have so much at heart.

Most respectfully submitted,

Burwell Akers	W. J. Jordan
Capt, Co. I	Capt. Co F
George H. Turman	A. Dickerson
Capt. Co. G	Capt. Co. A
Jackson Godby	H. Slusher
Capt. Co. B	Capt. Co. D
Jno. J. Wade	Jas. C. Taylor
Capt. Co. E	Capt. Co. C
Jno. S. Deyerle	S. H. Griffith
Capt. Co. K	Capt. Co. H

Brig. Gen. Humphrey Marshall
Commanding First Brigade,
Army of Eastern Kentucky. [110]

This missive was an extraordinarily unusual and even unprecedented request for a transfer out of the combat zone in wartime by a unit of an army that was on the very eve of an important battle that could possible settle the fate of Eastern Kentucky. This was a clear case of insubordination and bordered on mutiny. In almost any other organized army then, and today, a similar letter would have likely resulted in court-martial charges being brought against the company officers, and if found

---

[110] ibid, pg. 52

guilty, result in imprisonment or dismissal of some or all officers involved.

Having said all that; it must be remembered that the Confederate Army was no ordinary army but was mostly made up of volunteers at this early point in the war. Most of the men and officers were from the same district or county, and often from the same neighborhood. Many times regiments were raised with the verbal promise, (such as the 21st Virginia Battalion at Pound Gap,) to soldier only in their home counties in their area of the state.

When considering these circumstances, it's not at all surprising to realize that these organizations of troops, which had elected their officers upon mustering into the army, to have those officers to argue for their wishes, just like any good elected politician would do. The leaders and commanders of both the Confederate and Union Armies were aware of limitations of such a hastily organized and largely untrained citizen-army and no doubt made allowances for it.

General Marshall's only reaction to the letter was written by him while at Martin's Mill, when he commented that if the Fifty-fourth Va. was granted its wish for transfer, the First Ky. Regiment, (then in Virginia), might be sent to its own state, to replace the Fifty-forth. In that, he showed some understanding, as well as some sympathy for their concerns.[111]

While Marshall's force was encamped at Martin's Mill, Col. Garfield received from Gen. Buell's Assistant Adj. Gen., O.D. Green, at

---

[111] ibid, pg. 49.

Louisville, Ky., a letter that expressed gratification and thanks for him and his command for the campaign in which they were engaged. Since it wasn't clear what Gen. Marshall's intentions were, General Buell had no definite instructions for how to proceed with the campaign. As Marshall may have gone into Western Virginia, or have taken the road from Prestonsburg or Piketon to Hazard in Perry County or Whitesburg in Letcher County, Buell directed Garfield to drive the enemy from the soil of Kentucky, and having done this, to act as circumstances may require. On this date, Colonel(Charles A.) Marshall's Sixteenth Ky. Volunteers, from Mayville Ky., was assigned to Garfield's command.[112]

On the same date as the previous letter, Col. Garfield received *General Orders # 4a* from Asst. Adj. Gen. James B. Fry, to officially thank Garfield and his command for "having driven the enemy from his entrenched position and forcing him back into the mountains with the loss of a large amount of baggage and stores and many of his men killed or captured."[113]

On Jan. 24th, Garfield ordered Lieut. Col. J.R. Brown and 130 men of the 14th Kentucky regiment to proceed the next morning to the cliffs of Little Sandy to capture or disperse a body of the enemy who were committing depredations upon the property of citizens. He was also empowered to arrest and bring in to headquarters all persons who are aiding or abetting the rebellion. They were to

---

[112]ibid, pg. 23
[113] ibid, Pg. 24.

89

take three days cooked rations and 30 rounds of ammunition with them also.[114]

Near the end of Jan., Garfield sent a detachment of 110 men to Piketon, who had a skirmish with a marauding band and captured several leading and active rebels, who were sent to Newport Barracks. In the pursuit, Judge Cecil, of Piketon, and a Dr. Emmet was severely wounded.[115]

The following incident illustrates how the rebels might have been uniformed in most skirmishes in Eastern Kentucky:

Following the skirmish at Jennie's Creek, in Johnson Co., in 1861, a detachment from the 1st Kentucky Cavalry was ordered to pursue the retreating Confederates. They captured a number of prisoners who showed surprising little fight and who turned out to be Union sympathizers. The prisoners were described as a motley body of men, dressed in variegated fashions, with 'bee-gum' hats, homespun pigeon-tail coats, red sleeve jackets, and hunting shirts. [116]

---

[114] ibid, pg. 39.
[115] ibid, pg. 34.
[116] E. Tarrent, The Wild Riders of the First Kentucky Cavalry (Louisville: A committee of the regiment, 1894) pg. 73, , Richard Francis, Mountain Men of the Confederacy, 1973.

Chapter Nine

Retreat to Letcher County

Many years before the War Between the States, the pathway that became known as Pound or Sounding Gap was a major route across the Cumberland Mountains for migrating animals searching for provender or for a warmer climate. What started out as a mere path at first eventually became tramped down smoother and wider as herds of deer, elk, bison, and other animals trekked up the Pine Mountain narrow opening and into what would in the future become Virginia on the southeast side of the mountain and Kentucky on the northwest.

After another unknown number of years had passed, the first Native American hunters naturally followed this same trail across the mountain to hunt these same animals for food. With all this animal and human traffic tramping through the Gap, a tolerable road soon existed for the first European to explore the area around the Gap and to make the existence of the Gap known to the rest of the civilized world.

The first known European to traverse the storied Cumberland Mountain pass was Christopher Gist, who was one of America's first explorers of the country west of the Alleghany Mountains. He was a surveyor, the son of Richard and Zipporah (Murray) Gist, and was a native of Maryland. Gist was a scholarly professional whose signature, journals, and maps indicated that he enjoyed an education superior to many of his peers of that day. [117]

The Ohio Land Company was organized in 1748 by leading capitalists and public men of England and Virginia whom had received a land grant from the King of England, and they in turn hired Christopher Gist (who came out of retirement in his Yadkin North Carolina home) to explore the their territory and to locate their lands.[118]

The following are the instructions given to Gist by the Committee of the Ohio Company on the 11th day of September, 1750, (in part) :

You are to go out as soon as possible to the westward of the great Mountains, and carry with you such a Number of Man as You think necessary, in Order to Search out and discover the Lands upon the river Ohio, &

---

[117]   J. Stoddard Johnson, First Explorations of Kentucky, page 85, Louisville, Ky., John P. Morton and Company, Printers to the Filson Club, 1898

[118] ibid, pg. 86

other adjoining Branches of the Mississippi down as low as the great Falls thereof: You are particularly to observe the Ways & Passes thro all the Mountains you cross, & take an exact Account of the Soil, Quality & Product of the Land, and the Wideness and Deepness of the Rivers, & the several Falls belonging to them, together with the Courses & Bearings of the Rivers & Mountains as near as you conveniently can: You are also to observe what Nations of Indians inhabit there, their Strength & Numbers, who they trade with, & in what commodities they deal, etc, etc............. You are to draw as good a plan as you can of the Country You pass thro: You are to take an exact and particular Journal of all Your Proceedings, and make a true report thereof to the Ohio Company.[119]

Gist set out on his exploratory trip in Oct., 1750. After exploring through several states, he eventually (it is believed) passed along the river known today as Red River, then up the North Fork of the Kentucky River, to today's Letcher County. On April 1st, 1750, Gist made this entry in his journal:

Monday April 1.---Set out the same Course about 20 M. (miles) Part of the Way we went along a Path up the Side of a little Creek, at the head of which was a Gap in the Mountains, then our path went down another Creek to a Lick where Blocks of Coal about 8 to 10 In: square lay upon the Surface of the

---

[119] ibid, pgs. 101, 102, 103.

Ground, here we killed a Bear and encamped.[120]

This entry in Gist's journal details his trek up to the head of the North Fork of the Kentucky River, then on up the mountain and through the pass known today as Pound Gap. This then is the area General Marshall decided to head to after the Battle of Middle Creek, and after he had stopped for a few days at Martin's Mill in Floyd County, Kentucky, to gather corn and grind into meal for his starving army.

While still encamped at Martin's Mill, Marshall on Jan. 20th, 1862, wrote a letter to Adj.. Gen. S. Cooper asking for 1,500 cavalry and a good artillery company, adding, "I have the guns at Pound Gap,") telling Cooper in the letter that he felt confident that the reinforcements would allow him to invade the Bluegrass country around Lexington. He added his opinion to the request, saying that "it (the advance) will result in great good to the general cause, even if I have to retreat from the country afterwards."[121]

On Jan. 19th, a Captain Stratton came to Martin's Mill from Virginia with himself, a first and third lieutenant, four corporals, and 15 privates, being part of a mounted company raised in Virginia for Marshall's command. He stated that his other lieutenant, sergeants, and some 25 men were on the way; that his company was completely formed, but didn't know when they could get out, as those he had were fired upon in Logan County, Va., (today

---

[120] ibid, 155l

[121] War of the Rebellion, Series 1, Vol.7, pg. 54

94

West Virginia) coming out. They proposed to enlist for three years or the war if they could get out. Marshall accepted the Captain and his company and administered the oath after "ministering the usual medical examination."[122]

Edward Pollard, editor of the Richmond, Virginia Examiner, didn't think very much of mountain recruits or mountain people in general. During the Civil War Pollard reportedly said that the mountains were "inhabited by an ignorant and uncouth population squatted among the hills." [123]

A short time after writing his Jan. 20th letter to Gen. Cooper in Richmond, the rebels encamped in Martin's Mill in Floyd County stuffed their meager belongings into their blanket rolls and knapsacks and headed into Letcher County. The route the rebels took back to Letcher County is uncertain but we do know that going up Beaver Creek was an option and their encampment at Martin's Mill was on Beaver Creek. This was the most likely route for at least some of his command.

From a letter written on Jan. 23rd, with the heading of; *Camp in Letcher County, Ky.*, General Marshall wrote Gen. A. Sidney Johnston at Bowling Green, Ky., and gave him the details of his Middle Creek fight. He wildly over estimated the Federal loss in the battle in this letter as over 200 killed and more than that wounded. Garfield's official report listed 1

---

[122] ibid.

[123] Edward A. Pollard, The First Year of the War, Richmond: West and Johnson, 1862, pg. 197, John K. Ward.--- Richard Francis, Mountain Men of the Confederacy, 1973

killed, 20 wounded, and 2 mortally wounded. The truth was probably somewhere in the middle of both reports.[124]

Marshall went on in his letter to ask himself a rhetorical question about the battle; Why did I not pursue if I thought I had the victory? My reasons are simple and straightforward:

First. I could not renew the engagement that night because it was too dark, had I been so inclined. I did not know how far the enemy had gone, and would not have followed under any circumstances with the inferior force.

Second. I did not follow because my men were exhausted from hunger, having had nothing to eat all that day, and they were weak, and would not have been capable of service another day without food.

Third. I did not follow because I did not know the strength of the enemy in reserve, and had no idea of risking by rashness what my troops had gained by gallantry. I had fought superior numbers with the advantage of position on my side; I had no intent to renew the engagement, giving superior numbers the advantage of choice of the ground.

But, general, the controlling, present, and moving reason was that my men had nothing to eat, and I could not tell that they could obtain it by returning with a fight against heavy odds between us and our chance of food. By sending horses forward to Martin's Mill, on Beaver (Creek), I procured meal and brought it back to my troops, who were engaged in crossing my train over the mountains dividing

---

[124] <u>War of the Rebellion</u>, Ser.1, Vol. 7, pg. 55.

Middle Creek from Beaver Creek. "The fact is I could not pursue the enemy, and the enemy, being already repulsed, never had any idea of pursing me."[125]

Marshall had only been in Whitesburg a few days when he received he received an order from Gen. S, Cooper, written on the 24th to: "Fall back to Pound Gap and report dispositions there made. Letter will go by Captain Wade." Marshall received this letter on the26th of January by courier.[126]

On Jan. 27th, Gen. Marshall replied from Whitesburg in Letcher County to Cooper's letter of the 24th:

General: I have to state that my infantry regiments are within twelve miles of the village of Whitesburg, on Rockhouse Creek and Carr's Fork of the Kentucky River, and the battalion of cavalry now under command of Lieutenant-Colonel Simms is in the vicinity. All the sick are gathered in the neighborhood, and they amount to more than 300, and are doing well, considering their late exposure to rain and cold. I think it will be best to keep them under shelter until the measles and mumps have run their course. Your order is to fall back to Pound Gap. I suppose my present position to be a substantial compliance, as there is no food for man or horse nearer to Pound Gap than my present position. Major Thompson, whose battalion occupies the gap itself, informs me that he draws all his supplies some 18 miles. I have now occupied Brashearsville without opposition. The whole country is dependent on

_____

125 ibid, pgs.56, 57.
126 ibid, pg. 58.

97

the salt wells at this place for salt. The Lincolnites had disturbed the manufacture, but now the manufacturing has commenced again. They can make forty bushels a day. I have here some 400 hogs to slaughter so soon as I have the salt made. There are salt wells at Whitesburg where ten bushels per day can be made. I mention these facts because they are of military importance as connected with subsistence. .... The snow is on the ground now about three to four inches deep. My men must now suffer gathering and shucking corn in the fields. They have no gloves and few blankets or overcoats.

I forward herewith the resignation of Major Richard Hawes as commissary of brigade, which I recommend for your acceptance. Now I have neither commissary nor quartermaster of brigade. .... The enemy has never advanced beyond Paintsville.

> H. Marshall,
> Brigadier General

[First endorsement]
Respectfully submitted to Secretary of War.

> S. Cooper
> Adjutant and Inspector General

[Second endorsement]
Send an officer, (commissary) to General Marshall and send some blankets for his troops, and inform Adjutant General what quantity is wanted.

> J. P. Benjamin

[Third endorsement]

Quartermaster General's Office,
Feb. 6, 1862,
Fifteen hundred great coats, 1,500 blankets, 1,500 pairs shoes have been sent to General Marshall.
Respectfully,
A.C. Myers,
Quartermaster- General[127]

On Feb.1st, Gen. received the order to fall back to Pound Gap from the courier that had been sent from Richmond, Va., the same day the telegraphed message was sent to "fall back to Pound Gap." The courier was a secondary way to ensure Marshall received the message in case the first message was delayed.

Marshall replied to Gen. Cooper on 2nd Feb., from Craft's,[128] to say that he was extremely embarrassed by the order to fall back to Pound Gap. He stated that the subsistence of the country about Pound Gap for 20 miles was literally exhausted. "The supplies for the rifle battalion now at Pound Gap are drawn with great difficulty over that distance (55 miles) and much complaint of the precariousness of the supply. Nor can I halt within 20 miles of Pound Gap on this side of the mountains with any chance of obtaining food for man or horse.

You can have no conception of the state of affairs here, general; starvation stares these

---

[127] ibid, Series 1, Vol. 52, pgs. 259, 260.
[128] Mr. Craft was probably living around Millstone, Kentucky, which is approx. six miles from the Gap.

people in the face. They are most adverse to parting with a peck of corn or a pound of meat, and daily the women beg for the retention of the means of sustaining themselves and their children. It is no sham or affected apprehension they feel; I much fear they only see what spring-time will startlingly reveal as a stern reality. It cannot advance our cause or make converts to it to starve the best friends we have in this population, and in this county we have many, indeed a considerable majority of the people.

I have reflected upon my duty under your order, especially in view of the reason given for its issuance; and the disposition I shall make of the force will be to pass the mountains and to arrange the regiments as near as they can be to Pound Gap, so as to obtain supplies. ....

Marshall learned from the courier, Captain Wade, that the Secretary of War, (J. P. Benjamin,) felt solicitous about the invasion of Virginia by way of Pound Gap and by way of Piketon. Marshall assured Cooper that the enemy was equally solicitous to preventing an invasion of Kentucky by the two routes named. Marshall wrote that he didn't believe that the enemy would ever attempt an entry into Virginia by way of Piketon while there was a considerable force stationed at Pound Gap, for the reason that the latter position would lie upon the flank of the advancing column. He surmised that the only invasion danger would be from a heavy cavalry force pressing in and destroying as it goes.[129]

---

[129] <u>War of the Rebellion</u>, Ser. 1, Vol. 7, pgs. 58, 59

After writing the above letter, Gen. Marshall rode from Craft's to Pound Gap and finished his letter that evening. He ordered Col. Trigg's 54th Va. to fall back to Gladesville, Va., and if supplies could not be had in that vicinity to cross Clinch River, if requisite to obtain them. Col. Moore's 29th Va. was also on the march from Whitesburg for the same destination. Simm's mounted battalion was expected in Pound Gap the next day, the 3rd of Feb., and Marshall would send it to Clinch River " without hesitation." Colonel Williams was still at the mouth of Rock House Creek, which was 10 miles below Whitesburg, but will be ordered to join the rest of the command at whatever point convenient supplies could be found or indeed possible. Marshall stated he wouldn't be surprised to have great trouble with William's 5th Kentucky on account of its removal into Virginia, for the men were nearly all from the mountain counties of Kentucky, and, according to Gen. Marshall, "they would prefer, I believe, even to be retreating through the mountains of their own state to any rest which could be offered to them in any other part of the country." He reported the regiment to still be entirely undrilled, and had been since the first enlistment of its soldiers. (The regiment was largely recruited in Oct.-Dec.,1861.) A note was here inclosed, a written proposition from Mr. Brashears, the owner of the salt- works near Whitesburg:

I propose and agree to lease to the Government of the Confederate States of America my track of land in Perry County,

Kentucky, embracing some 4,000 acres, with privilege of using the machinery there in situated and of making salt there and of cultivating the land, and with the privilege of cutting the timber and mining the coal, for the term of three years, from the first day of May next, for the sum of $2,000 for the whole term, payable in equal installments annually, and with power to said government to assign this lease and to locate troops on the land and otherwise to exercise all acts of ownership for the term through his agents, servants, officers, or assigns.

The acceptance of this proposition by the President or Secretary of War is to be considered as making this contract complete, on my being notified thereof by General Marshall, or any other agent of the government, and a copy hereof furnished to me, signed by the President or Secretary, at any time prior to the 1st of May, 1862; possession to be given at that time or as much sooner as the other party chooses to take it.

Witness my hand and seal at Whitesburg, Letcher County, Kentucky, this 1st of February, 1862.

R.S. Brashears.

Witnesses:
H. Marshall
J.S.C. Taylor, M.D.

[Indorsement]
It is not recommended to decide on this question at present, as it remains open until the 1st of May. Moreover, this department has

made preparations for furnishing salt in less precarious localities and sufficient quantities.

L. B. Northrop,
Commissary General Subsistence
February 17, 1862[130]

The salt-works at Brashearville (now Cornettsville,) in Perry County, were owned by the father of Captain Samuel Ray Brashears, Co. H, 10th Kentucky Mounted Rifles, which was organized in Whitesburg in September and October, 1862, by Benjamin E. Caudill, who was before then a Captain in Company F, 5th Kentucky Infantry , William's Regiment.

On Oct. 19, 1862, a Home Guards unit from Harlan, Kentucky, known as the Harlan Battalion, attacked B Company of the 10th Ky., and ransacked the salt works, stealing even "the largest pone of corn bread I ever saw," according to Lieutenant Clabe Jones, who was in the battle and who wrote a autobiography after the war. He estimated the pone of bread to weigh around 50 pounds!

Captain David Caudill of B Co. was wounded in the action and an estimated one killed on each side, with estimates ranging as high as 5 rebels killed and several wounded.[131]

---

[130] ibid, pgs. 60, 61
[131] Jones,Clabe,Autobiography;
www.bencaudill.com/leatherwood_battle.html

Chapter Ten

Marshall at Gladesville

In obedience to orders from Gen. Simon Cooper, the Confederate Adjutant General, the little army of Humphrey Marshall had fallen back from Whitesburg to Pound Gap (and beyond) by February 8th, 1862. The Kentucky River line that Gen. Marshall selected for defense was threatened by the fact that General Zollicoffer had been defeated at the Battle of Logan's Cross Roads (also known as the Battle of Fishing Creek, and the Battle of Mill Springs) on Sunday, January 19th, 1862, just 9 days after the Battle of Middle Creek. Zollicoffer himself lost his life in this battle, which was the largest in Kentucky up to that date.

With the defeat, the Confederates moved out of the state into Tennessee, leaving the southern border of the state open to invasion, with the exception of Cumberland and Pound Gaps. Pound Gap became even more important as a gateway for invasion by the Federal forces and the move was likely caused, in part, by a need to strength their hold on the gaps and to consolidate their meager forces available to guard the mountain passes.

When Marshall's troops moved to Pound Gap, he himself continued on to the town of Gladesville , or Wise Courthouse, (now Wise) in Wise County, Virginia. This was the nearest Virginia town of any size close to the Gap. The distance was between 10 and 15 miles, with one of the worst roads in the mountains to travel on between the Gap and the town.

Edward O. Guerrant, Marshall's new Asst. Adj. General, left Whitesburg on Feb. 7th to catch up with Marshall. Guerrant went through the Gap that same day, noticing that some rough log pens had been built and filled with rock and sand as breastworks or fortifications for the defense of the Gap. On the summit and on beyond the mountain down to its foot were rude log huts the soldiers had constructed as winter quarters.

His description of the road from the Gap to Gladesville is revealing: "At the foot of the mountain on the V'a side commenced the most desperate roads—I had ever yet beheld—I will not say I never expect to see worse for I thought I had reached the maximum on Indian Creek & up Troublesome & Quicksand, (in Kentucky) but only say I cannot imagine worse roads than the 8 or 10 miles beyond the Gap toward Wise C. H. or Gladesville. The mud is almost "swimming" except where brush has been thrown in & there it is almost impossible."[132]

---

[132] Guerrant Diary entry for Feb 7th, 1862.

Guerrant also observed that there were eight cannon and accompanying caissons positioned in the Gap when he passed through. He and his party arrived at Gladesville on the 8th after spending the night in two different houses, owned by two brothers named Hall, who lived about 5 miles from the foot of Pound Gap toward Gladesville. Their bill for both the houses that night was $15.00 in gold. The corn for the horses was sold to them at $20.00 per barrel. The home owners represented the country as perfectly destitute—impoverished by the army. "No Union men (Lincolnites they called them) in this country," the Hall's assured Guerrant and his party.[133]

Guerrant got his first glance of Marshall at a distance in Gladesville and pronounced him "about the size of Uncle Joshua."-- Marshall's cavalry had relocated from Kentucky to Powell's Valley in Lee County and Guerrant headed there from Gladesville. He commented that the view from the "little Stone Gap" at the entrance to Powell's Valley surpassed anything I had yet seen. "As far as the eye could reach, the narrow valley—with its stream of sparkling water wending through it like a silver wire—was hemmed in on each side by the tallest mountains. On tops of the mountains I beheld great dark clouds lying lazily—realizing the idealities of schoolboys' eulogies on cloud capped m'ts—etc."[134]

From Gladesville Marshall reported that the Virginia side of the mountain was much more difficult than the Kentucky side. Corn in

---

[133] ibid
[134] ibid Diary for Feb. 8th, 1862.

that village was hauled 30 miles for common uses, and was selling at $2.00 per bushel, or $10 per barrel. For that reason, he had caused the two Virginia regiments to pass behind the Clinch River, and had directed Colonel Simms to forage his mounted battalion in the county of Scott or Lee, some 30 miles from Gladesville. He also directed Colonel William's Kentucky regiment and Radcliffe's company to come no further into Virginia than the Pound, (4 miles beyond the Gap) and he allowed Williams to occupy the Kentucky side of the mountains in Letcher, Harlan, or Pike County if he preferred to; keeping these two points in view: 1st, subsistence, 2nd, the protection of Pound Gap and Stone Gap. [135]

In November, 1861, Gen, Marshall had appointed Dr. Basil C. Duke as chief of the medical staff of his brigade.[136] Dr. Duke wrote a letter on Feb. 11th from Gladesville to Gen. J.E. Johnston with some news and some good things to say about Gen. Marshall. He reported to Johnston that the enemy was now at Piketon in force with about 6,000 men. They had brought up provisions for 10,000 men via the Sandy River in steamboats of a larger class than had ever navigated the Sandy before. With the men and provisions came enough horses and wagons to make an inland expedition on Pound Gap within the next ten days. Dr. Duke mentioned that spies had come in the day before with these observations. In the present condition that the rebel army was in Dr. Duke was sure this was the darkest day of the army's

---

[135] <u>War of the Rebellion</u> Series 1, Vol. 7, Pg. 866.
[136] ibid, pg. 703.

existence. For the very first time since the organization of the army, he doubted their ability to repel the foe. *How can our small, starved force meet such an enemy? Colonel Williams is at our old camp, near Robinson's at Pound. He looks as cheerful in the presence of all these difficulties as if no great events were passing. He says the ragamuffins (5th Kentucky Inf.) are ready and willing to dispute the ground from Pound Gap to Abingdon. General Marshall looks danger in the face with as much composure and coolness as any man I ever saw. He is certainly one of the finest military men in the Confederacy. His troops love him dearly and will at all times make a gallant fight under him, but we feel this line has been neglected, for some reason, by the department. We must have 10,000 men on this line or we will all go to the devil...... Our men are suffering very much for the want of provisions---many of them sick. Colonel Williams had at one time 394 of his command down at one time, and that was on the march from Middle Creek to Whitesburg. I had nothing but a few old wagons without covers, and some sixty old broken down horses to transport them on. It rained every day during our march, and that in torrents, and strange to say we have only lost two (sick) men...Colonels Trigg's and Moore's regiments are at or near Castlewood. They are further from Pound Gap than the Yankees are. John T. Ratliff of Carter County, has just come in with a new company of 100 men; that company is Company A, of a new regiment. I hope you will get Colonel Williams commissioned brigadier general at once and send it to him. Nothing would please Kentucky so much...* B.C. Duke [137]

In a letter to General S. Cooper written the same day and from the same town as Dr. B. C. Duke's letter, General Marshall informed Cooper of the 6,000 to 7,000 enemy troops in Piketon that two different spies had informed him of. One of the spies was from Louisa; the other had two sons in William's regiment and was from Prestonsburg.

Marshall also informed General Cooper that Theophilus T. Garrard (Colonel, Third Ky. Regiment, U.S.) with a heavy force, was moving towards the Poor Fork of the Cumberland River. He surmised that Garrard was making his movement to combine his advance with that of Garfield in order to make a heavy and immediate assault upon Pound Gap. Thus a move from the Stone Gap on one side of Pine Mountain and a move from Piketon from the other side would assail Pound Gap in front and rear.

Marshall advised Cooper that Col. Moore and Col. Trigg had fallen back to Clinch River for supplies and that his mounted battalion (Simms) had fallen off 55 miles from Pound Gap to obtain food and forage. He had left Major Thompson and his 350 "special service men" at Pound Gap, and at the Pound, Colonel Williams and his 500 men, while the enemy has from 5,000 to 6,000 within 37 miles of his forces. He asked Cooper for at least 10.000 men to be able to "move instantly so as to destroy the force at Piketon, break up that

---

[137] ibid, Series 1, Vol.52, pgs. 270, 271.

column, and drive it into the Ohio River, so as to free your frontier and cripple the enemy before he cripples you."

He ended his letter to Cooper by asking him a series of questions:

1st. Have I, as brigadier-general of the Confederate States Army, a right, without direction of the Department, to call out the militia of the neighborhood or surrounding states when, in my judgment, the emergency demands it?

2nd. Have I the right to prevent supplies which are necessary to my army from passing out of the country I occupy by exchange or sale between private persons?

3rd. Have I the right to prevent individuals professing friendship to the Southern Confederacy from passing into Virginia from Kentucky, or *vice versa*, now that Kentucky is one of the Confederate States? [138]

On Feb. 13th, Marshall ordered Captain Witcher to take his company of mounted men to the Louisa Fork of the Sandy to watch the country between Grundy, Va., and Piketon, Ky.

He also directed Captain Jeffress to take the six pieces of artillery from Pound Gap to behind Clinch River. (Castlewood) At the Gap there was no company to man them, and no horses to draw them, which exposed them to danger without the possibility of doing service. He proposed to move all the stores behind the Clinch River, yet to hold Pound Gap as long as possible with the 350 men still there. The exposure to the weather and other factors since Middle Creek was causing the loss of even more

---

[138] ibid, Vol. 7, pgs., 872, 873, 874.

of Marshall's men. Lieutenant Tribble of Stoner's company had died a few days since, after returning from the Sandy River area. Private Shawhaw and several others of the mounted battalion had died also. Col. Trigg had lost 5 men and Col. Moore 2 men. Colonel Williams had lost 10 men due to disease since returning. There were also 110 men in the hospital at Gladesville on February 13th.[139]

Guerrant met Marshall face to face for the first time on Feb.12th and gave a description of the General; Gen. Marshall is about such a sized man as Uncle Joshua Owings (Guerrent's Mother's brother of Montgomery County Kentucky) and somewhat resembles him—being fuller in the face, & under the waistcoat—with one eye cocked. His voice is very strong & course. Rough & dictatorial in his conversation—but impressed me as being a man of considerable talent & decision of character.[140]

Marshall was confident that the Federals were collecting supplies and men at Piketon for an invasion of Virginia through Pound Gap with the object of hitting the salt-works and the railroad. With this in mind, he once again asked for supplies and men enough to drive the enemy to the out of Eastern Kentucky and to the Ohio River.

As to supplies, he figured they could be had in sufficient quantity for 5,000 to 10,000 men by bringing them 50 miles to the rear of Clinch River where they could be located to cover both roads and the salt–works at

---

[139] ibid, pg. 879.
[140] Guerrant diary entry, Feb. 12th, 1862.

Saltville. Colonel Trigg of the 54th Virginia had reportedly left his regiment when they crossed the Clinch River and had gone to Richmond. His object was to obtain clothes for his regiment, but he had gone without leave. Marshall commented that he had no hope of preserving any Virginia regiment since Col. Stuart's 56th Virginia had been successful in getting from unwelcome service. [141]

There were few farmers left to carry on farming activities since the beginning of the war, but what few that were left were bound to have been unhappy when Marshall set some guidelines for purchases made from them and also decreed what should be done with surplus crops. He set the price of corn at 75 cents per bushel, 40 cents for shelled oats, $1.00 for wheat, rye, or barley. He also directed that where there was a surplus beyond the wants of the farmer, that surplus should be taken, if not sold at the prices listed above. (These prices were less than half the regular going price for these products.) A certificate was to be left for the amount of commodities taken, so that the Department or Congress may fix the rate of "just compensation to which the party may be entitled."[142]

He also directed that men feeding cattle near the road to Pound Gap take their stock elsewhere, as he had levied on all the hay, grass, and small grain, which would be needed to feed public animals on his line of march. He felt that some men were feeding hogs and cattle in Scott and Lee Counties under the hope of

---

[141] War of the Rebellion, Ser.1, Vol. 7, 883, 884.
[142] ibid, 884, 885.

realizing high prices in the spring and summer from the Army. He commented that if he had the command he would seize and bacon all their hogs and beef or he would make them carry the stock south of the railroad. He stated that the owners were getting all the supplies out of the way (of the army) under the hope of future private gain and they should be stopped at once.

On Wed. Feb. 19th, Marshall had received information that the Yankees, 1,400 strong, were moving upon Pound Gap. Marshall immediately ordered Col. William's regiment to proceed to the Gap and recalled the regiments of Trigg and Moore. He sent to the Gap and brought away the Yankee prisoners, clothing, the cannon, etc. Two soldiers died in the hospital at Gladesville on this day.[143]

On Feb. 25th, William's left their camp at the Pound and marched through Gladesville towards Clinch River, leaving Thompson and his battalion to watch Pound Gap. Three days later, Gen. Marshall left after dinner for Castlewood in Russell County where most of his troops now were. From here, Marshall decided to travel to Lebanon, Va., in Russell County, and establish his headquarters there.[144]

On March 8th, General Marshall wrote a lengthy letter to Confederate President Jefferson Davis, mentioning to him that with the week he had been at Lebanon, and the three weeks he had spent in Wise County,

---

[143] Guerrant, diary entry, Feb. 19th, 1862.
[144] ibid,Tues.Feb. 25th, Fri., Feb. 28th, Mar. 4th., 1862.

made a month in all since he had left Pound Gap. He told Davis that he had every opportunity to study the people of Virginia and he had come to the conclusion that they were no better than the people of Kentucky on the other side of the Cumberland Range. He related how he had made a speech at Lebanon "to try to wake them up to the duty of enlisting, but they stand as stolidly to accept the draft as if they had no interest on earth in the subject of war."In a word, they were doing nothing, willing to do nothing which submits them to loss, and threatening to "be for the other side" if they are not indulged, or are molested. He assured Davis that this feeling is but the surface of the difficulty the country faces. "Under all this the soil here is just as it is in Northwestern Virginia." He had found that Wise County had whole districts of the county as false as could be (to the Confederacy) and in fact, he had learned from the leading men of the county that the enemy at Pikeville[145] had been furnished with the names of the leading men in Wise as to: such to be killed, such to be transported, such to be sworn and let go.[146]

Marshall asked Davis for the power for commanders to call out the militia so young men would be compelled to either come into camp or join the enemy. He stated he believed he could bring into camp 5,000 men in his five county section who would otherwise not join at all. He stated to Davis that 7,000 or 8,000 men comprised the enemy force in Pikeville and

---

[145] He used the correct name here.
[146] War of the Rebellion, Series 1, Vol. 52, pgs. 283, 284.

114

"meditates a speedy movement Virginia." He said he had sent a letter to the Adj. Gen. asking for re-enforcements to provide a total of 5,000 infantry and 1,500 cavalry to deal with such a large enemy force. He said it was easier to overcome the 8,000 then at Pikeville than to drive out 12,000 in sixty or thirty days from this time.[147]

---

[147] ibid, 285

Chapter Eleven

Skirmish at Pound Gap

While General Marshall and his Army of Eastern Kentucky were having problems with supplying their needs in the mountains of Kentucky and Virginia, Colonel Garfield's men were also having their share of supply problems. Garfield had moved on the 22nd of February to Piketon, taking with him the 22nd Kentucky, along with the 40th and 50th Ohio. That night the river rose 60 feet and destroyed nearly all his stores. [148]

On the next day, from Camp Brownlow in Piketon, Garfield sent a force under Captain Garrard of the 22nd Ky. Volunteers to proceed to where the main road from Pound Gap intersects with the Elkhorn Creek. From there he was to proceed down the Elkhorn to its mouth, scouting the valley thoroughly, and then return to Piketon.[149]

---

[148] War of the Rebellion, Series 1, Vol.10, part 2, pg. 9.

[149] ibid.

The object of the expedition was to drive out or capture a "predatory band of rebels under the command of Captain Menifee, who is acting as scouts for Marshall." Garfield also instructed Garrard to "take possession of all arms of active secessionists in the vicinity through which he would pass, and to bring to the headquarters in Piketon all who are found in arms or actively aiding the rebellion." He instructed Garrard to return within four days.[150]

In a letter to Capt. J.B. Fry on March 7th, Garfield reported that his command had in a great measure recovered from the great flood in this (Sandy) valley, though the exposure to it caused a large increase in their sick list. Since his arrival in Piketon, he had sent out several scouting parties and was now able to fully report on the situation in the area.

As his advance reached Piketon, Marshall's remnant force had left Whitesburg and passed hurriedly through the Pound Gap. Garfield reported that he had captured a few stragglers, and deserters were coming in daily. With the exception of a few bands of robbers, which he expected would be dispersed in a few days, "there is no enemy in Eastern Kentucky."

Garfield gave Fry a breakdown of Marshall's forces in Virginia: his cavalry force has gone to Blountsville, Tenn., and is in a very demoralized condition; their horses are nearly worthless. Colonel Trigg's Virginia regiment is encamped on Coffee Creek, in the vicinity of Lebanon, about 20 miles from Abingdon, Va. Colonel Moore's (Virginia) regiment is on

---

[150] ibid.

Clinch River, 10 miles this side of Lebanon. Colonel William's (Kentucky) regiment, which came down this valley 1,500 strong, is reduced to about 700, by battle, sickness, and deserters, and is on the border of Wise County, Virginia. About 20 miles beyond the (Pound) Gap two whole companies, refusing to leave Kentucky, deserted and dispersed when the regiment passed through the Gap. At the same time the battery of artillery which was stationed at the Gap was removed to the vicinity of Abingdon. Another battery had already gone as far as Lebanon with Colonel Trigg.

There are still stationed at the Gap five companies of Virginia State Militia under a Major Thompson. General Marshall and staff are at Gladesville, where he seems to have little interest in the army, and little control over it. He had lost a large number of his wagons and in his retreat has ruined and lost a large share of his horses and mules.[151]

Garfield informed Fry that McLaughlin's squadron of Ohio cavalry had joined him at Piketon. Also the Fourteenth Kentucky was at Paintsville, part of the Sixteenth Kentucky was at Louisa, and the remainder at Catlettsville.

He commented that there had been a marked change in favor of the Union among the citizens of Buchanan, Wise, Scott, and other counties. At the foot of the Cumberland Mountains several public meetings had been held to express their attachment to the Union.[152]

---

[151] ibid, pgs. 17, 18.
[152] ibid, pg. 18

The dispositions of Marshall's forces in Virginia as given by Colonel Garfield were so precise that one almost feels that Garfield had been present when Gen. Marshall gave the orders. It's obvious that the spying system in Eastern Kentucky and Western Virginia was paying off for the Federal forces. It's a good indication that the ardor felt for the Confederacy in the beginning of the war was on the decline in the second year of war.

The Confederate mountain boys were especially beginning to be soured on the war, as sickness, disease, lack of food, lack of clothing, and battle losses increased. One of those mountain boys that became sick and started home was Confederate Private Madison Pigman, who became sick with typhoid and rode towards his home a short distance away. When he awoke a day later, he learned his horse had carried him home where his family found him asleep, still in the saddle, in front of his home.[153] To recover from an illness at home gave a soldier a much better chance at recovery than did lying in a log make-shift hospital on a cold ridge-top of the Cumberland Mountains.

From Camp Brownlow, in Piketon, Col. Garfield wrote Brig. Gen. W.S. Rosecrans, (who commanded the Department of West Virginia), on March 10th that he had three regiments of infantry and one squadron of cavalry with him, and had rations enough for two months there and in Paintsville.

----

[153] E. Merton Coulter, The Civil War and Readjustment in Kentucky, 1926.; Mountain Men of the Confederacy, Richard Francis, 1973

Garfield informed Rosecrans that Colonel Carter, commanding Twelfth Brigade, was at Cumberland Ford, within 6 miles of Cumberland Gap, where 5,000 rebel forces were fortified. Carter was urging him to co-operate and suggested that Garfield move through the Pound Gap to attack the 5,000 rebels at Cumberland Gap in their rear.[154]

A few days after his letter to Rosecrans, Garfield learned that General Marshall had ordered the militia of Wise, Scott, and Lee Counties to muster on the 15th, with six day's provisions, and aid in guarding the mountain passes at the Cumberland and Pound Gaps. In order to prevent a concentration of rebel forces at Pound Gap he left Piketon on the 14th with a detachment of infantry from the Fortieth Ohio, under Colonel Cranor; the Forty-second, under Major Pardee; the Twenty-second Kentucky, under Major Cook, amounting in all to 600, and 100 cavalry under Major McLaughlin, and packing a few days' provisions on mules, proceeded up the Big Sandy, and reached the foot of the Cumberland Mountains a few miles below Pound Gap in the night of the 15th.[155]

When the Union troops reached the headwaters of Elkhorn Creek just below Pound Gap, they encamped there to await the dawn and the struggle to wrest the Gap from Thompson's reported 500 "special service" troops who were spending that night in their log cabin shelters that they and the 5th Ky. Inf.

---

[154] War of the Rebellion, Series 1, Vol. 10, part 2, pg. 28.

[155] ibid, pg. 33.

had constructed under the orders of General Marshall.

All the approaches to the Gap were steep, and except for the main wagon road, were mostly bridle paths that even horses would have difficulty climbing with the snow that was falling that night and the next day. Garfield was presented with a major problem by those conditions, as well as the fact that none of his men knew the country around the Gap and it's out of the way trails that might allow his command to slip up on the rebels.

Garfield offered money to several local citizens to lead his men up the bridal paths but most refused. Some time that night a man appeared in Garfield's camp and offered to lead the way up the mountain, not by bridle paths, but by "squirrel trails."This man was thought to be Vincent Bently, about 70 years of age and a Letcher County resident. When questioned by Garfield, he wanted no money, but only wanted to come and go as he pleased. Another reason was to "rid the kentry of a set of muderin' thieves, as is carryin' terror and death inter every poor man's home in all the valley." Another name mentioned as the guide was a Mr. Jordan.[156] Whoever it was, he was obviously someone who knew the mountain well.

It's not known whether the rebels knew of the arrival of the Federals that night, but the weather conditions of fog, sleet and snow most likely prevented the sentries perched on the

---

[156] Batch, The Life of President Garfield, p. 200; The Civil War in Buchanan and Wise Counties, Jeffrey Weaver, H.E. Howard, Inc. Lynchburg, Virginia, 1994.

rocks and peaks on the summit at Pound Gap from detecting the Yankee force. Anyone who has had occasion to travel across the mountain today during a snowstorm or even during rainy conditions are very much aware how quickly and completely the elements of weather can prevent seeing but a few feet in front of you. Those conditions completely eliminated any advantage the high peaks provided for observation of the roads leading to the Gap by the Confederates.

The Confederates had two forces with which to defend their camps and the Gap. On top of the ridge was Major Thompson's 350 to 500 men of the 21st Va. Battalion, and at the bottom of the mountain on the Virginia side, Captain Campbell Slemp was in charge of a small force to protect the cabins of the Confederate camp which were built there. (Today the little community of Almira is located there.)

Early on the morning of the 16th of March, Garfield ordered Major McLaughlin to advance directly up the main road leading to the Gap and attack the rebels in front, while the infantry were led by an unfrequented path (by the civilian guide)to the summit of the mountain one mile to the left (north) of the Gap. He divided the infantry into two columns, and ordered Colonel Cranor to lead one column to the farther foot of the mountain, and thence ascend the Gap road from the other side, while the remaining column would advance along the summit towards the Confederates in the Gap. Garfield thus hoped to attack in front and by the flank at the same time, and to cut off the retreat of the Rebels by the Abingdon road. This plan was upset when Cranor's column missed the path that they should have used halfway down the south side of the mountain and didn't discover their mistake until the head of the column was too far past it as to cause great a delay in the attack in case they should be sent back.[157]

McLaughlin had a heavy snow storm and many cut trees in the road blocking his path up the main road, which the cavalry cleared as they advanced.

As they advanced nearer the Gap, one of the sentries stationed on Sentry Rock gave a shout of the enemy's presence. The rifles and shotguns of the Rebels sounded through the mountain side as the Federals made an attack, only to be repulsed by the Rebel fire from the log fortifications across the road in the Gap. After a sharp skirmish, the Federals were forced back down the mountain. This action had sufficed, however to draw the attention of the rebels to that quarter while allowing the 42th Ohio under Major Pardee, and the 22nd Kentucky under Major Cook, to come along the summit from the north without being noticed. The rebels then formed a battle line and put up a sharp resistance. After half a dozen volleys from the Yankees, by which at least one of the rebels was killed and several wounded, the rebel line broke and the whole line of battle fled in some confusion, and took refuge among the ravines and thick undergrowth of the mountains. The Federal skirmishers followed

---

[157] War of the Rebellion, Series 1, Vol. 10, part1, pgs. 33, 34.

them until they were completely scattered. As soon as the cavalry re-ascended the hill Garfield sent them down the main road in pursuit of the Confederates. The cavalry pursued them for about six miles before calling off the chase.[158]

Captain Slemp's small force at the base of the Virginia side of the mountain was soon overwhelmed and was forced to join the retreat on the Abingdon road.[159]

Major Thompson, in his March 21st report of the battle, stated that he had notice on the evening of the 15th that the enemy was approaching his position at Pound Gap, and that he was then about 17 miles distant from the Gap. Because of the dark and cloudy night, along with a slight mix of rain and snow, and "with the guidance of well-informed citizens and scouts, most of them from Kentucky, and a part of them from Virginia, the enemy had made a night march and it is believed that during the night of the 15th had marched a strong column to the south side of the mountain, so as to attack me in front and rear and to cut off my retreat." [160]

Thompson said that his scouts that had discovered the night march on the 15th was cut off by that march and were unable to deliver any information of the movement to him.

---

[158] ibid.

[159] Addington, Luther F., The Story of Wise County, Virginia , The Over-Mountain Press, Johnson City, Tennessee, 1992.

[160] War of the Rebellion, Series 1, Vol. 10, part 1, pg. 41.

He reported that on the morning of the 16th, at about 9 o'clock, his pickets were attacked in front of the Gap by a company of cavalry and about 200 infantry coming up the main road. He then ordered the companies of Captain Maness and Lieutenant Miller to meet them, who met them with alacrity and drove the enemy back with the loss of, as he believed, several killed.

After the first attack had been repelled Thompson withdrew Captain Maness and his company and posted them to the right of the Gap and re-enforced him with Captain Pridemore's company. Very soon thereafter their position was assailed with another strong column of the enemy. (This was Cook's and Pardee's regiments.) Maness and Pridemore contested their position for an hour with great gallantry. Thompson dispatched a portion of Captain Russell's company, under Lieutenant Marcum, to re-enforce Captain Maness, but the thickness of the fog caused them to pass between two columns of the enemy and they were cut off from Captain Maness. When Marcum's column discovered their dangerous condition, they crossed the mountain to the north and re-crossed to the south side of the Gap.

At this time Thompson received a dispatch from Captain Slemp, who had been posted with a small force at the cabins at the southern foot of the mountain, both as a reserve and to watch and report any approach of the enemy from points on the right, reporting that he was attacked by a superior force of the enemy and could not hold his position without re-enforcements. Finding himself now attacked and overpowered from the rear and front, and that if he remained on the crest of the mountain he would be surrounded and cut off, Thompson ordered a retreat to the foot of the mountain by the left, and his forces were re-united at Poindexter's, about 4 miles from the Gap. He made a stand there, prepared to give battle if assailed.

Thompson's command remained at that point until after dark, when he ordered them to fall back to Gladesville, the nearest point at which they could obtain food, having been without sustenance since the morning. After dark, Thompson returned with a picked body of 20 men to watch the movements of the enemy. He approached near enough to discover that they were burning both camps, destroying two or three damaged wagons and some small personal property and stores, which consisted of the clothing of his men, their blankets, and cooking utensils, and some inconsiderable quantity of soap and salt.

On the morning of the 16th, when he was attacked, about one-third of Thompson's command was on detached service and 30 were on the sick list. With the exception of Captain Slemp's command, he had only an effective force of 175 men to meet "1,400 or 1,500 infantry and 100 cavalry." [161] [162]

After the battle Thompson retreated to Gladesville, then to Guest's Station. (Coeburn).

---

[161] Garfield actually had a total of 900 men.

[162] War of the Rebellion, Series 1, Vol. 10, part 1, pgs. 41, 42.

Garfield's troops occupied the camps of the defeated rebels that night and burned their quarters the next morning, consisting of 60 log huts and three larger buildings which were used for quartermaster and commissary stores and a hospital. He reported that he had captured their muster rolls and other official documents, together with a number of important letters. He said he suffered no losses in the battle while the rebels lost 7 killed and wounded.[163]

The following is a letter from an unidentified Federal soldier with his perspective of the battle as they attacked the rebel breastworks:

*A loud echoing shout burst from the long line, as with fixed bayonets it swept down through the ravine and up the hill. There was no backbone to contend with, however, for as our bayonets appeared over the hill, scarce an enemy was in sight. A few straggling ones could be seen tearing through the laurel underbrush, as we sent a ringing volley after them , killing one and wounding sever*al.[164]

From the other side, a rare letter (in part) from a member of the 21st Virginia Battalion had his own perspective of events following the skirmish at Pound Gap:

Guesses Station, Wise County, Va.

March the 23rd 1862

---

[163] ibid, pg. 33.

[164] Letter to the Cincinnati *Gazette,* dated March 19,1862 from an unidentified soldier; Jeffrey C.Weaver, The Civil War in Buchanan and Wise Counties, Manu. By H.E.Howard, Inc., Lynchburg, Virginia, 1994

Dear and affectionate wife the opportunity presents itself to send you a few lines more for fear you have not received several letters I started to you... I am enjoying good health yet all tho we have seen a rough time but our company faired well to what the other companys did they left nearly all of thire plunder and we got the most of our bed clothes and the companys is scattered for a mile or so at Houses Some at a barn and build fires under the sheds. Our company Stays at some houses but we are Scroughed So we can Scarcely cook or Eat or Sleep around the fires William H. France and Edward Pennington & myself has slept in a room where there is no fire last night was cold and we filled up a kettle with some fire and Oak bark we faired tollarable well we will indeaver to manage the best we can for our selves in any way that is honorable and right....

Write all about the affairs at home.
To Nancy Pennington Tobias S. Pennington[165]

From Gladesville, Major Thompson wrote to General Marshall shortly after the Pound Gap action: *I got out with all my men. I fought them nearly an hour and a half, until my retreat was nearly cut off. Then I was forced to retreat. The enemy was 2,500 and*

---

[165] Letter from Tobias Pennington to his wife, Nancy, Southwest Virginia Historical Society, Jonesville,Virginia; Jeffery C. Weaver, <u>The Civil War in Buchanan and Wise Counties</u>, Manu, by H.E. Howard Inc. Lynchburg, Virginia, 1994.

100 cavalry. My men are entirely without tents or blankets.

On March 19th, General Marshall wrote General Robert E, Lee that he had a cavalry force on the Louisa road within two miles of the state line and within 25 miles of Pike(ville), which he intended to order to burn Garfield's supplies at Pike(ville) "if the thing can be affected."

On March, the 20th, he sent a report to an unidentified general. In it he commented that "one can pass from Whitesburg to Gladesville, 15 miles west of Pound Gap, and save 10 miles between the places." Marshall had at one time sent his sick on horseback through that route, and had driven a lot of hogs through the same pass. He said that "one can drive wagons from the Pound, 4 miles this side of the Gap, through to Cumberland Ford, 15 miles in front of Cumberland Gap." He had sent wagons down on the Poor Fork of Cumberland after corn and they had returned to the Pound laden. Hence he had moved all the public property away from Pound Gap. Thus when the enemy came to the Gap, "there was nothing there but two or three disabled wagons and a few bushels of salt and something of that sort," said Marshall. [166]

---

[166] <u>War of the Rebellion</u>, Series 1, Vol. 10, part 1, pgs. 35, 36.

BATTLE of
POUND GAP
MARCH 16, 1862

UNION CAVALRY

CONFEDERATE INFANTRY

CONFEDERATE BrestWorks

PINE MT.

Ky.

VA.

MILLER

RUSSELL

2ND BRIGADE

PRIDEMORE

COOK

PRIDMORE

CRYHOFF

STEMP

LETCHER CO.

WISE CO.

CONFEDERATE CAMP

(ALMIRA)

(HOYSE GAP)

... TO Pound

UNION CAMP
(NIGHT OF THE 15TH)

ELKHORN CK.
(JENKINS)

→ TO PIKETON

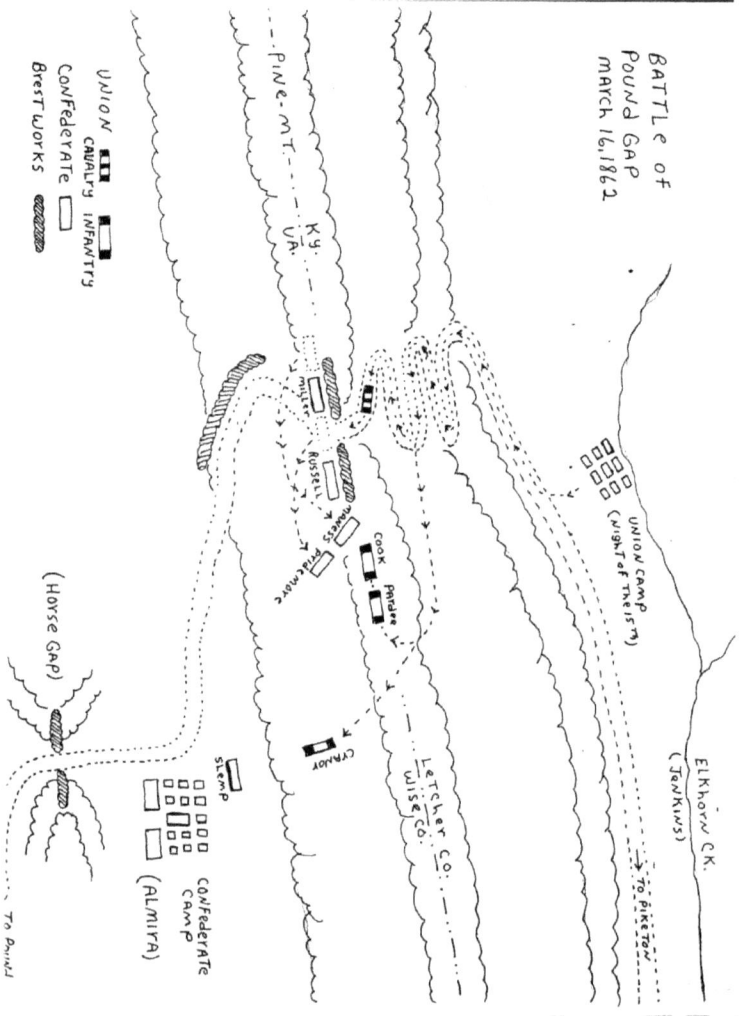

Sketch by David Lucas

130

Old Pound Gap Road-Virginia Side of
Mountain.

Old Pound Gap Road- Kentucky Side.

131

Picket Observation Post- Raven Rock

Another View-Raven Rock

Pound Gap Battlefield, Border between Virginia and Kentucky.

Pound Gap Monument on Battlefield

Pound Gap Battlefield Memorial

Confederate Encampment of 1861-1865, Whitesburg, Kentucky, Mouth of Sandlick Creek.

Confederate Cemetery, Westwood Section, Whitesburg, Kentucky.

Confederate Casualty, Battle of Cynthiana, Ky. June 11, 1864, Westwood Cemetery

IN MEMORY OF

3 SGT
JOHN T. KELLY
CO H
13 KY CAV
CSA
1842
KIA
CYNTHIANA, KY
JUNE 11, 1864

135

North Fork of Kentucky River, Whitesburg, Ky.

Major General John Hunt Morgan

Colonel Benjamin E. Caudill, Tenth Kentucky
Mounted Rifles

Captain Robert Bates, 7th Battalion
Confederate Cavalry

Captain Martin V. Bates, 7th Bn.
Confederate Cavalry, (left), 7' 2½"
tall. Average size man in middle.

Captain Martin V. and Anna Swan Bates.
Martin 7' 2 ½"—Anna 7' 5 ½"

Chapter Twelve

A Call for Militia

President Davis wrote Gen. Marshall on March 13th,1862, that after consultation with Gen. Lee, whose letter would soon follow Davis', that he would receive authority to call out the militia in his district. Not only would he have the power to call out the militia, but also over the courts by proclamation of martial law, if he found it necessary.[167]

The very same day Gen. R.E. Lee wrote Marshall, inclosing authorization to call out the militia "in the counties in which you are operating." Lee cautioned Marshall that should he call out the militia, take measures not to interfere with the counties in which Gen. (Henry) Heth is operating.[168]

In his report to Adj. Gen. Cooper on Mar. 13, from Lebanon, Va., Marshall called his attention to the special service battalion then at

---

[167] War of the Rebellion, Series 1, Vol. 10, part2, pgs. 321, 322.

[168] ibid, pgs. 322, 323.

Pound Gap, "those special men" as he put it. He advised Cooper that they should be disbanded immediately and embraced in the call for the militia. He allowed as how the battalion could not be induced to muster for three years as he was led to suppose they would.[169]

Lieutenant-Col. Simm's had recently resigned from command of Marshall's mounted troops, and Marshall had re-organized by adding a battalion of five companies, (Thomas', Clay's, Holliday's, Stoner's, and Cameron's,) to the battalion of mounted rifles, and requested his assistant adjutant general, Charles Duncan, be commissioned as major of the First Mounted Rifles of this brigade. Captain Witcher and Captain Stratton each had a company of 64 mounted men that were all Virginians that could be made into an efficient corps if the companies were made out. (Filled up). If a new battalion wasn't approved, Marshall informed Cooper that he would keep both companies as independent squadrons of mounted rifles, "for it does not suit to mix solders from different states in the same corps of volunteers."[170]

From Lebanon ,Virginia, on March 14th, Marshall issued General Orders No. 6, which directed that hereafter all passage and communication across the Cumberland range of mountains between Kentucky and Virginia, either way, within the boundaries of Lee, Wise, and Buchanan Counties, shall cease, unless the

---

[169] ibid, pg. 323.
[170] ibid, pgs. 323, 324.

140

same shall be conducted under military passport from brigade headquarters.[171]

The order went on to say that "unless a man is coming from Kentucky to join the army and to assist to defend his country and to secure the independence of the Southern Confederacy he had better remain at home.".....No distinction of persons will be made in the execution of this order. No ties of friendship or relations of kindred shall justify an infraction of it. No plea of business or of interest will serve to avoid its force. The man who is detected hereafter in stealing through the lines of this army, knowing that he is violating this order, shall be treated as a spy summarily.[172]

By order of---

H. Marshall
Brigadier-General, Commanding

On March 19th, Marshall called out the militia with the following order:

Special Orders, Brigade Headquarters
No. 38, *Lebanon, Va., March* 19, 1862;

Official information having reached me that the troops of the United States have taken Pound Gap and have invaded the State of Virginia in force, by virtue of authority with which I am vested, both by the President of the Confederate States and the Executive of the State of Virginia, I do hereby order the whole body of the militia of Virginia, resident within the counties of Lee, Scott, Wise, Grayson,

---

[171] ibid, pg. 37.
[172] ibid

Carroll, Buchanan, Russell, Washington, Smythe, Wythe, and Tazewell to rendezvous immediately , fully armed and equipped, at the respective places herein designated; that is to say, the militia of Washington, Russell, Grayson, and Scott, at the Old Court, in Russell County; the militia in Lee and Wise at Guest's Station, in Wise County; the militia of Buchanan, at Grundy; the militia Smythe and Carroll, at Saltville; the militia of Wythe, at Wytheville, and the militia of Tazewell, at the mouth of Indian Creek, in Tazewell County. Colonels in command of regiments will move them by companies as rapidly as possible to the places of rendezvous hereby appointed. At such places a board of surgeons will examine and certify to the cases of persons exempt for disease, and the rest will there be mustered into the service of the Confederate States.

By Command of Brig. H. Marshall:

J. Milton Stansifer

Acting Assistant Adjutant-General[173]

Confederate Strength of Brigade
Marshall's Brigade, March 19, 1862

Trigg's 54th Virginia	424
Moore's 29th	189
William's 5th Kentucky	400
Thompson's Battalion	200
	60
Infantry	1, 213
Shawhan's cavalry company	60
Bradley's Batn. Mounted Rifles	200

---

[173] ibid, pg. 39.

Witcher's Batt. Mounted Rifles	56
Stratton's co. of Mounted Rifles	25
	___
	281
Jeffress' battery, six pieces	60
	___
Total Strength	1,614 [174]

By Wed. March 19th, 300 or 400 militia were present in the town of Lebanon, Va., and General Marshall made an hour's speech to them. At least one man, Edward O. Guerrant, was disappointed in his abilities as an orator on that day, and thought he "didn't try." Guerrent commented that Gen. Marshall had ordered out the militia in ten counties, "which ought to make 10,000 soldiers."[175]

Volunteer companies of militia had been organized in some counties since the beginning of the war. One of those counties was Scott Co., Va. which had set up volunteer companies in each district to wit:

There shall be one or more Volunteer companies of not less than forty men in each captain district, two lieutenants and four sergeants respectively, which officers shall be elected by the men of the companies, and confirmed by the court. Each man shall be armed with his own rifle, musket, or shotgun, or with arms of like character loaned or furnished him by the citizens of each district

---

[174] <u>War of the Rebellion</u>, Series 1, Vol. 10, part 1, pg. 40.

[175] Guerrant, diary entry for Mar. 19th,1862

from the home stock on hand or otherwise. In like manner he is to furnish, have procured for him, a sufficiency of ammunition. The companies shall be divided into platoons extending from the center to the extremities of the district, and shall act as a general patrol within their proper bounds, and under their proper officers, at least once a month, or oftener if necessary. A report shall be made of the operations of the company and of the order and security of the citizens to the central committee by the captain in writing.[176]

General Garfield's successful effort to rid the Sandy Valley of General Marshall's brigade of Virginia and Kentucky Rebels made the Ohio General and politician stand out as a man that could overcome the elements, (the great flood of Feb., 1862,) the lack of resources, and poor transportation facilities, to win two battles with the only rebel army in far Eastern Kentucky.

His new-found fame would eventually help him in his bid for the White House, but for now, he would have to be satisfied with a new job and a promotion to Brigadier General. His promotion was dated Jan., 10th, 1962, the same day the Battle of Middle Creek was fought.

After driving the rebels from Pound Gap, Garfield had spent the night at the base of the mountain before returning to Piketon the next day. While at Piketon, he learned of his promotion, but there was one problem to be solved before he could wear the new star. With

---

[176] Court records of Scott County; <u>History of Scott County</u>, Robert M. Addington, 1932, Reprinted 1992 by The Overmountain Press.

the need of an appropriate civil official to swear him in, it soon became apparent that there weren't any civil officials in Pike County that could administer the oath of office to Garfield. This problem was solved when John C. Charles, Sr., a justice of the peace, was finally procured to swear in the new General in Piketon. [177]

On March 24th, Garfield Received orders to go down the Ohio River to Louisville, then by land to Bardstown, Kentucky, with three regiments of troops. General Buell had made the decision to withdraw Garfield from Piketon in anticipation that it might become necessary to strengthen the Cumberland Gap garrison. Garfield would command the column of re-enforcements to be sent there, including the three regiments he was bringing from Eastern Kentucky. Two regiments would remain at Piketon.[178]

General Buell, Commanding General of the Department of the Ohio, was in Nashville, Tennessee, when he issued Special Orders No. 69, which placed Colonel Jonathan Cranor in command of the portion of the Eighteenth Brigade still left in Piketon when now *General* Garfield and his three regiments left for Bardstown. The forces Cranor would have in his command were the Fortieth Ohio, Colonel Cranor; Sixteenth Kentucky, Colonel C.A. Marshall; and the First Squadron Ohio Cavalry, Maj. William McLaughlin. Cranor's orders were to remain in Piketon until the

---

[177] Scalf, op. cit.,201. ; Preston, John David, The Civil War in the Big Sandy Valley of Kentucky, Gateway Press, Inc., Baltimore, 1984

[178] War of the Rebellion,1, Vol. 10, part 2, pg. 59.

145

weather would permit him to move his whole force, together with camp equipage and stores, to Prestonsburg. Cranor was cautioned, "for urgent reasons to allow no soldier or officer to be quartered in any house or other building." He was to keep company and battalion drills on a regular schedule with the whole command. [179]

By March 28th, Gen. Garfield and his three regiments were in Bardstown, Kentucky, and out of the Eastern Kentucky Mountains. He was successful in the east and would go on to be very successful as a member of the western armies. General Marshall of the Army of Eastern Kentucky probably wasn't too sorry to see him go.

General Marshall was having some success with his calling out of the militia, but there were still signs of dissension in the ranks. Fifteen Rebel soldiers were sent after a party of militia who had refused to serve and were hiding out in a cave in Russell County, Virginia. Prisoners engaged in various crimes were being brought in every day. Marshall was very lenient with them, even towards the most vicious. [180]

Marshall was seeing some movement from his calling out of the militia in the eleven Western Virginia Counties, not all of it the kind that would help the Confederates. Some of the movement was towards the enemy instead of the ranks of the Rebels.

On March 24th, Marshall wrote Gen. Cooper that his call out of the militia had

---

[179] ibid, pg. 67
[180] Guerrant diary entry, Mar. 31st, 1862

produced a strong movement toward the enemy. Marshall had received a note from Major Bradley at Osborne's Ford that;

"Many of the Union men from the region of Estillville have been going out in squads to Kentucky, it is believed, for the purpose of joining the enemy."

Marshall agreed with that assessment:

"This, I think is true. Several squads have certainly passed out in that direction, one of them of from 40 to 50 men. From this county (Russell) a good many have gone. In one case a Kentuckian carried off 7 or 8 with him on the night he first saw my order to prepare the militia. I am in possession of a letter he left behind which should hang him. I hear from Buchanan that the Union men are quite bold. I know that there are a great many in Wise County. My information is that there are many in Washington (County) and that in the lower part of Lee they march through with drums and fifes and with colors flying."

Marshall went on to say that he now had over 500 in camp and drilling daily in the school of the soldier. He thought that the militia of Wise and Scott would not make up more than one full regiment. If Washington and Lee is added in, the whole wouldn't furnish more than two full regiments, although he even doubted that. In fact he had information that the Lee County militia had comparatively no arms or ammunition. The same facts exist in Wise County also. Marshall in this letter asked General Cooper if the Government might be able to furnish any arms? He also reported the enemy as still at Pikeville.[181]

General Lee answered the letter written by Marshall on the 24th requesting arms for the militia by informing him that there were no arms available:

Headquarters,
Richmond, Va., March 30, 1862
Brig. Gen. Humphrey Marshall,
Commanding, &c., Lebanon, Va:

General: Your letter of the 24th instant to the adjutant and Inspector General has been referred to me. In reply, I have to say that all the arms we have at our disposal here are being put in the hands of the troops going into the field, and at this time there none that I can furnish you with. You will make a requisition for such as you require, and all that can be obtained shall be sent to you. You have authority to purchase such private arms as you can obtain. I applied to the Governor, but he had none to furnish to your men.

Such is the scarcity of arms that (we) are having pikes made. If they will be of service to you, they can be sent you. As for ammunition, you will make a requisition for such kind and quantity as you need, and it will be sent to you.[182]

One week to the day after General Lee wrote his letter to Marshall, General Grant and General Albert Sidney Johnston met in a great battle at Pittsburg Landing on the Tennessee

---

[181] War of the Rebellion, 1, Vol. 10, part 2, pgs. 360, 361.
[182] ibid, pg. 374.

148

River (better known as the Battle of Shiloh) which convinced both sides that they were in a war that would be bloody and relatively long before the issue was decided. That Sunday and Monday, April 6th and 7th, 1862, was the largest battle, up until that time, fought on the American continent. The 23,000 causalities convinced even the most die-hard skeptics that this was a war that neither side could afford to lose. Too much blood had already been spilled for either side to quit before they were made to. That there was still three more years of hard fighting to do and many more lives to be lost was in the future for both the Federal Union and the Southern Confederacy, and was known only to God, but one thing was for certain; the fighting would go on in the mountains of Eastern Kentucky and Western Virginia and in the rest of the divided country.

In a letter to Gen. Lee on April, 10th, Gen. Marshall related that he had met and addressed the militia in person in Tazewell, Smyth, and Washington Counties, that had answered his call to duty. On the same trip he had also met the militia in Scott, Grayson, and Carroll Counties. A good number of the militia had volunteered for the war while assembled. The organizing and assembling of the militia had allowed Marshall to ascertain the approximate reliable militia strength of the country in which he was operating. This would allow him to have it placed in readiness for service should the need arise again. "The number organized will not exceed 3,000 nor fall short of 2,000," he wrote.

The news he had received of several regiments at Piketon being sent to Western Kentucky justified him in giving permission to the militia to return home to plant their crops after their organization was complete. Accordingly, he had already dismissed them all except those from Lee, Wise, Buchanan, and Wythe Counties. Those from Wythe he intended to dismiss as soon as he got to Wythe County to meet Gen. Heath.

The conscription had mostly been confined to young unmarried men, but about seven married men had been drafted because they positively refused service because they thought their property should protect them from service. In one case the party had taken the oath of allegiance to the enemy while in Kentucky engaged as a schoolmaster.

Marshall had set the classification as the most just in the draft was; 1st, on the unmarried men of the country; 2nd, on married men without children; 3rd, on men with families whose age subjected them to duty. He noted that he did call on them from the ranks as justified.

He had raised in this way in Russell County a company, under Captain Smith, of more than a hundred rank and file (118), a company of cavalry (64 rank and file), who elected Otis Caldwell their captain, and a squad of 71, who wanted want to elect their officers. With these volunteers taken from the Russell County militia, the remaining 405 men were organized into four companies and dismissed to their homes. The new volunteers were put into the field at once for the war. Marshall only actually drafted a total of five men for the war. They were the only single men left in the two Russell County regiments after all the other single men volunteered, and Marshall "knew of no good reason why they should not volunteer."

From Tazewell County, Marshall raised two companies of 100 men each for the war; from Carroll County one company of 100 men; from Grayson, one company of 100 men; from Scott, 200 men, or about that number. He demanded 300 men from Wythe County, 250 from Washington, 250 from Smythe, 200 from Lee, 100 from Buchanan and McDowell, and 50 from Wise.

Since Wythe County was Colonel Moore's home and Marshall was in part trying to fill up Moore's 29th Virginia Infantry, he sent Inspector-General Stansifer and Colonel Moore to Wythe, but they had limited success, although they did manage with Marshall's assistance to fill up the 29th Virginia entirely.

Marshall Proposed to renew from the Pound Gap Battalion the enlistments for three years or the war of all that want to change from special service to general service. If successful, there would be enough new and old material to form a new Virginia regiment.[183]

---

[183] ibid, pgs. 410, 411,

Chapter Thirteen

On to Princeton

From Lebanon, Virginia, on April 25th, Gen Marshall wrote Gen. Lee that he re-enrolled 197 men of the 29th Virginia and added 73 recruits which brought the total manpower of that regiment to 382 men in six companies, but with the recruits from the militia, he had also added three more companies to the regiment to fill it up. The companies added were Company G, (from Russell County, Captain Smith), 197 rank and file; Company H (from Tazewell County, Captain Bruster), 105 rank and file; Company I (from Russell County, Captain Dickenson), 80 rank and file; and Lieutenant March was now *en route* for camp with 100 men from Carroll, Wythe, and Grayson Counties, bringing the strength of the 29th Va. to 774. This number did not include deserters, 22, in arrest, 3, detached, 1, and in the hospital, 1. This would bring the total number of men in the 29th Va. on that date to 801 men.

Gen. Marshall brought the Pound Gap special service battalion to the court-house in Russell and allowed them a few days of rest, then personally made a speech to them trying to instill some *esprit de corps* among them, and attempting to convince them to enlist for the war. The first day he managed to raise a company of 94 men from the battalion, who organized on the spot, electing Captain Slemp as their captain. The next day 67 more men began a company, of which Captain Pridemore expected to be their captain when the number of men expanded to 100, and on the same day 51 more began a company for Captain Russell. All of these men were from Scott and Lee Counties entirely. Marshall had managed to obtain the 212 men from his skeleton special service battalion, (21st bn.) and he commented on them that "I have never seen finer material in my life." There were only two men over thirty years of age and those were in Captain Slemp's company of 94 men. The rest were between 18 and 23 years of age. All of the men of the battalion were mustered for pay that day and all were given a thirty days furlough. All who had not chosen to re-enlist had been put into one company under Captain Maness and all boys under eighteen and men over forty-five were discharged from the army.[184]

Marshall reported that the counties north of Russell County had displayed a disloyalty as bad as any of those in

---

[184] <u>War of the Rebellion</u>, 1, Vol. 10, part 2, pgs. 444, 445

Northwestern Virginia, and throughout his district there had been signs of the same spirit. The sheriff of Russell County had informed him that 900 Virginians had been sworn into the service of the enemy at Pikeville since the proclamation of the Governor of Virginia. One of his captains (Ratliff) who was in Lebanon to pick up guns, informed Marshall that two-thirds of Buchanan and McDowell Counties are against the Confederacy. Marshall thought that one-half of Wise County were of the same persuasion. The desertions from Lee, Scott, and Russell had been very numerous; scouts had informed him of the continual passage of men from Virginia into Kentucky.

Depredations were constantly being committed in Lee County by East Tennesseans, and threats were being made from Harlan County, Kentucky, to lay the country waste. In Lee County, Va., the militia had recently had several engagements with Unionists from Tennessee passing over into Kentucky. A courier brought Marshall word that the militia had had a conflict with the enemy, killing 25, and taking 75 prisoners, who were sent to Cumberland Gap. In Buchanan County, the Union men had surprised Captain Ratliff , killed one of his men, took two prisoners, and stampeded about 50 of his men, who lost their weapons, some ten or a dozen of them being country rifles of their own private property. He issued more rifles to the company, and directed that the marauders be driven out of the district.[185]

---

[185] ibid, 448.

On May 3rd, Marshall received word from Colonel Jenifer of the 8th Virginia Cavalry that the enemy had taken possession of Princeton, in Mercer County Virginia, on the evening of the 1st of May. The General immediately dispatched May's 5th Cavalry Bn., Moore's 29th Va., and a section of artillery, all under the command of newly promoted Brig. Gen. John S. Williams, to Liberty in Tazewell County. Colonel Trigg's 54th Va. was sent to Saltville, as the enemy was also threatening the Salt Works there.

The 5th Kentucky passed through Lebanon early on the morning of the 3rd, "looking finely & in fine spirits." The regiment had 9 drums with them. Col. Moore's 29th Va. passed through Lebanon at 4 p.m. on their way to Liberty, in Tazewell County.[186]

On Sunday, May 11th, at night, General Marshall and his staff climbed atop Flat Top Mountain on the road to Liberty, Va., and gazed down upon the camps of his army which lay encamped far below in the deep valley with the blazing of their campfires, which was the "grandest sight I ever witnessed," according to one member of Marshall's staff. They passed down the mountain and through the camps and went on to (militia) General Bowen's house which they reached at 11 o'clock at night on the 11th.

On the 12th, Marshall put his army on the road to Jeffersonville, (or Tazewell Court-House).That evening the army camped two miles beyond the town and rested there for the next two days. While encamped there a soldier

---

[186] Guerrant, diary entry, May 3rd, 1862.

had tried to escape the coming battle and died when he took off running and ran into a post, killing himself. Doubtless the fear of the coming battle out-weighed that of being branded a coward.[187]

Friday, May the 16th, Marshall's army started early on the road from Jeffersonville for Princeton Court House in Mercer County, where they expected to soon meet the enemy. The distance was 17 miles and the whole way nothing but desolation was encountered, except for a few pickets of the enemy who fired on the Confederate skirmishers as they reached the Cross-Roads road. The march was through an almost primeval wilderness, of impenetrable under- growth and but 2 or 3 houses were seen the whole 17 miles.

About six miles from Princeton the advance ran into the enemy and the engagement commenced. Marshall ordered his battalion and cavalry and mounted rifles forward and they went in without delay, being encouraged by Gen. Marshall. The pickets chased the enemy clear to Princeton and were in turn chased back. Another mile of advance brought the rebel army into contact with the skirmishers of General Cox's Federal forces. Soon, the fighting commenced in earnest. Gen. William's regiment moved in the center as the advance towards the town continued, with Trigg's 54th Va. on the right and Moore's 29th Va. on the left. The Rebels drove Cox's force back on the town, fighting very valiantly but they could not withstand the onset and fierce

---

[187] ibid may, 11th, 12th,15th.

rushes and loud huzzas of the Ragamuffin Regiment. (5th Kentucky)

Guerrant described the scene thus :

"By the side of the road—in which he had fallen—lay the gigantic corpse of a Zouave—apparently a German—all stark in death. The avenging ball had struck him just below the corner of the mouth & passed clean through his head—killing him instantly. He belonged to the Ohio Piatt Zouaves—His corpse was nearly black when I saw it.--& I pray I may never see another such sight. A little further down lay another of our enemies wounded—prayed Gen'l Marshall to have him cared for. The Gen'l promised he would. Here we came to a large hill which was cleared—except a few old dead trees &c. remaining. All over this ground lay the dead & wounded Yankees being more exposed to the fire of our troops." [188]

When the Federals were driven from this position they retreated to the town which was about two miles distant. When the fighting first started Captain Leonidas Elliott of the 5th Kentucky had been mortally wounded and would expire the next day. Three or four others had been slightly wounded but that was the extent of the losses of the rebels here. The loss of the Federals was 16 or 18 killed and several wounded, (according to Guerrant) besides what they carried off.

As darkness settled over the battlefield Colonel's Trigg and May were ordered to enter the town under cover of darkness. Eventually the whole brigade moved cautiously down the road to await the result of May's and Trigg's

---

[188] ibid, May 16th,, 1862

157

advance. When intelligence was received of the desertion of the town, the whole of the rebel forces occupied the town.

As they entered the outskirts, General Williams was ordered to advance with the battalion of cavalry to pursue the enemy. As they entered the town they were ambushed and Henry Weedin of Captain Holliday's company was killed.

The town was now a charred and blackened ruin, with only a house here and there standing. The town had been burned by Colonel Jenifer of the 8th Virginia two or three weeks earlier when the Federals first entered the town. On their retreat the Yankees had left 50 or 60 tents standing, some of them with candles still burning in them.

The rebel soldiers procured candles and began rummaging through the town and camp of the departed Federals, looking for blankets, oilcloths, hats, caps, guns, shoes, coffee, crackers, and anything else of value, and the enemy had left plenty.

The Confederates had eventually settled down in the town, and some had caught an hour or two of sleep when they were suddenly aroused and made to leave the town in order to occupy one of the commanding hills and prevent being flanked by the enemy who reportedly on their way there. They left Princeton just at daybreak and had been on their hill just a short time when the Federals appeared in the broad, open, and level field between the rebels and the town.

About 500 Federals marched out on the field and remained there in full view of the

Confederate Army for about one-half an hour. The Rebel battery was drawn up on the hill, with a commanding view of the town and field. Trigg's and Dunn's forces, (a battalion of recruits), were drawn up in the ravine just behind the six cannon of Captain Jeffress' battery. Gen. William's 5th Ky. was placed half a mile to the right, with part of his regiment on the left in the undergrowth.

Colonel Wharton, of the Rebel forces, had been ordered by General Marshall to be in Princeton by the night of the 16th but hadn't yet arrived. As Marshall arrayed his forces on the hill near Princeton, he received word that Wharton would arrive by 9 a. m., which he did. Wharton had positioned his men on Marshall's right flank and proceeded to open immediately on the enemy with his one piece of artillery.

Soon after, the enemy's battery, which was stationed near the ruins of the Court House in Princeton, opened fire on Jeffress' six pieces with shot and shell. Jeffress' battery immediately responded to the enemy with both sides booming away. The noise of the cannon was terrific, but most of the Yankee cannonballs were sailing harmlessly over the hill, but about 35 struck on the hill where the rebels were stationed. Despite the close calls and all the noise, none of the rebels were killed or wounded by the Federal missiles, many of which failed to explode. The townspeople later reported that the rebel cannon had hit a fence with one cannonball that killed nine Federals.

About 10 a.m. Wharton's command was furiously attacked by an estimated 1,000 Federals who had crossed the river behind

Wharton, but they were soundly defeated and scattered, with the claim by the Rebels that 50 or 60 of their dead and more than 100 wounded being left on the battlefield.

A flag of truce soon appeared from the town, asking to bury their dead and to remove their wounded, but General Marshall refused. Despite his refusal, some other officer had allowed it, as the enemy were already engaged in burying their comrades, so Marshall decided to allow the enemy ambulances to pass along his right and pick up their wounded also.

The remainder of the day the two armies lay in sight of each other and no other sounds of musketry was heard but an occasional round of cannon fire was exchanged. During the night the enemy vacated Princeton, taking the Raleigh road. Bradley's battalion of mounted rifles, (275 men) was ordered to follow him.

Seventy one of the Federal wounded who were too badly wounded to move were left in Princeton. Federal surgeons were left in attendance and a chaplain was permitted to stay with them. Twenty nine Yankee prisoners were captured by the Rebels and sent to Abingdon, where three others were already confined. Other items listed as captured by the rebel army was about 35 miles of telegraph wire, horses, mules, saddles, pack saddles, medical instruments, medicines in panniers, tents, a few stores, 18 head of cattle, a number of wagons, and some excellent muskets and rifles.

General Marshall reported casualties of four killed and 10 wounded. General Cox of the Union forces reported 23 killed, 69 wounded, and 21 missing.[189] The Army of Eastern Kentucky numbered 2,195 of all forces when the battle began, but Wharton's command added 800 men to the total, making 2,995 the actual number of men in Marshall's army.

Cox's Federal command probably numbered somewhere between 500 and 1,500, as he reported only three regiments as being in the battle, the Twenty-eighth Ohio, and parts of two other regiments, the Thirty-fourth and Thirty-seventh Ohio regiments.[190]

Marshall's little army of Cumberland Mountain Confederates had performed well in this, their second battle involving several hundreds of troops on both sides. While their causality rate had been low at both Middle Creek and Princeton, they had seen enough of war to know what fighting was all about, and were becoming somewhat seasoned troops. The men that were weak in body, mind, and spirit had quit and gone home, or into hiding by the second year of the war. The mountain boys of Kentucky and Virginia were learning how to make war with the best of them.

On June 1st, 1862, Marshall's army was still encamped about two miles from Jeffersonville, in Tazewell County, resting and engaged in recruiting their ranks. That very day they mustered in a company of Partisan Rangers from McDowell and Buchanan counties, under Captain Harman.[191]

---

[189] War of the Rebellion, 1, Vol. 12, part 1, pgs.513-517 ; Guerrant, diary, May, 16th,1862

[190] War of the rebellion, 1, Vol. 12, part I, pgs. 503, 514, 515.

[191] Guerrant, diary entry, June 1st, 1862.

Also on that day, Colonel Cranor of the Federal Eighteenth Brigade in Piketon took advantage of the lack of Confederate troops in far Southwestern Virginia to send in the 40th Ohio for a raid through the Pound Gap. Proceeding through the Gap and up "one of the most desperate roads in the mountains," they entered the village of Gladesville, and soon met up with a small detachment of Lee County's 94th Militia, who were easily subdued. Alexander Orr, J. N. Russell, and John M. Smith were captured and taken to Camp Chase, Ohio. [192]

County Clerk Morgan T. Lipps and Alexander Smith, commonwealth attorney, were also captured in the raid. Smith was released immediately, but Mr. Lipps was taken to Piketon, and later to Louisa, and then released after three months.

"Elder" Lipps had that afternoon bridled and settled his horse, and in his shirt sleeves had rode over to Gladesville to have his horse shod in preparation to go hold one of his weekend meetings. As he was riding home he unexpectedly ran into the Federal soldiers who took him captive. He asked them permission to be detailed to go home and get his shirt and they agreed to allow him to do so.[193]

---

[192] The Civil War in Buchanan and Wise Counties, Jeffrey C. Weaver, H.E. Howard, Inc. Lynchburg, Virginia, 1994

[193] Addington, The Story of Wise County Virginia, 1956.

Chapter Fourteen

On to Kentucky

After the Battle of Princeton, at least 71 Federal wounded were left in that town that were too badly wounded to move. On May 20th, a Federal chaplain from the Thirty-fourth Ohio approached a Rebel post bearing a flag of truce with a note from Union General Cox, accusing Gen. Marshall of leaving his wounded adversaries without proper arrangements to attend them.

The next day, General Marshall wrote to Gen. Cox and expressed his outrage that he would be accused of abandoning the wounded prisoners to their own mercy. Marshall related how he himself had visited the wounded and left his own surgeons, along with some Federal surgeons to attend to them. Marshall offered to exchange the wounded left there for a like number of Confederates then on parole in Virginia.[194]

General Cox replied to Marshall's letter on May 22nd and allowed as how that the order for treating the Federal seemed to not have been carried out by Marshall's subordinates. A large supply of Medicines, bandages, lint, etc. left with them by the Federals had been carried away, he had been informed, and no adequate provision for food for them had been made either. He expressed his wish that the Federal wounded be moved within their own lines to alleviate their miseries and he would extend the same courtesy with Confederates who may be found in the same situation.[195]

The Chief Surgeon of Marshall's Army of Eastern Kentucky, Basil C. Duke, received a note from Marshall making inquiries about how he had provided for the Federal wounded left at Princeton. Dr. Duke sent an answering note on May 23rd, saying that he left with the surgeons (of the enemy) medicines enough for all their purposes, taking none of their surgical and none of their bandages or lint. Besides, upon examination of the stock of dressings, he had left the steward of the hospital all the lint and dressings he had upon the field. Provisions of bacon and flour was all he had on hand, which was left in a sufficient amount to serve their purposes.[196]

Marshall's army would enjoy a couple of months rest after Princeton, with some recruits joining his ranks while encamped in Tazewell.

---

[194] War of the Rebellion, Series 2, Vol. 3, Pg. 566.
[195] ibid, pgs. 570, 571.
[196] ibid, pg. 587.

Witcher's cavalry also had a brush with the Federals in Logan Co. Virginia, in which Witcher himself was wounded, but not dangerously. Witcher was taken to Jeffersonville, Va. to recuperate from his wound.

On August 13, 1862, General Edmund Kirby Smith began his move into Southeastern Kentucky by way of the Cumberland Gap, while Major General Braxton Bragg's army entered Kentucky further west in early September. Smith fought a major battle in Richmond, Ky. while moving towards Lexington and achieved a hard-fought victory over Federal General "Bull" Nelson's forces there.

Brag's forces defeated a federal force at Munfordville and bagged 4,000 prisoners, 4000 small arms, several pieces of artillery, and munitions of war in large quantities.[197]

It was an auspicious start for the invasion of the Bluegrass State, but one that would turn sour at Perryville, Kentucky, where Bragg would be defeated there By the Federal Army of Major General Don Carlos Buell, on October, 8th, 1862. The battle was the largest ever fought in Kentucky, with Federal casualties reaching 4,211 (845 killed, 2,851 wounded, and 515 missing) and Confederate total losses of 3,396 (510 killed, 2,635 wounded, and 251 missing,) which makes the butcher's bill total 7,607 men. The total likely is even higher, as burial records for at least 70 additional dead have been identified.[198]

---

[197] Perryville, Noe, Kenneth W., pg. 70, The University Press of Kentucky, 2001

[198] ibid, 344.

On August 18th, in a letter to the Sec. of War, from Abington, Va., Marshall wrote that he had received a telegram from Gen Kirby Smith urging him to be ready to move into Kentucky to co-operate and to hold all in readiness for a moment's warning, which he will give by telegraph. General Loring, the District Commander in Southwestern Va., is detaining his (Marshall's) regiments, which is a clear violation of the understanding they had. "Can you not restore my corps, so that I can progress with my special instructions? Recruits come to me here from Kentucky. I want some Enfield rifles."[199]

In an undated letter to the Secretary of War, Marshall asks again for 5,000 men and 5,000 stand of Enfield rifles and muskets be sent him "at once, and I will move them forward by degrees as I get the men to use them, but I don't want any mistake about having them at hand when I need them."

He mentions in the same letter that there is a man by the name of (Captain) Menifee in Kentucky who is recruiting for General Floyd's state line, and has gathered some 300 men in the mountains. "He has committed violence on private property, taking all the property, for instance from a store of a citizen of Kentucky town, and is now moving forward on my line of contemplated movement, I have no doubt plundering and exciting the whole country."[200] (This store was owned by Colonel John Dils of the 39th Kentucky

---

[199] War of the Rebellion, Ser. 1, Vol. 16, part 2, pg. 763.
[200] ibid, 765.

166

Infantry, U.S., which was supposedly robbed of several thousands of dollars' worth of merchandise by Captain Menifee and Capt. Caudill, who would later be Colonel of the 10th Kentucky Mounted Rifles.)

General Kirby Smith notified Marshall on August 20th that he was moving from Barboursville, Ky. to Richmond, then to Lexington on the 25th. He asked Marshall to move forward rapidly into Morgan County and co-operate with him. He added that, "I feel assured that the president will approve of your so acting."[201]

The next day, Marshall reported to Gorge W. Randolph, the Sec. of War, that he has one regiment already in Piketon (the 5th Ky.,) and shall order his cavalry forward without delay. He asked that General Loring be ordered to relieve Trigg's 54th Va., so that he could move forward. He asked Randolph for the arms he had requested and to re-enforce him if possible.[202]

By September 7th, Marshall was ready to head to Kentucky to try to co-operate with Smith and Bragg in their Kentucky invasion. Marshall's army now consisted of the 5th Kentucky regiment, (700 men) 43rd Tenn., (750) 21st Va. Bn., (350) 54th Va., (750) 29th Va., (700) Mounted Rifles, (350) Shawhan's Cavalry, (150) Georgia Bn., 500), and 12 cannon, Jeffrees' Battery (six pieces), and Capt. Davidson's Battery, (four pieces) besides the Va. Cavalry (400). The army extended from

---

[201] ibid, 767.
[202] ibid.

Abingdon, Va., to Mount Sterling, Ky., a distance of 200 miles.[203]

The Rebel Army of Eastern Kentucky passed through Pound Gap on the 9th, where the appearance of the burned encampment (destroyed by the Yankees during the March 16th battle) at the Gap "renders the very picture of desolation." On the mountain Marshall and staff passed the trains and Davidson's Battery and rode on to Craft's at the mouth of Millstone, where they turned off the main road and traveled up Millstone a mile to Jesse Bates' home where they stayed for the night.

The next morning Marshall passed from Millstone over into the head of Rockhouse, then crossed another mountain to the head of Beaver. From there they advanced to Prestonsburg, which they reached on Sept. 12th.[204]

When Marshall turned up Millstone Creek on Sept. 9th, the 43rd Tenn. Reg. and the 21st Va. Bn. had continued on down the Kentucky River to Whitesburg, the little county seat of Letcher County, Kentucky. Whitesburg, in the U.S. census of 1860, had just 350 residents and very few buildings. It had a water mill below the town on the Kentucky River, 3 or 4 general stores, a jail, a hotel, a couple of flour mills, a few lawyers, a couple of churches, and a few other proprietary entities, plus the courthouse, which brought all the legal business conducted in the county to its streets.

---

[203] Guerrant diary entry, Sept. 7th, 1862.
[204] ibid, Sept. 9th, 10th, 11th 12th.

Those streets were unpaved, but there were wooden sidewalks on each side of the street which helped keep the mud off shoes when rain turned the streets to mush. Loaded wagons would sometimes become so mired in the miserable mud holes that a team of horses or mules would have to be hitched to the stranded wagon and pull it up the street to the peak to get it started down the other side.

On the west side of Whitesburg the Confederates had a hospital near the mouth of Sandlick Creek where Marshall had left his sick soldiers when he had to pull back to Pound Gap just after Middle Creek. Some of his army had also encamped there at that time.

Just about the time the 43rd Tenn. And the 21st Va. Bn. Came through Whitesburg on the 9th of Sept., Colonel Benjamin E. Caudill was in Whitesburg recruiting men for the new Confederate Regiment which would become the 10th Kentucky Mounted Rifles, and would later, in March, 1865, be re-designated the 13th Kentucky Cavalry Regiment.

Caudill's effort to raise a regiment of mountain men for a mounted force would be entirely successful, as a total of nine companies with a total of 1,134 men would enlist in the months of September and October 1862. Eight companies were composed of men mostly from Letcher County, with a sprinkling of volunteers from Perry, Pike, and Floyd Counties. One company, K, was recruited in Virginia in August, 1863 when the army was scattered throughout the western counties of Virginia.

Unfortunately, some of the new recruits deserted even before the regiment left

Whitesburg, but the majority were true to their word and served the Confederacy until the end of the war. Also, the recruits of Company F of the new regiment came largely from Floyd County, Kentucky.

Colonel Benjamin Caudill had been in the Confederate Army since the muster of the 5th Kentucky Infantry in November of 1861.This was the regiment raised by John S. Williams, who became the colonel of the regiment when it was mustered in on that date. Captain Caudill was the commander of Company F of that regiment.

At the same time that Colonel Caudill's 10th Ky. was being organized, the 14th Ky. was being recruited in the Big Sandy Valley, along with Field's Partisan Rangers. These three new Confederate units were made possible because of Marshall's move back into Kentucky, along with the invasion by General Bragg and Smith, who were giving the Federals fits in the central part of the state.

Roster, Field and Staff, 10th Kentucky:
Caudill, Benjamin F., Colonel, Nov. 2nd, 1862
Caudill, David J., Lt.Colonel, Nov. 2nd, 1862
Chenoweth, Thomas J., Major, Nov. 2nd, 1862
Strong, Hiram, Surgeon, Nov. 2nd, 1862
Whipple, George S., Surgeon, Feb. 14th, 1865
Newton, Moore, .Q.M. ....
Collier, J.W. , A.Q .M. Nov. 2nd, 1862
Strong, E.C., A.Q.M. Nov., 2nd, 1862
Craft, John, A.Q.M. Nov. 2nd, 1862
Hope, Robert A., Adjutant Sept. 1861 P-burg
Craft, J.H., Adjutant Nov., 1st., 1861
Booth, A. J., Ord. Sgt. Oct. 13th, 1863

On October 25, from Catlettsburg, Ky., Colonel John Dils, Jr., of the Federal 39th Ky., reported to Major General Wright in Cincinnati that the Sandy Valley and adjacent counties were overrun with marauding guerrilla bands. He said that Witcher's band was the most formidable of the marauders; his fields for "operating for thieving" is near Grayson Court-House, Ky., with a force near 1,000, mostly mounted, and in addition (General)Marshall is in Salyersville, Magoffin County, with a large force of 10,000, (actually about 3,000) with a part of that force (William's 5th, 700) at Prestonsburg, Floyd County, on Sandy River, 75 miles from Catlettsburg. He reported that John B. Floyd was also at Logan Court-House, Va. (now West Va.) with 1,500 men.

Dils reported his force at Catlettsburg as 400, with 200 recruits reported to be above on the Sandy River, and no difficulty getting all the men he wanted for his regiment if they were relieved.[205]

On Sept. 13th, Marshall's command was still in Floyd County when Kirby Smith wrote him urging him to come to Paris, Ky., as rapidly as possible. The enemy was then concentrating his forces at Louisville and Covington, and "it is of the highest importance that our forces should be united with the least possible delay."

By Sept. 26th Marshall and his command had finally reached Mount Sterling, Montgomery County, Kentucky, where Generals Marshall, Smith, Heth, Ledbetter, and Churchill had a meeting to plan their next move. The next day, Marshall's command marched to Owingsville to try to cut off Federal

---

[205] War of the Rebellion, Ser. 1, 16, part 2, pg. 614.

Colonel Morgan's retreat from Cumberland Gap, which had been caused by Kirby Smith's entry into Kentucky in middle August. Morgan's men had had a rough time of it, being out of supplies and trying to subsist off the poor country he had traveled through.

Morgan managed to escape the Confederate forces and Marshall was ordered to march on to Lexington and Frankfort, where Richard Hawes, the Confederate Governor designee for Kentucky, was scheduled to be installed as governor by General Bragg on Oct. 4th, only to be interrupted by the appearance of the Federal forces across the Kentucky River on the Shelbyville road. The Confederates quickly retreated to Versailles, Ky., west of Lexington. The Confederate Army and General Bragg would then meet General Buell and Union Army at Perryville on Oct. 8th.

General Marshall's forces marched to Lexington, Nicholasville, and nearly reached Danville but were too late to participate in the battle of Perryville.

On Oct. 13th Marshall's army was encamped near Bryantsville, Kentucky, when they got word to march back to Pound Gap and home. At 10 o'clock that night they reached Lancaster, where Marshall and his staff had a supper of pickled pork and cornbread while occupying an abandoned home on the outskirts of Lancaster.[206]

The 5th Kentucky Infantry, now under Colonel Hiram Hawkins, had been mustered in at Prestonsburg, Kentucky during the months of Sept. and Oct., 1861. The date of their official

---

[206] Guerrant, diary, Oct. 14th, 1862.

entry into service was October 21st of that year. That were told at the time of their enlistment that their term of service was for one year only. In their retreat from Central Kentucky, the reg. was at Hazel Green, Ky., moving towards Pound Gap, on Oct. 21st, 1862, when their one year enlistment was up.

In a letter to the Confederate Secretary of War, dated Nov. 5, 1862, Marshall advised him of what had been done concerning this regiment :

"They refused to reorganize. In my march from Kentucky the subject of their re-enlistment was frequently discussed. Once I made some remarks to them urging them to re-enlist, and promised all the twelve months' men furloughs of thirty days if they would re-enlist. At McCormick's, on the 18th of Oct., I had two companies of the regiment brought to my headquarters, and promised to furlough them then if they would re-enlist, and I obtained but two re- enlistments from the two companies. Someone then suggested that they desired to change to mounted service, and I agreed if they would make up companies of 80 men, I would accept them as cavalry, give them the furlough, and they could, at its expiration, rejoin me as mounted corps; all had no effect. The men said they had been in service about twelve months, and when their time was out they wanted an honorable discharge, and after a little rest they would re-enter the service, for they knew they could not stay at home. I could not then move them.

173

At Hazel Green, the 21st October, the regiment was not turned out to march. I went to see about it. They said their time was out, and they would not march out of Kentucky willingly. I found that desertions had been going on frightfully, and that the deserters carried off their arms and accouterments and ammunition. I determined to save what remained of these, and considering that if they were disbanded and paid they might rejoin, but if they deserted they never would, I determined at once to muster the twelve- months men for pay and to discharge them, and did so. The commissary returns show the regiment drew at Bryantsville, Ky., just before the retreat commenced, 1,047 rations: they stacked at Hazel Green 300 muskets. I took away from them these arms, and mustered them out on the spot."

This incident with the 5th Kentucky was a common problem when regiments enlisted for only a short time period during the Civil War. There were many instances when some soldiers refused to serve even one day longer when their enlistments were up, even on the eve of battle. As the war dragged on, only enlistments for the war were allowed, with bonuses to enlist and the fear of being drafted spurring some to enlist so as to be able to choose their service and regiment.

Marshall mentioned the success Colonel Caudill had achieved at Whitesburg, enlisting nine companies of mounted infantry with which he drove the Home Guards through

174

several counties. He told the Secretary that these new soldiers had also commenced to desert when they understood that they were expected to leave Kentucky immediately. He had therefore directed Col. Caudill to remain in Kentucky with his command until further orders. Four mounted companies, under major Johnson, Caudill's nine companies (600), and three companies under Colonel Hawkins (385 men) remained in Kentucky when Marshall's command crossed Pine Mountain and through Pound Gap on Oct. 30th, 1862. These men were occupied in guarding the country from Whitesburg to Prestonsburg, thus keeping the roads open for possible recruits who wanted to join the Confederate Army. Dispatches from these units to Marshall on Nov. 2nd gave the enemy's location as still being in Mount Sterling, in central Kentucky. By Nov. 3rd, Gen. Marshall's headquarters were once again re-established in Abingdon, Virginia. His venture into Kentucky was now over.[207]

On Nov. 12th, Secretary of War G.W. Randolph sent this message to Marshall:

General Marshall, Abingdon;
Keep your promise to the twelve months' men, and do what you think best. Can you not employ your cavalry in driving hogs out of Eastern Kentucky?[208]

---

[207] O.R. 1, 20, pt 2, pgs. 389-392
[208] ibid, 392.

Chapter Fifteen

Carter Comes Calling

On Nov. 8th, the Sec. of War wrote to Marshall to inform him of complaints about stragglers from the 5th Kentucky with arms in their hands, who were plundering, and stealing horses, and Camron's Kentucky battalion, Miller's Rangers, and Everett's Rangers were marauding in Washington County, Virginia. He advised Marshall to use force, if necessary to protect the people of the country.[209]

Marshall wrote Randolph on Nov. 18th about his suggestion of driving out hogs from Kentucky, using his mounted force. Marshall feared it would not be a welcome task for the men to do this; but his own opinion was that such service could not only be performed but would be the most useful in which these men could be engaged. The Virginia troops on the other hand, would not willingly enter Kentucky

---

[209] O.R. 1,20, pt. 2, pg. 394.

after all that has transpired. The Kentucky troops ardently desire to return to Kentucky and they have no doubt but that a very large force can be raised there with any fair assurance that they will be permitted to operate in that state.

He allowed as how his failure to bring infantry recruits out of Kentucky was a signal failure, but he wanted the President and Sec. of war to understand the cause of the failure. He blamed the cause on the fact that no sort of chance was afforded him to come into contact with the people of Kentucky; he did not even get within 40 miles of his own home. He did manage to bring out, from his own section, one regiment of cavalry, nearly 800 strong, all recruits, both officers and men. His battalion of mounted rifles grew from 300 to 700 strong. He also thought he would be able to make a full regiment of mounted troops, 1000 men, from the recruits.

He had forwarded the muster rolls of the nine companies of infantry recruits Captain Caudill had enlisted in Whitesburg; and has managed to save 3,000 men from the wreck. Colonel Hawkins had been at first been left on the Sandy with his regiment (while retreating from Kentucky). Now he has retreated into Virginia before a superior force, which occupies Piketon, Ky., 900 strong. He informed Randolph that the men he left at Whitesburg "have been constantly engaged with the Home Guards (About 600 strong, from Harlan County, Kentucky), and , I hear, successfully engaged generally, though the other day a party of 40 came into Whitesburg and murdered several of the citizens, burned the houses of Captain Caudill and of his father and brothers, and carried off his wife a prisoner."[210]

In another letter to Assistant Secretary of War Hon. J. A. Campbell, Marshall admitted that after he arrived at Abingdon on the 13th of Nov., one of his battalions of riflemen had halted five miles outside Abingdon; Everett's company of same in the environs of town. Three or four days afterward, Messrs. White, Rev. Johnson, Campbell, and Cummings called on him and made complaint that the mounted riflemen were entering Mr. White's corn-field and taking corn he could not spare; some were shooting hogs, burning rails, etc. He informed Hon. Campbell that he had written an order in their presence reprobating such practices in the most emphatic terms.

Marshall gave the price of corn in the Abington area as; corn $3.00 per bushel, pork at $25.00 per hundred weight, hay at $2 per hundred weight, which would fix the price of land at $1,000 or $1200 per acre. "I gave my disbursing officers instructions to pay $1.50 per bushel for corn, and $1 per hundred weight for hay, and if the articles could not be purchased at this price to report the matter to me and to not take where there was any doubt of the ability of the owners to spare without the inconvenience of his own family, stock or property."[211]

Colonel John Dils jr., of the Federal 39th Kentucky, reported to Gen. Horatio Wright that a Confederate force had advanced to Coal

---

[210] ibid, 407-410.
[211] ibid, 400, 401.

Grove, 8 miles from the Federal Camp Finnell, but they had fled their encampment about one hour before Dil's men reached there. Dils pursued them and reported the capture of 75 rebel prisoners, 150 guns, 3 wagons, a lot of tents, horses and mules. He pursued them to within 20 miles of the Pound Gap, but his men being marched down, the others got away.[212]

On Dec. 4th another engagement took place at Piketon between the 39th Ky., and the Confederates of Col. John N. Clarkson of the Va. State Line Cavalry about 4 miles below Prestonsburg at Wireman's Shoal's. Clarkson's command was composed of detachments of the First, Second, and Third Regiments of the Virginia State Line Cavalry. His force reached Piketon on the 4th of Dec., where they were informed that several boats were on their way up the Sandy River, loaded with large supplies of ammunition and clothing intended for the Federal troops stationed at Piketon. He moved his column immediately down the banks of the river, and discovered nine loaded boats, attended by a strong guard.

The information of the approach of the Rebel force had already been carried to the boats by a Union sympathizer in the area, and the boat crews and their guards were ready for them. A spirited contest ensued between the adversaries, and continued for about one hour's duration, when the 300 or so Federals were routed by the rebels.

Colonel Clarkson reported 2 men killed and 7 wounded. He gave the loss of the enemy as at least 25 killed and about the same number

---

[212] O.R. 1,20, pt1, pg.7.

wounded, and 25 prisoners, which they secured. He gave the supplies captured from the boats as, 500 rifles and ammunition, with all the accouterments necessary for 800 or 1,000 men. "The clothing of every description captured was sufficient to equip the greater portion of the force under my command." A large amount of sugar, coffee, and salt was aboard the boats, and was nearly all brought away by the Rebels.

Two of Clarkson's Captains were painfully, but not dangerously wounded, but Clarkson was able to convey them back to Virginia with the Rebel force. Lieutenant Hampton of the enemy force was reportedly killed in the battle.

In their three day incursion, Clarkson's men had traveled 140 miles, captured property to the amount of $250,000, captured 25 prisoners, 100 cattle, more than 150 horses, and many negroes. [213]

Colonel Dils of the 39th had a different take on the battle; he admitted losing the boats to capture, but not until "14 or 15 of them had been killed." He admitted to only two men of his command as being killed, and his losses in supplies of 50 to 100 rifles, 7,000 rounds of ammunition, 300 suits of fatigue uniforms, a small lot of commissaries, 1 tent and two push boats.[214]

A movement on the Salt-Works and the railroad in Western Virginia had been planned by the Federals as early as Nov. 25th, 1862, but

---

[213] ibid, 32, 33.
[214] ibid, 31, 32.

it wasn't until Dec. 19th, that arrangements for the raid were completed and the necessary orders given for the movement of the troops. Major General Horatio G Wright had given the job of fitting the expedition out to Major Gen, Granger in Lexington, Kentucky, and Granger had chosen Brigadier General Samuel P. Carter, a native of the area, to carry out the raid.

Carter gave the order for the assembling of his forces while at his headquarters in Lexington. The troops were to assemble near the mouth of Goose Creek, Clay County, Kentucky. The units involved consisted of two battalions of the Second Michigan Cavalry, Lieutenant Colonel Campbell, the Ninth Pennsylvania Cav., Major Russell, and First Battalion Seventh Ohio Cavalry, Major Reaney. Carter left Lexington on the 20th for Goose Creek. Col. Charles J. Walker of the Tenth Kentucky, U.S.A. was put in charge of the cavalry brigade.

The troops were ordered to move without baggage, with ten days' rations and a hundred rounds of ammunition. A supply train accompanied the force for 60 miles, then transferred the forage and rations to a mule train. On the 22nd, the command came up on the two battalions of Second Michigan and Ninth Pennsylvania at McKee, Jackson County, Ky., where the whole force was detained a day waiting for the supply train and pack saddles. On the 22nd a junction was effected with the remainder of the troops (First Battalion Seventh Ohio Cavalry) at Heard's on Goose Creek. Carter was surprised to find that his whole force amounted to only about 980 men, with a considerable number of them in the field for the first time. From there, the marches were slow due to the roads being merely bridal paths along the banks of creeks and over steep mountains.

It wasn't until the 28th that they reached the foot of the Cumberland Mountains (on the north side) opposite Crank's Gap, which was 12 miles south-east of Harlan Court-House. There, the horses were fed, a day's forage was prepared, and the pack train sent back under charge of a detachment of the Ky. State Guard. The summit of the mountain was reached before sunset, with the field of their operations with its mountains and valleys spread out before them. After a consultation with the officers of the command, Carter decided that his force was too small to divide it into two columns as had been planned.

Soon after dark, the descent of the south side of the mountain began, hoping to make a long march before daylight, but owing to the steepness, narrowness, and roughness of the way, the rear of the column didn't reach the foot of the mountain until 10 p. m., having been four hours in the descent. Hearing of 400 rebels being in Jonesville, just 5 miles distant, Carter crossed through a gap in Poor Valley Ridge, and crossed Powell's Valley, about 5 miles east of Jonesville. At daylight, Waller's Ridge was reached , which was about 22 miles from the foot of Cumberland Mountain. No one knew of their presence until some of the officers allowed some of the men to visit the town of Stickleyville where a number of Rebels belonging to Trigg's 54th Va. mistook them as friends and wondered within the Federal lines and were captured.

In a short time they were again on the road and went across Powell's Mountain and through Pattonsville. Before sunset they reached Clinch River, 12 miles from Estillville, (now Gate City) Scott County, Virginia.

In Estillville someone told them that a considerable force of rebels was in possession of Moccasin Gap, and were prepared to resist the Federal's passage. Carter dismounted the Michigan battalions and sent them through the Gap. They advanced with caution, only to find the Gap undefended, with the Confederates reported to have fled towards Kingsport, Tennessee. A Rebel Lieutenant and several soldiers were then captured on the south side of the Gap on the Blountsville road.

The Federals moved forward during the remainder of the night as rapidly as they could over the unknown roads, picking up Rebel soldiers here and there. A portion of the command became separated from the main body due to the darkness of the night. A small force of Rebel cavalry fired on the Yankees, killing a sergeant of the Second Michigan and captured two other soldiers who had wondered from the road.

At daylight, Carter's command reached Blountsville, Sullivan County, Tennessee, and took possession of the place, capturing some 30 men of the Rebel Fourth Kentucky Cavalry Regiment, who were in the hospital, and paroled them.

Hearing that Colonel Slemp and his 900 men, Colonel Giltner and his 4th Ky. Cavalry, and a battery were in Bristol, Carter decided to bypass it and move towards the railroad bridge in Union, Tenn., and accordingly sent forward Colonel Lieutenant Campbell with a portion of the Second Michigan, under direction of Col. James P.T. Carter, of the Second East Tenn. Inf., towards Union with orders to take the place and burn the railroad bridge across the Holston River. When General Carter reached Union the town was in the possession of the Federals and the 600 foot long bridge was slowly burning. The 150 rebel troops of the Sixty-second North Carolina had surrendered without resistance .

The prisoners were paroled and by the afternoon they were on their way back to North Carolina. "Their joy at being captured seemed to be unbounded," wrote General Carter later.

The stores, depot, niter, some salt, tents, barracks, arms and equipment, and a wagon bridge across the river at Union were destroyed by the Federals. While the destruction was underway, a detachment was sent under the command of Colonel Walker, under the guidance of Colonel Carter, towards the Watauga Bridge, at Carter's Depot, 10 miles west of Union.

On reaching the station, two companies of the Sixty-second North Carolina resisted the Federals but were soon broken and fled to the woods. The Federals loss here was 1 killed, 1 mortally and 1 severely wounded, and 2 slightly wounded. The Federals put the rebel loss at 12 to 16 killed. The Railroad bridge across the

Watauga River, some 300 foot in length, was put to the torch, and entirely destroyed; also a large number of arms and valuable stores. A locomotive that was captured there was run into the river, destroying one of the bridge piers as it went into the river.

Because the alarm had now been given, and the troops being worn out, the decision to return to Kentucky was made. The Federals left Watauga at midnight, the 31stof Dec. and reached Kingsport, at the mouth of the North Fork of the Holston River at sunset. After feeding and resting a short time, and issuing a meat ration to the men, they were back on the road again. They passed some 8 miles north of Rogersville, and reached Looney's Gap, in Clinch Mountain, late in the afternoon; passed through without opposition, and about 11 p. m. of January 1st, 1863, reached a place in the edge of Hancock County, Tenn., where forage could be obtained, and bivouacked for the night.

Soon after daylight on the morning of the 2nd of Jan., they marched towards Jonesville, Lee County, Virginia, with the intention of reaching the foot of the Cumberland Mountains on the Kentucky side before they halted. The march was impeded by bushwhackers, (Lt. Colonel E.F. Clay's Third Ky. Confed. battalion of mounted rifles, 300 strong, and Major Johnson's Company of Mounted Rifles, 100 strong)., who constantly annoyed their front and rear. Just before reaching Jonesville the rebels opened fire from the hills in front of the town with two companies of skirmishers.

When the Federals reached Jonesville late that afternoon, they were attacked by Johnson and Clay. Meanwhile Colonel Giltner's 4th Kentucky had arrived , along with General Marshall, who ordered Giltner to move his 4th Kentucky to a small hill south of town where the Federals had first made their appearance.

The Federals then sounded "boots and saddles" on their bugles and left the village immediately. The rebel skirmishers passed across the village and struck the woods, which they penetrated until they came to the Harlan road, leading across the mountain and into Harlan County, Kentucky. Because of the darkness and the many chances for ambush by the retreating Federals, Marshall refused to order his men to take up the chase.

The Federals marched through Crank's Gap at 11 p. m. on the 2nd of January, and reached the foot of the north side of the mountain where they bivouacked, with the men being completely worn out, having been in the saddle the last five days and seventeen hours, having been out of the saddle but thirty hours he whole time.

At the time of Carter's entry into Virginia in his raid, Marshall's command was widely scattered over the Southwestern section of Virginia, with the mounted force having to hunt forage for their horses. Marshall adopted the road from Abingdon to Pound Gap as his line of defense, and all the roads leading to Estillville (Gate City) as his main lines of observation.

He had (H. L.) Giltner's 4th Ky. cavalry regiment at Lebanon, in Russell County, Major

V.A. Witcher's mounted battalion (34th Va.), was at Chatham Hill, in Smyth County, Colonel C. Slemp's (64th Va,) regiment of infantry (about 600 strong) was within 2 miles of Bristol, Lieut. Col. Clay's Third Kentucky Mounted Rifles was at three springs, within 5 miles of Bristol, and Major Johnson's battalion of mounted rifles (250) was at Kingsport, or its vicinity.

Colonel Hiram Hawkins' 5th Kentucky Infantry was then at or near Abingdon, Va., and Colonel (Ambrose C,) Dunn had command of a small force of re-enforcements that arrived by train in Bristol.[215]

Marshall reported his whole command numbered between 1,400 and 1,500 men of all arms to meet Carter's invasion. As Carter had reported his force at 980 men, Marshall had nearly double the number of men that Carter had to accomplish his mission. Since Carter didn't accomplish all that he had set out to do, it's not difficult to give General Marshall full credit in his repulse of the Union forces.

The total casualties for the Union forces during the five days were:

2 killed, 2 wounded, and 15 missing, for a total of 19.

The total Confederate casualties were not given in the reports after the raid, but were thought to be very light, excepting for the captured, which numbered 138 Rebels, according to Union reports. At the battle at Union, Tenn., Federal General Carter claimed 12 to 16 Rebels were killed in action, but this figure was likely not correct.

---

[215] ibid, pgs. 85-131.

One incident of the raid generated some controversial discussions concerning the killing of a Federal prisoner captured by a mounted picket detail from the Third Battalion Kentucky Mounted Rifles, of Lieut. Colonel E.F. Clay's command. In his after action report, Col. Clay explained that he had ordered Company A of his battalion to scout the roads leading from Estillville by which the enemy might approach his camp, and watch his movements. The scout sent on the Reedy Creek road had advanced about 6 or 7 miles when they met three of the enemy's cavalry--one a sergeant. Two of the Federals were made prisoners by the scout, and the other was shot from his horse by Major Thomas Johnson, who was not a member of Clay's command, but who had just overtaken the scouts while on the road from Abington to join his own command. The two prisoners were sent to Clay's camp, accompanied by Major Johnson, who was very much excited, and yet holding his pistol in his hand. Col. Clay questioned the prisoners, and learned from the sergeant that one Federal had stopped to fix something about his saddle, and that he, (the sergeant) had stopped back to bring them up to rejoin their command, having been placed in the rear of his company by his captain for that purpose. This had led to their capture and the shooting of one of his men by Major Johnson.[216]

Lieutenant H.H. Duncan, commander of Co. A, Third Battalion Kentucky Mounted Rifles, gave his version of the shooting of the prisoner in a report to Lieutenant-Colonel Clay:

---

[216] ibid, pgs. 120, 121.

_____ 1863

Sir: By your order, I submit the following report:

It was on the night of December 29, 1862 that, by your order, I was ordered to take a part of one company and scout down the Kingsport road, as it was reported the enemy's cavalry was coming in the neighborhood. I had gone some 7 miles and stopped the main body, and sent pickets 1 mile in front, with orders to stand until relieved. This was about two hours before daylight. The pickets in the mean time, hearing horsemen advancing, sent one of their number back to me to know what to do, as Colonel (Major Thomas) Johnson's command was encamped in the neighborhood, and they fearing to fire for fear it was Johnson's men falling back. I was sitting in the road, mounted, with my men, when three men rode up to us from the rear, who afterward proved to be Col. Johnson and two of his men. At or about the same time three of the enemy rode up and asked if the front of the column was ahead. I asked what column. They replied the Ninth Pennsylvania. I then replied that we were Confederate troops, and ordered them to surrender, which they did, as I ordered my men to prepare. At or near the same time I heard a pistol shot, which I afterward learned was Colonel Johnson's. He shot one of the prisoners. We then fell back and stationed pickets. I then delivered the prisoners over to you (Colonel Clay). Colonel Johnson was a prisoner himself until he let himself be known.

Then was about the time of taking the enemy. These are the facts, as well as I remember.

Yours, respectfully, H.H. Duncan

Second Lieut. Co. A, First (Third) Batt. Ky. Mounted Rifles.

Lieutenant- Colonel Clay. [217]

Major Isaac B. Dunn made a report of the incident also, and he backed Major Johnson's actions. He related that Major Johnson ordered the three Federals to surrender but the sergeant made a motion to draw his pistol, when Major Johnson fired and killed him; the other two surrendered, and were made prisoners; and were sent to Colonel Clay's camp.

---

[217] ibid, 122.

Chapter Sixteen

Marshall Exits the Scene

Colonel John Dils jr. of the Union 39th Kentucky Regiment, sent a scout of 40 men from Peach Orchard in Lawrence County, Ky., to Pike County in early Jan., 1863. The scout had a little skirmish with some Confederates, killing 2, wounding 1, and capturing 1 prisoner belonging to guerrilla parties, " all bad men." They reported the nearest rebel force as being at Whitesburg, Letcher County, Kentucky, 12 miles from Pound Gap; about 300 there. (This force was Colonel Benjamin Caudill's Tenth Ky. Mounted Rifles, who had been left in Letcher County by Marshall to watch the mountain gaps.) Dils had learned, he said, that Marshall had not more than 600 men at Abingdon to guard the railroad, and he (Dils) was anxious to strike them a blow; but he "can't move until we (the 39th) are mustered in, and we want good guns; so we can try our hand."[218]

It might have been just as well that Colonel Dils wasn't allowed to "try his hand," as Gen. Marshall had nearer 1,000 of his mounted troops encamped around Abingdon, instead of the 600 Col. Dils had heard about.

"Troops of the Line" in Brigadier-General Marshall's command, February 18, 1863; Headquarters Holston Springs, Va.:

Fifth Ky., Col. Hiram Hawkins.
(10th) Ky. Mounted Infantry, Col. B.F. Caudill.
64th Virginia, Colonel Campbell Slemp.
4th Kentucky Cavalry, Col. Henry L. Giltner.
1st Kentucky Mounted Rifle Bn., Lieut. Col. E.F. Clay.
2nd Kentucky Mounted Bn., Maj. Thomas Johnson.
Jessee's (Ky.) squadron, Capt. E. Trimble.
Ky. Partisans (one company), Capt. William J. Fields.
Louisiana Mounted Rifles, Capt. O.P. Miller.
27th Virginia Battalion, Partisan Rangers (two companies), Capt. J.S. Collings.

---

[218] O.R. 1,20,pt.2, pg. 310.

Virginia Cavalry (one company), Capt. J. A. McFarland.

Davidson's battery, Capt. G.S. Davidson.

Jeffress' (Virginia) battery, Capt. W.C. Jeffress.

On detached service.

9th Georgia Artillery Battalion, Maj. A. Layden.

29th Virginia, Col. A.C. Moore.

54th Virginia, Col. Robert C. Trigg.

27th Virginia Battalion, Lieut. Col. H.A. Edmundson.

34th Virginia Battalion, Maj. V.A. Witcher.

Marshall's total muster-roll on this date was 7,667 troops. He gave his total effective force as 5,769.[219]

In his report on the number of troops in his command, Marshall enclosed the following letter;

(Indorsement) [sic]
HOLSTON SPRINGS, SCOTT COUNTY,VIRGINIA, Feb. 18, 1863.

The Sixty-fourth Virginia Regiment has been formed since Mr. Seddon came into office, and is composed of men raised in Lee, Scott,

---

[219] ibid, 1, 23,pt.2, pgs. 638, 639.

and Wise Counties, Virginia. One battalion of the regiment has not been drilled a month. The Fifth Kentucky Reg. is composed of recruits raised in Kentucky last fall. Both of these regiments are going through with the mumps and measles, and together, would not now parade for a fight more than 600 men. The troops were very sickly at Jonesville. Among other diseases, the small-pox broke out (it was said), and several officers and men have had it. While a great many of my recruits ran away from the pestilence, I left 125 men in hospital at Jonesville, and have about 40 under charge of an employed physician here.

Of the enumerated 790 mounted riflemen, Jessee's squadron of 150 have not more than 30 men mounted, and is composed of new recruits (exchanged prisoners), and have not received much camp instruction, I have not desired to mount them until spring, on account of the scarcity of forage. In Miller's company of 40, only a few have horses.

The Virginia mountain line, from the extreme eastern picket thrown out from Cumberland Gap to the eastern termination of the Department of East Tennessee, is at least 175 miles long. You see within the only force protecting it.

H. Marshall
Brigadier-General. [220]

---

[220] ibid, 639, 640.

On March 17th, 1863, a letter from Adj. Gen. S. Cooper informed Maj. Gen. D.S. Donaldson, Comdg. Dept. of East Tennessee, that Gen. Marshall had informed Cooper on March 3rd that he proposed to make an expedition into Kentucky with his command, by Pound Gap, and that he would have 1,500 mounted men ready for the movement in a week and when he enters the State will be joined by 300 more waiting his arrival.

The proposition of General Marshall had been favorably considered by the Department, with a view of making a diversion in favor of operations in Middle Tennessee, and for collecting supplies in the region of Kentucky in which the command moves, for the use of the armies; horses, mules, cattle, etc., thus collected, may be driven on the hoof, and the other articles could be transported in wagons. [221]

General Marshall did in fact start his mounted command towards Pound Gap on Friday, March 13th, with Colonel Giltner's 4th Ky. and Maj. Johnson's 2nd Bn. Of Kentucky Mounted Rifles in the van. By March 17th, Gen. Marshall was in Whitesburg, Letcher County, Ky., with Colonel Giltner's regiment camped near town. Not a pound of meat or bread was available there for the hungry 600 men of Giltner's regiment.

---

[221] ibid, pg. 705.

When Marshall's command left Whitesburg, Colonel Caudill of the 10th Kentucky went with the General as far as the head of Caney Fork on Beaver.[222]

One week later, on March 24th, Marshall's command had advanced to within eight miles of Louisa, Ky., when a reconnaissance by cavalry discovered the Rebels advancing rapidly towards the town with the intention of surprising the Federals there. Col. G.W. Gallup was in command of the Fourteenth Kentucky Infantry, who had first discovered the rebel force advancing. As soon as the skirmishing began, Gallup gave orders for his men to fall back to a prepared position where four 6 pounder artillery pieces were in place, skirmishing as they withdrew.

The Rebel skirmishers followed the Yankees through the wheat and corn fields, with Everett's company and a company of Clay's battalion deployed as skirmishers in a skirt of woods. Soon two companies of the 4th Kentucky (Alexander's and Whitaker's) were ordered to charge the enemy, with General Marshall himself charging with them. The charge was successful and the Federals took off towards town where they rallied behind their fortifications.[223]

Although in favor of attacking the town, the high hill the rebels would have to climb, along with the artillery and

[222] Guerrant, diary entry, March 17th, 1863.
[223] ibid, March, 25th.

strong defenses, convinced Marshall to give up on taking the town of Louisa. He gave as his excuse also that he had only 900 men, while the enemy could muster 1,700 or 1,800 defenders. In actuality, the Federals claimed to have only 750 effective fighters, exclusive of the Second Battalion Tenth Kentucky Cavalry, who were armed only with pistols and sabers, which according to Brig. General Julius White, "was useless in this mountainous region, except for guard or outpost duty."[224]

Marshall's force back-tracked and marched 8 miles towards Paintsville the same day as the battle at Louisa, and made 9 miles the next day. On March 28th they reached Paintsville and headed west towards West Liberty, reaching there on the 30th.[225]

Captain Reed had been sent with Marshall's forces to procure supplies for the Department of East Tennessee. He returned on April and reported that Marshall was, on the 5th of April, at Hazel Green, Ky., with 1,800 to 2,000 men. Reed reported that Marshall was intending on marching to Winchester, Ky., but he had collected no supplies and his men were not in a very fine state of efficiency, there being much straggling. Reed reported that the enemy, 2,880 strong, had come up to Paintsville from Louisa, and their cavalry had advanced

---

[224] O.R. 1, 23, pt.1, pg. 196.
[225] Guerrant, dairy entry, 27, 28, 30, March,

to Salyersville. Marshall had left his infantry in Virginia, but had ordered 600 of them to follow him into Kentucky through Pound Gap at a later date.

Brigadier General Davis, who was then the Commanding General of the Dept. of Tennessee, ordered the 600 infantry of Marshall's to stop at Pound Gap instead of proceeding into Kentucky, fearing they would be overpowered by the enemy who were between them and the force with Marshall. Gen. Davis then changed his mind and ordered them to proceed as Gen. Marshall had ordered. He also ordered 60 cavalry to Pound Gap to co-operate with the 10th Ky. that had remained near the Gap.[226]

By the 14th of April, Marshall's mounted men were in Harlan County, Ky., having traveled up the Middle Fork of the Kentucky River on their way back to Virginia. Much bickering had taken place among the soldiers, especially the officers, about Marshall's advance into central Kentucky. A few officers had actually resigned and gone home while in Kentucky and others were threatening to do so. Marshall had tried to stifle the dissent by talking to the soldiers one company at a time in order to motivate them but eventually the dissatisfaction caused him to head for Virginia.

From Harlantown,(now Harlan), Harlan County, Ky., Marshall wrote to

---

[226] O.R. 1, 23, pt. 2, pgs. 751, 752.

Brig. Gen. D.S. Donelson, Commanding East Tennessee, on April 18th, 1863, that in obedience to Donaldson's order, he had moved all his available cavalry from the valley of the Holston, about the 14th of March, on the way to Kentucky. He had found it impracticable to obtain stock or hogs (in Kentucky).He had been able to subsist his force, however, on the country through which he had passed. His horses had been cut down to nothing by the venture. He had had none of the co-operation promised him. No enemy had been met in force anywhere except at Louisa, and there he had not engaged them. He had not procured any recruits, and had found that the people manifest no desire against Lincoln's rule. He was now in the valley of the Cumberland, in front of his district, because "there is nothing to live on in the district itself." The people of Harlan County had been very hostile to his men, "and I propose to familiarize them at least with our faces, and to render communications easy from Cumberland Gap by this point to Whitesburg and the Sandy."[227]

On April 20th, Marshall's men left Harlan C. H. and traveled up the Poor Fork of the Cumberland River, then over the Mountains, reaching Whitesburg on the 21st.

General Marshall left on leave on May 1st and Colonel Trigg of the 54th

---

[227] ibid, pgs. 777, 778.

Va. was sent by Major- General Dabney H Maury, then commanding the Dept. of East Tenn., to command Marshall's forces, who were then scattered in Harlan, Perry, and Letcher Counties. [228]

On the day Trigg took command of the forces in Kentucky, Maj. Gen. Maury wrote him that it was very important that he should give his immediate attention to the condition of the forces under his orders, which now occupy Perry, Harlan, and Letcher Counties. "They appear to be too much scattered, and there is every reason to believe that after their recent service they will require unusual attention on the part of the commander to insure discipline and efficient action. Hold your command completely ready for active service, with 100 rounds of ammunition to the man."

When General Marshall left on leave on May 1st, he traveled to Richmond, Virginia. The fact that he had received word of his being replaced by Brig. Gen. William Preston of Kentucky probably was the reason for his trip to Richmond. The rumor that his officers and men had lost confidence in his leadership had evidently gotten back to Richmond and they felt that a change in leadership was necessary.

The Adjt. and Inspector General's Office published the official orders that relieved Gen. Marshall from command

---

[228] ibid, pg. 809.

and his replacement by Brig. Gen. William Preston on May 9th, 1863. Gen. Marshall received orders to report to General Joseph E. Johnston for assignment.[229]

On June 4th, the newly installed commander of the Department of Southwestern Virginia, Gen. W. Preston, received a telegram from his chief of staff ,V. Sheliha, that a regiment of Federal mounted infantry had passed into Harlan County on the 3rd of June, via Moore Creek; "they may intend entering Southwestern Virginia."[230]

The movement of the Union cavalry seemed to be intended as a demonstration on Big Creek Gap instead of Harlan County, as a telegram from Maj. Sheliha shows: The report of General Gracie's scout in Harlan County removes any present apprehensions.[231]

General Marshall headed off to Tennessee to command a brigade with General Joseph E. Johnston's army, and his successor, General Preston, was now charged with keeping the Federals from the salt-works and railroad in the Dept. of Southwestern Virginia.

Marshall had been assigned to the job in late 1861, when his command consisted of only the 21st Battalion of Virginia Volunteer "special troops" at the Gap, who had a verbal clause in their

---

[229] ibid, pg. 828.
[230] ibid, pg. 862.
[231] ibid, pg. 874.

enlistment terms that prevented them from having to leave the Gap and the State of Virginia. Another of his regiments he had inherited was the 29th Virginia Infantry Regiment that had only six companies and 300 men. The 5th Kentucky Infantry Regiment was a regiment in name only when Marshall traveled to Prestonsburg on Dec.1st, 1861. Only a portion of them had even been mustered in and they had had no training what-so- ever to speak of.

Marshall had managed to take this nucleus and mold them into a fine brigade of over 7,000 mostly veteran soldiers that had met the enemy and held their own in several battles and skirmishes in the 1½ years he spent with his brigade. He had done his best with what he had and that was all a country could ask of a man.

Marshall was born in Kentucky on January 13, 1812.He was a West Point graduate and a Mexican war veteran. He resigned from the Confederate Army in 1863 and served in the Confederate Congress as a representative from the border State of Kentucky. After the war, he was elected as a senator from Kentucky in the United States Senate.

Chapter Seventeen

Federals Raid East Tennessee

After General Marshall traveled to Richmond for new orders in early June, he learned that he would be reporting to General Joseph E. Johnston at Jackson, Mississippi, to take command of a brigade. Marshall made a trip there by railroad to confer with Johnston and to make a decision as to whether he would accept the transfer or submit his resignation.

After catching up with Johnston at Jackson, Marshall was offered by Johnston command of a division or a brigade, but Marshall made the decision to hand in his resignation instead. By June 11th Marshall was back in Abingdon getting ready to go to Richmond, Va., for "law and a newspaper."[232]

Gen. Marshall's replacement, General Preston, was already in Abingdon dispensing reports and orders. He sent a telegram to his boss, Major- Gen. Jones, Commanding Dept. of Western Va., (in Dublin, Va.)., of reports of an enemy regiment of cavalry hanging around Harlan, Kentucky, with the possible goal of an advance into Southwestern Virginia.

In return, Gen. Jones directed Brig. Gen. John S. Williams, who was now at Saltville, Va. under the command of Gen. Jones, to give all

---

[232] Guerrant, diary entry, June 11th, 1863.

the aid he could to Gen. Preston if the enemy moved upon him. Instead of on Saltville, the Federal force under Gen. Burnside made a move on East Tennessee, prompting Gen. Jones in Dublin, Va., to order his forces at Saltville and Glade Spring to hold themselves in readiness to move at the shortest notice with Gen. Preston's forces. This notice was given because of a report received the morning of the 7th that the enemy had two mounted regiments then at Pound Gap.[233]

General Burnsides' raiding force from Somerset, Ky. had hit East Tennessee instead of the salt-works in Saltville, Virginia, but Gen. Jones had prepared his forces to move to protect the salt works had it became necessary to do so. The importance of the salt-works to the Confederacy throughout the war cannot be overestimated. There was, of course, no means of refrigeration in those days, except with blocks of ice in winter time; therefore the preservation of beef, bacon, and other meats with which to feed the armies and the general population was, in a great measure, dependent upon the Confederacy's ability to hold the salt works and keep the manufacturing process going.

Maj. Gen. Ambrose Burnside was in command of the Federal Department of the Ohio, which was headquartered in Cincinnati, Ohio. Burnside ordered Col. William Sanders, of the 5th Ky. United States Cavalry, to lead an expedition into East Tennessee to destroy the East Tennessee and Virginia Railroad and do as much damage to the enemy as possible.

---

[233] O.R., 1,23,pt.2, pg.870.

Colonel Sanders left Mount Vernon, Ky., on June 14th, 1863, with a force of 1,500 men, composed of detachments of different regiments as follows; 700 of the First East Tenn. Mounted Infantry, under Col. R.K Byrd; 200 of the Forty-forth Ohio Mounted Infantry, under Major Moore; 200 of the One hundred and Twelfth Illinois Mounted Infantry, under Major Dow; 150 of the Seventh Ohio Cavalry Volunteers, under Captain Rankin; 150 of the Second Ohio Cavalry Volunteers, under Captain Welch; 100 of the First Kentucky Cavalry Volunteers, under Captain Drye, and a section of Captain Konkle's battery, First Regiment Ohio Artillery Volunteers, under Lieutenant Lloyd—for the East Tennessee and Virginia Railroad.

These forces took the Mount Vernon road to Williamsburg, Ky., on the Cumberland River, a distance of 60 miles, with a train of wagons, containing forage and subsistence stores to accompany them. From Williamsburg, they followed the Marsh Creek road to near Huntsville, Tennessee.

Hearing that a small party of rebels was stationed at Wartburg, Sanders sent a force of 400 men from the First Tennessee Mounted Inf. to surprise and capture them, and afterwards followed with the whole command. The surprise was complete, capturing 102 enlisted men and 2 officers, together with a large number of horses, 60 boxes of artillery ammunition, several thousand pounds of bacon, salt, flour, and meal, some corn, 500 spades, 100 picks, besides a large quantity of other public stores, and 6 wagons with mule teams. The prisoners were paroled and the property destroyed. Some of the Rebels escaped, giving notice of the approach of the Federals at Knoxville, Kingston, Loudon, and other places.

Reaching within 3 miles of the Loudon bridge on June 19th, Sanders learned that three regiments of Rebels with a reported 8 pieces of artillery, had been digging ditches and rifle pits for three weeks there to prepare for just such a raid on the bridge. For that reason, Sanders by-passed the bridge and went instead to Lenoir's Station, which place he reached at 8 a. m., arriving there after the departure of the Rebel troops. Here they captured a detachment of cavalrymen, with three 6-pounder iron guns, 8 officers, and 57 enlisted men. They burned the depot, a large brick building, containing five pieces of artillery, with harness and saddles, two thousand five hundred stand of small-arms, a very large amount of artillery and musket ammunition, and artillery and cavalry equipments. They also captured 75 Confederate States mules and horses. They decided not burn a large cotton factory found there, as it furnished the Union citizens there with cloth to make clothing. After the Federals left Sanders learned later that, " it was burned by mistake or accidently." As they advanced to Knoxville, the Federals destroyed the telephone wire and railroad track at points one mile apart.

At 7 p.m. on June 19th they encountered Rebel pickets and drove them to within one mile of the city. At daylight on the 20th, they moved up to the city limits on the Tazewell road, finding the enemy well posted on the hills and the adjacent buildings, with eight or nine pieces of artillery. The streets were barricaded with cotton bales, and the batteries were protected by the same material. The rebels were estimated at 3,000, including citizens who were impressed into service. After one hour's skirmishing, Sanders withdrew, capturing near the city two pieces of artillery— 6 pounders,-- the tents, and all the camp equipage of a regiment of conscripts, about 80 Confederate States horses , and 31 prisoners.

The Federals started for Strawberry Plains, following the railroad, and destroying all the small bridges and depots to within four miles of that place. At Flat Creek, a "finely built" covered bridge was burned and also a county bridge.

They crossed the Holston River on a bridge, only to find the enemy with four pieces of artillery waiting for them on the other side. After an hour's skirmishing, the Rebels loaded up on a train with a locomotive that had been waiting with steam up, and escaped, leaving all their guns (cannon) which were five in number. They also left 137 enlisted men and 2 officers as prisoners, also a vast amount of stores, ammunition, and provisions, including 600 sacks of salt, about 70 tents, and a great amount of camp equipage in Federal hands. They also destroyed the "splendid" bridge over the Holston River, over 1,000 fcct long, built on eleven piers. With the trestle work included the bridge was over 2,100 feet in length.

On June 21st, at Mossy Creek, New Market, and vicinity, they destroyed several cars, a large quantity of stores, several hundred barrels of saltpeter, 200 barrels of sugar, and a large amount of other stores. The Federals also destroyed the bridge at Mossy Creek, which was over 300 feet long. Also destroyed was a saltpeter factory and the machinery of a gun factory.

Heading for Roger's Gap and home, the Federals found the rebels had blockaded the Gap with fallen timber and the Gap guarded by infantry and artillery, with all practicable gaps also being blocked and guarded. Sanders determined to abandon his artillery, and move by a "wood path" to Smith's Gap 3 miles from Roger's Gap. There, the guns, carriages, ammunition, and harness were destroyed and left. A regiment of cavalry was driven from Smith's Gap, "only a bridal path," to clear the way for escape. After escaping the Gap, 170 Federals got on the wrong road and didn't rejoin the command until they reached Kentucky.

Sanders and his command reached Boston, Ky. and safety on June 24th. Many of their horses had given out and not enough were available to mount the men, many having to walk.

The losses suffered by the Federals on the raid, as reported by Colonel Sanders, were :

2 killed, 4 wounded, and 13 missing.

461 Rebels were captured and paroled.[234]

Major General Simon B. Buckner was in charge of the Confederate defense during the

---

[234] O.R. 1, 23, pt.1, pgs.384-389.

Sanders raid, and he made the following report to Adj. Gen. Simon Cooper in Richmond:

Knoxville, June 24,1863

General: The enemy's cavalry escaped through Chalder's Gap, with loss of a few prisoners and horses, and their artillery and baggage. They are beyond the mountains. The railroad and small trestles will be in order to the Holston in four days. The cars can cross the Holston, on a trestle-bridge I am building, within two weeks. After that time there will be no delay or transfer of freight. After four days hence the only transfer will be in crossing the Holston, where, if necessary, I will send a small steamer.

S. B. Buckner; Major General

General S. Cooper

[Indorsement]

June 26, 1863.

Engineer Bureau:

Do you understand how General Buckner can so speedily renew the bridges? It makes the damage to us less serious than supposed. I should be pleased to see you on this subject.

J.A.S. (Seddon)

Secretary.

Even though June, 1863 had seen the resignation of the commander of the Army of Eastern Kentucky, the new commander, Brig. William Preston, had handled himself well during the East Tennessee raid of the Federals. At least one of the Rebel Army's Captains was making himself known in Eastern Kentucky at this time also. Captain P.M. Everett and his Company B, Third Battalion Kentucky Mounted Rifles, of Lieutenant Colonel E.F. Clays regiment, made a productive raid from Camp Old Russell Court-House (Castlewood, Va.), into Eastern Kentucky. The purpose was to ascertain the strength of the Federals and their location.

In a report to Major General Simon B. Buckner, Commanding General of the Dept. of East Tennessee, Capt. Everett reported that he had successfully returned from his incursion into Eastern Kentucky on June, 23rd. He had fought with the Fourteenth Kentucky Regiment of Cavalry, (U.S.), near Mount Sterling (under command of Colonel De Courcy), and had killed twenty one of the enemy, wounding six, and capturing seventeen prisoners. At Flemingsburg, he captured and paroled a captain in the U.S. Navy. Everett then proceeded to Maysville, in Mason, County, Kentucky, on the Ohio River, and captured 50 Federal horses, 330 guns, (rifles) and 25 pistols. Among the guns captured were around 150 new Enfield rifles belonging to a new company in the process of formation. Also captured at Maysville was one piece of artillery (a 12 pounder) which formally belonged to General Zollicoffer, (killed at the Battle of Mill Springs in 1862) which Everett spiked and left. The small arms were destroyed and the Government horses supplied the place of broken down mounts in his own command.

As they returned from Maysville, Everett ran into the Federal forces and had this to say of his fight at Mount Carmel and Fox Spring:

"I dispersed an organization of Home Guards, under Col. Charles Marshall, at Mount Carmel. Said organization numbered about 170 men. At Fox Spring (I) engaged a company of Home Guards, under Major_____ Pennebaker, Capts.___Evans and ____ Curtis, and 1 private. Some 15 miles from the last named place I encountered a force variously estimated at from 800 to 1,500 men under command of Brig. Gen. DeCourcy. Said force consisted of mounted infantry, cavalry, and one full battery of artillery, who attacked me both in front and rear simultaneously. The fight lasted for a short time, when seeing that it was impossible to overcome the superiority of their numbers, and exposed to the fire of artillery, which was so posted as to command the position which I held, I drew off my forces and came by easy marches (not being followed at all) to this place. Up to the engagement last mentioned I had never lost a single man killed or captured."

Everett reported only two wounded in the two clashes, Lieutenant (William L.) Flood and Private Wells, both wounded at Fox Springs. He claimed to know of 27 Federals killed, who had fallen into their hands, and 30 paroles of prisoners had been taken by Captain Blackburn.

Everett sent back a detachment under Lieutenants (Alexander H.) Darnell and (George W.) L'Aile to hunt up any stragglers of his command and "to bring them all out; also to take charge of those whose horses had given out." Everett reported his total loss as around 30, including killed, wounded, and missing.

211

He reported two infantry regiments and two cavalry regiments of the enemy at Louisa, numbering about 1,000 men. At Mt. Sterling the Federal force included the Fourteenth Regiment Kentucky Cavalry, 300 men, and the Twenty-fifth Massachusetts Infantry, 400 men; at Lexington was one Massachusetts regiment infantry, 600 men; at Paris, one regiment Mich. Infantry, 400 men; at Big Hill, (Madison County) two regiments cavalry, 400 men each. Everett also reported that the rest of the (Federal) infantry has left Kentucky by way of Louisville, supposed for Vicksburg.[235]

The Federal force facing Everett and his Company B, Third Battalion Ky. Mounted Rifles, was in command of Colonel De Courcy, with overall command being handled by Brig. Gen. Samuel D Sturgis, commanding First Div., Twenty third Army Corps. Sturgis sent De Courcy to contain the Rebels with the Eighth and Ninth Michigan Regiments of Cavalry, under Lieutenant Stockton; the Tenth Kentucky Cavalry, under Lieutenant Colonel Maltby, and a detachment of the Fourteenth Kentucky Cavalry, under Captain Bowman, with sections of the Eighth Michigan and Tenth Kentucky Batteries.

De Courcy had a different take on the rebel casualties, reporting 3 killed, "a good many" wounded, and more than 100 taken prisoner, including 1 captain, 2 lieutenants, and 4 sergeants.He also reported recapturing all the property stolen at Maysville by the Rebels. [236]

---

[235] ibid, 1, 23, part 1, pgs. 383, 384.
[236] ibid, pg. 381, 382.

By June 23rd, Everett and his raiders were back in Virginia, "broken down and very much scattered."[237] His raid had taken a toll on both men and horses.

---

[237] Guerrant, diary entry, June 23rd, 1863.

Chapter Eighteen

Second Gladesville Raid

When General Marshall returned from his unsuccessful raid into Kentucky in April, 1863, he established himself at Harlan Court House and scattered his command to watch the gaps in Harlan County, Pound Gap, and Cumberland Gap, to prevent any incursion into Eastern Kentucky and Southwestern Virginia.

The Tenth Kentucky Regiment Mounted Rifles, of Colonel B.E. Caudill's command, was scattered throughout Letcher County and in Whitesburg, guarding the salt-works at Brashearville, and keeping an eye on Pound Gap for incursions by Federal forces. On May 14th, Colonel Caudill and his regiment were ordered to Pound Gap.[238]

Colonel Caudill afterwards moved a portion of his 10th Kentucky Regiment to Gladesville, Virginia, in Wise County. and established his command in and around the court-house there.

---

[238] Guerrant, diary entry, May, 14th, 1863.

The removal from Pound Gap of Caudill's command and leaving it practically unguarded was unfortunate timing as the next few days would prove. The Federals were planning a move to attack Caudill's regiment at Pound Gap and Gladesville, ; then move upon the railroad at or near Bristol, and destroy as much of it as practicable "unless it should appear too hazardous an undertaking."

On the 3rd of July, 1863, General Julius White, U.S. Army, commander of the District of Eastern Kentucky, set in motion an expedition to try to bag Caudill's men and destroy the railroad at Bristol. He marched from Beaver Creek with six companies of the Sixty-Fifth Illinois Infantry (two mounted), Second Battalion Tenth Kentucky Cavalry, one squadron Ohio volunteer cavalry, one company Fourteenth Kentucky Infantry (mounted), and two mountain howitzers. under command of Lieutenant Wheeler, of Company M, Second Illinois Light Artillery. At Pikeville, 20 miles south of the Beaver Creek assembly point, the main force was joined by a part of the 39th Kentucky Infantry (mounted), in all about 950 men. From Pikeville Gen. White proceeded up the Louise Fork of the Sandy River with about half of his entire force; directing that the Second Battalion Tenth Kentucky Cavalry and the Ohio squadron, (McLaughlin's), all under command of Major John Mason Brown of the Second Battalion, Tenth Kentucky Cavalry, proceed by a rapid march through the Pound (or Sounding) Gap to Gladesville, Virginia, for a demonstration or an attack upon the enemy under Colonel Caudill at that place.

Upon reaching the Gap, Major Brown's force found it unguarded, with the road to Gladesville open to invasion. Some little skirmishing did occur on the way to Gladesville, but Brown's men advanced to within a few miles of Gladesville on the night of July 6th before deciding to halt and await daylight before attempting the attack on the town. While waiting, their chaplain spoke to the men and offered prayer, as they expected that some might lose their lives in the attack. While darkness still prevailed, the men mounted their horses and headed towards the village.

With the break of dawn, the Federals charged into town, completely surprising and carrying the place by storm, beating in the doors and windows of the court-house with axes, from which the enemy were firing, and compelling his surrender after fifteen minutes of close and desperate fighting, during which the Federals claimed to have killed 20 rebels and wounded 30 more. (Wildly exaggerated.)

After gathering the captured rebels together, the total captured was 18 commissioned officers, including Colonel Caudill, commanding the regiment, and 99 enlisted men. (Later amended to 127 total). The camp equipage, stores, arms, and ammunition of the command were destroyed. Major Brown, Tenth Kentucky Cavalry, then turned his prisoners towards the Pound Gap for the long trip towards Pikeville and Louisa and the Camp Chase prison camp near Columbus ,Ohio.[239]

---

[239] O.R. 1, 23, pt. 1, 818, 819

When the fight was over the prisoners were loaded into wagons and started towards the Gap. After moving through the Gap the Federals pitched their camp on the Kentucky side of the mountain and commenced building a pen about 10 feet high with which to keep their prisoners secure. The pen then had guards placed around it. The intention was to stay the night, but before too long a bugle sounded for "boots and saddles" and the command to fall in was given. It turned out that a (false) report of Rebel cavalry coming from Saltville prompted an early start towards Pikeville,

The prisoners were placed on horses, with guards walking by their sides to keep them from absconding. The next day the Federals rode while the rebels walked.[240]

Rumor had it that the reason the Confederates had been caught so unaware on the morning of the 7th of July, 1863, was that there had been a ball that night and that the officers and men had been enjoying themselves just a little too much and had gone to bed just a little too late, as many of them were still in bed when the enemy came charging into the center of town.

Colonel Caudill had been an exemplary soldier since he joined the 5th Ky. on Nov. 1st, 1861, as Captain of Company F of that regiment. As the Colonel of the Tenth Kentucky, he had managed to hold his command together while fighting the battle of inadequate proper food, and with almost no

---

[240] The Story of Wise County, Virginia ,pg. 108, Addingdon, Luther F. 1956.

equipment or clothing coming from the Confederate government to sustain them.

Gen. Marshall had also done his best to acquire the materials needed for war from the Confederate government, but he had fought mostly a losing battle. Now both Marshall and Caudill was out of the war for the hearts and minds of the people of Eastern Kentucky and Southwestern Virginia, albeit only temporarily in Colonel Caudill's case.

After spending a year in captivity in Fort Delaware, located on Pea Patch Island on the Delaware River, he was "one of the first 50" sent to Morris Island, Charleston, South Carolina in June, 1864, as hostages to try to halt the cannon fire of the Confederate forces that had been firing on Union forces. Also sent with him were two more mountain Rebels from Wise County, Colonel A.S. Vandeventer, of the 50th Virginia Infantry Regiment, and the Major of the same regiment, Major L.J. Perkins, both of whom were captured in 1863.

Caudill would be exchanged in 1864 and would return to duty with the 10th Ky., which, after all, carried a regimental flag emblazoned with a white cross on a blue field with the words, "Caudille's Army" proudly sewn on it.

Caudill was also held for a time in the Johnson's Island prison camp in Sandusky Bay, on Lake Erie, Ohio, in 1864. While there he wrote a letter to his wife, Martha L. Asbury Caudill, that was much more political than personal:

(The spelling and punctuation is presented as written in the original letter).

"Margaret, you cannot amagine the many desires I have for peace so that I with the rest of pore soldiers could be discharged and return to our loved ones at home and be governed with such a government that our forefathers left us, but political demagogs has destroyed that form of government and braut on this uncalled for war, and now a military despotism rules the people and forces the brother to spill the brothers blood when the majority of the people north and south is opposed to the war, and if the people was permitted to speak at the poles, this war would cease and the constitutional Union restored. Margaret, the subgigation of a free people never can be affected. As we fite for all that makes life desirable, we want our lands and property and especially our liberty and the suspencion of the right of habas cobras and passage of the confiscation bill. Then after we went into armies to defend our homes and property, next comes the proclamation of the liberating all of the slaves in certain states and calles on the army and the navy to defend and protect the slave in every effort he would make to obtain his freedom indevering to excite survill incerection. With these extremes tha have united our people that if tha could have been protected with their rites the war would have been over and the Union restored long sinse, but till eavil is checked time will only reveal the end. God grant some meanes may be devised to bring all to their senses and that and honorable peace may take place. Send me some

stamps. Yours,   B.E.   .
Caudill[241]

One gets the feeling when reading these words today that Colonel Caudill was well aware that every word in his letter would likely be read by prison officials and censors before mailing it. His letter strikes a conciliatory tone that most likely was purposely worded by Caudill to help his case for exchange. Prison commanders were during the war notorious for using food and mail privileges to control the prison population. Officers were subjected to the same king of scrutiny as the enlisted men, if not worse, and no one wanted to lose their ability to keep in touch with their relatives and friends at home. For that reason, the true feelings of the prisoners, both north and south were seldom expressed.

Caudill does manage to put a lot of the blame for the war on the freeing of the slaves, the suspension of habeas corpus, and the passage of the confiscation bill, (Confiscation Act of 1861, passed by the U.S. Congress) which allowed the seizure of property used to support the Confederate cause. In late 1862 Caudill had suffered having his own home and that of his father and brother burned by Union raiders and his wife arrested to boot. No doubt but that the war had exacted a high cost on Colonel Caudill and left a bitter taste in his mouth. The fact that he became a well-known preacher after the war likely signified that he had come to an understanding with himself, his former enemies and with his maker.

---

[241] diary, Caudill, Benjamin E.

The loss of 127 men by the 10th Ky. left the regiment with a much reduced force in its active ranks: a mere shadow of its former self.

When Colonel White detached part of his force to pass through Pound Gap and to capture Colonel Caudill's men at Gladesville, he moved the remainder of his force, all under Colonel Cameron, commanding brigade, up the Louisa Fork of the Sandy River. The purpose of the foray was to seek out and attack a regiment of Rebels under Colonel A.J. May, said to be posted near the State line, (between Virginia and Kentucky), and also for the purpose of diverting the attention of rebel forces from the movement of Major Brown, (at Gladesville) by a demonstration in the direction of the Salt-Works.

After advancing to a point near the State line, Col. Cameron found that May's force had retreated to a point some 60 miles distant, and within supporting distance of other Rebel forces greatly superior to Cameron's force. The roads in the area were also wholly impracticable for field transportation, and the country was totally bare of subsistence for men or animals.

With these obstacles to attempting to capture May's Rebel force, Gen. White detached Col. Cameron with the remaining mounted force to attempt capture of a body of the enemy on Tug Fork, about 25 miles distant, and White himself returned to Pikeville with the infantry and howitzers, from which point he could support the movement on either flank(Coloncl Cameron's or Major Brown's) should it become necessary. As Cameron's men moved towards tug Fork, he was attacked by a rebel force on Pond Creek, and was engaged with them for several hours. The Federal units involved in the fight consisted of detachments from the Thirty-ninth Kentucky Infantry, under Lieutenant- Colonel Mims, and from the Sixty-fifth Illinois Infantry, under Captain Kennedy, all boldly charging up the precipitous mountain sides with the greatest gallantry.

The Rebel force was completely routed, leaving 5 dead on the field, with many more wounded, and 20 prisoners, who fell into Federal hands. Colonel Cameron's command sustained no loss in the skirmish at Pond Creek.

The total loss of the move up the Tug Fork, the attack on Gladesville, and the Pond Creek battle was 9 wounded, none severely. The wounded were all suffered by Major Brown's mounted force in their raid through Pound Gap and the attack on Gladesville. The Tenth Kentucky had 6 wounded and the First Ohio Squadron (McLaughlin's) had 3 wounded.[242]

Brig. Gen. Preston wrote Adjutant Gen. Cooper on July 11th, from Abingdon, giving a breakdown of the Federal forces opposing him in the Sandy Valley:

Headquarters Preston's Brigade
    Abingdon, Va., July 11, 1863.
General S. Cooper
Adjutant and Inspector General:

---

[242] O.R. 1, 23, pt.1, 818, 819.

General: I learn that the exigencies of the service may require the union of the departments under command of General Bragg and Major-General Buckner. When you ordered me to relieve General Marshall in this department, you anticipated the difficulty of administering the affairs of the district intrusted [sic] to my command, and authorized me to communicate directly with the Department. Major–General Buckner, to whom I reported, from a similar view, gave me plenary authority in this district. I recall these facts, as in my judgment the difficulties will be greatly augmented if this portion of Virginia be included in the new department. The main vulnerable point here is Saltville, which produces 10,000 bushels of salt per diem, and which is of vital consequence to the Confederacy. The approaches are through Pound Gap and Louisa Gap, in Northeastern Kentucky. The enemy have already along the Sandy 4,000 or 5,000 men, menacing a raid on Abingdon and Saltville. The 10th and 14th Kentucky, the 39th Illinois (Kentucky) and some Ohio troops, about 1,500 strong, are intrenched [sic] at the mouth of Beaver, (Martin, Ky.), between Pound Gap and Prestonsburg. They attacked and captured a picket of mine near Pound Gap. My force is not much more than one-half of that Gen. Marshall had for the defense of the district. Colonels Trigg's, Leyden's, and Moore's regiments, the best disciplined and instructed troops I had, have been withdrawn. The remainder are wretchedly armed, and have a large territory to guard. To atone, as far as possible, for these deficiencies, the only remedy will be prompt and energetic action on my part, without waiting for orders from a remote point...........

I am general, very respectfully, your obedient servant, W. Preston, Commanding District.[243]

Brig. General Preston's First Brigade, Department of Southwestern Virginia, included the following units as of July, 31st, 1863:

5th Kentucky, Col. Hiram Hawkins.
10th Kentucky, Maj. J.T. Chenoweth
64th Virginia, Col. C. Slemp
4th Kentucky Cavalry, Col. H.L. Giltner.
Fields' Company Kentucky Cavalry, Capt. W.J. Fields.
1st Kentucky Mounted Riflemen (battalion), Lieut.Col. E.F. Clay.
2nd Kentucky Mounted Riflemen (battalion), Lieut. Col. Thomas Johnson.
Jessee's squadron Kentucky Mounted Riflemen, Captain G.M. Jessee.
27th Virginia Battalion Mounted Riflemen , Lieut. Col, H.A. Edmundson.
Davidson's battery, Capt. G.S. Davidson.
Jeffress' battery, Capt. W.C. Jeffress.[244]

On July 23rd, General Buckner's Chief of Staff, V Sheliha, in Knoxville, Tennessee, wrote Gen. Preston that Buckner intended marching Sunday morning (August 2nd) on the enemy that was stationed at Louisa and Beaver Creeks. Preston was directed to hold

---

[243] ibid, pt. 2, pg. 906.
[244] ibid, 945.

600 infantry, his two batteries, and 1,000 cavalry in readiness to march at any moment. He was also ordered to furnish transportation necessary to haul 80,000 rations, 400,000 rounds of ammunition for small arms, and 3,000 rounds for artillery. He was directed to inform the headquarters at Knoxville the most reliable and latest information relative to the position of the enemy at the above mentioned points.

Gen. Buckner also wanted to borrow the two fully equipped Napoleon guns at Saltville and to furnish Maj. Gen. Jones in their place, four 6 pounder guns.

On August 1st, Gen. Preston received a notice that the contemplated move into Kentucky had been postponed for the present, chiefly in consequence of a report received from Colonel Clay (of the 1st Kentucky Mounted Rifleman Battalion).[245]

Not only were the regiments of the rebel mountain districts having difficulty keeping the soldiers in ranks from deserting, especially when stationed near their home counties, but other Confederate units were experiencing the same problem in keeping their men from quitting and going home. Sometimes these soldiers received letters from home encouraging them to quit the army.

The following letter is from a woman then living in Madison County, North Carolina, to a soldier in the Sixty-fourth North Carolina Volunteers. This is only a specimen of similar epistles received by men of the north Carolina

---

[245] ibid, 939, 947.

regiments, especially the ones stationed too near home.

Marshall, Madison County, North Carolina,

July, 20 (?) 1863.

H.W. Revis:
Dear husband; I seat myself to drop you a few lines to let you know that me and sally is well as common, and I hope these few lines will come to hand and find you well and doing well. I have no news to write to you at this, only I am done laying by my corn. I worked it all four times. My wheat is good; my oats is good. I haven't got my wheat stacked yet. My oats I have got a part of them out, and Tom Hunter and John Roberts is cutting to-day. They will git [sic] them cut to-day.

I got the first letter yesterday that I have received from you since you left. I got five from you yesterday; they all come together. This the first one I have wrote, for I didn't know where to write to you. You said you hadn't anything to eat. I wish you was here to get some beans for dinner. I have plenty to eat as yet. I haven't saw any of your pap's folks since you left home. The people is generally well hearat. [sic] The people is all turning to Union here since the Yankees has got Vicksburg. I want you to come home as soon as you can after you git[sic] this letter. Jane Elkins is living with me yet. That is all I can think of, only I want you to come home the worst that I ever did. The conscripts is all at home yet, and I don't know what they will do with them. The folks is leaving here, and going North as fast as they can, so I will close.

Your wife, till death, Martha Revis [246]

Martha Revis mentioned in her letter a man named Tom Hunter, who was helping stack her wheat crop, even as she was writing her letter to her husband. Mr. Hunter enclosed a note of his own in the letter, possibly at the urging of Mrs. Revis, so as to help her persuade her husband to quit the rebel army and come home:

I pen a line, sir. I am well, and is right strait out for the Union, and I am never going in the service any more, for I am for the Union for ever and ever, amen. I am doing my work. There was 800 left to go to the North, so will tell you about it in the next letter; so I will close.

Your brother till death. Hurrah for the Union! Hurrah for the Union, Union!

Thomas Hunter.

What a remarkable letter from a wife to a husband who is already homesick and hungry and who is barely able to tolerate serving even a day longer under the conditions that soldiers of that day and time had to endure, especially soldiers of the southern armies. Of course the people left at home had their own struggles to cope with, with their husbands in the army and the responsibility of raising their children and feeding their families falling on the woman of the family.

---

[246] ibid, 951.

This letter was written in July, 1863, right after the two devastating defeats suffered by the south at Gettysburg and Vicksburg. The waning of the southern hopes of independence after these two major defeats did nothing to boost the morale of Southerners, and as the sample letter shows, low morale and outright treason began to invade the minds of even those who were at first "all in" for the war and the independence it could possibly bring for the southern people.

It's no wonder that as defeat after defeat began to mount up, even the most extreme measures of punishment were not a sufficient deterrent of desertion as the war went on. When frequent executions failed to stem the flow of dissertations, another tact was tried, as evidenced by this General Order published by General Bragg in Chattanooga, Tennessee.

Headquarters Department No. 2,
Chattanooga, Tenn., August 6, 1863.

General Orders
No. 1.

I. In pursuance of the proclamation of the President of the Confederate states, the general commanding hereby announces that a general pardon and amnesty has been granted to all officers and men now absent from their commands without leave who shall, with the least possible delay, return to their proper post of duty within twenty days after the first publication of the proclamation in the State in which the absentee may be at the date of the publication.

II. The benefit of this amnesty and pardon is extended to all who have been accused or who have been convicted and are now undergoing sentence for absence without leave or desertion, excepting those only who have been twice convicted of desertion. The general commanding orders that all parties entitled to the amnesty and pardon hereby offered be released from arrest and their punishment remitted. They will return to their respective commands without delay.

III. Those who desert or absent themselves without leave after the publication of these orders will not be entitled to the benefit of the amnesty and pardon granted by the President.

By command of General Bragg:
George Wm. Brent,
Assistant Adjutant –General[247]

---

[247] ibid, pgs. 954, 955.

Chapter Nineteen

Morgan's 1864 Raid

At the beginning of the Civil War, the mountain people of Eastern Kentucky, East Tennessee, and Southwestern Virginia had a decision to make, either siding with the people of their heritage, the southern people, or going with the national government they loved so much and which their forefathers had fought so hard to establish. The oddity is that the most southern of the three states, Tennessee, was the one that tended to support the U.S. government, while the two more northerly lying of the three states contained two mountainous areas that supported the south.

Southwestern Virginia supplied part of the men for several battalions and regiments during the war, including;

The 7th Battalion Confederate Cavalry;

22nd Virginia Cavalry;
50th Virginia Infantry Regiment;
51st Virginia Infantry Regiment;
French's Battalion Virginia Infantry;
21st Virginia Battalion (Colonel Thompson's "special service" troops.
64th Virginia Infantry Regiment;
27th Virginia Battalion;
54th Virginia Infantry Regiment;
29th Virginia Infantry regiment;

Several other Confederate units had whole companies or parts of companies containing Southwestern Virginia mountain men in their ranks.

The Confederate units which were made up of entirely or nearly entirely of Eastern Kentucky mountain men are these:

10th Kentucky Mounted Rifles (1862)
13th Kentucky Cavalry (March, 1865)
14th Kentucky Cavalry Regiment;
5th Kentucky Infantry Regiment;
1st Battalion Kentucky Mounted Rifles;
1st Battalion Kentucky Cavalry;
Field's Company Partisan Rangers.

Several Eastern Kentucky men joined Federal units. Some of these are:
39th Kentucky Infantry Regiment;
10th Kentucky Infantry Regiment;
10th Kentucky Cavalry Regiment;
14th Kentucky Volunteer Infantry;
1st Regiment Capital Guards Battalion;
19th Kentucky Infantry Regiment;

231

45th Kentucky Mounted Infantry;
40th Kentucky Mounted Infantry;
Harlan Battalion.

Several other organizations of both sides had men from the Kentucky and Virginia mountains in their ranks. The units listed above are far from complete lists, as men from the region traveled throughout the state, especially at the beginning of hostilities, to join various outfits, so as to "not miss out on the fighting."

Pound Gap's western opening was on Letcher County land, so this county was naturally inclined to want to protect the Gap with its own men, especially since most Letcher County citizens sided with the south. At the beginning of this book I mentioned that Eastern Kentucky's heritage was of a southern tilt, since most of the county was settled by Virginians, South and North Carolinians, and Tennesseans.

When the Tenth Kentucky Mounted Rifles were organized in Whitesburg by Col. Benjamin E. Caudill in Sept. and Oct., 1862, a large number of local men flocked to Whitesburg to fill up the regiment. They probably had several reasons for enlisting at that time, but the fact that Col. Caudill was a local mountain man who might possibly be able to keep the regiment close to home had to have been one factor encouraging enlistment. In fact, the Tenth Kentucky did manage to stay in their home county for a large amount of their service, especially during the first two years of the regiment's existence.

232

One of the few times they were called on to leave the friendly confines of Pound Gap was when Colonel Caudill and 126 others of his command were surprised and captured by the Federals at Gladesville, Virginia, on July 7th, 1862. After Caudill was captured, Major Chenoweth became their commander, even though their ranks were much reduced then by desertions, sickness, casualties, and captures.

In August, 1863, Brig. General Preston turned over command of his First Brigade, Army of Western Virginia, to Colonel H.L. Giltner. This was the brigade to which the 10th Kentucky Mounted Rifles belonged. Col. Giltner wrote the following letter to General John S. Williams, who by then commanded a brigade of troops in Saltville, Virginia:

Headquarters, Preston's (Giltner's) Brigade,
Abingdon, Va., August 25, 1863.

(General Williams:)

General: I inclose you a copy of the telegram placing me in command of the remaining troops of the brigade. I should have answered your communication of yesterday to Captain Martin, acting assistant adjutant-general, with reference to the strength and disposition of the troops remaining here of the brigade at once, but for the fact that I was desirous of receiving intelligence from Brigadier-General Preston with reference to the Tenth Kentucky Regiment, Lieutenant- Colonel Prentice's and Captain Field's commands,

233

which had been solicited of him before the receipt of your note.

The Fourth Kentucky Regiment of cavalry is now in the vicinity of Lebanon, and has 501 effective men present for duty. Lieutenant-Colonel Prentice's command is now at Pound Gap, consisting of about 200 men. Captain Field's company, Partisan Rangers, is also at Pound Gap, with 76 effective men. Captain Davidson's battery is within 2 miles of this place. He has 91 men present for duty. Major Chenoweth is at Whitesburg, Ky., with about 133 men. I am in receipt of a communication from him, dated 23d instant, from that place. Major Chenoweth, Lieutenant Colonel Prentice, and Captain Field's commands have all been ordered to withdraw from their present positions to Castle Wood.

Respectfully, your obedient servant,
H.L. Giltner,
Colonel, Commanding Brigade. [248]

On May 9th,1864, Colonel George W. Gallop, of the 14th Kentucky Infantry (U.S.) reported that Major Wise, (Smith) Eleventh Michigan, left Louisa on that morning for Pound Gap and his scouts had a run-in with some of Gen. John H. Morgan's scouts; captured 6 horses. His telegraph operator and instruments, and 1 private; and killed two others. He mentioned in the same report that one hundred and twenty five veterans of the 14th desire furloughs; "can they be given; if so who gives them"?

---

[248] O.R., 1, 30, pt.4, pg. 606

The three squadrons that Major Smith left Louisa with included Companies A and F of his own Eleventh Michigan, and one company of the Thirty-ninth Kentucky of Col. Mims Regiment. They passed through Paintsville, Middle Creek, Forks of Beaver, and head of Mud Creek, arriving at Pikeville in the evening of May 11th. They procured forage there and proceeded to Pound Gap, passing inside of Rebel breastworks built in the Gap. Hearing that there were some forty five Rebels encamped on Rockhouse Creek, Smith moved to that place, marching from sunrise until 1a.m.; resting two hours and pushing on again at 4 a.m.; and charged into the enemy's camp about 11a.m. of the 13th instant. The Rebels ran for three miles, pursued by the Federals, who captured 1 captain, 1 lieutenant, and five horses with equipments, and killing one horse. Smith's horses were so worn out by the trip there that they were unable to follow them any further, but immediately started to return to Louisa, marching by Beaver Creek, Prestonsburg, and Paintsville. He reported no enemy at the Gap nearer than four miles, where a small picket was placed to prevent refugees from leaving Virginia, but Smith's orders didn't call for passing through the Gap, so he left the picket unmolested. On his return he learned that Colonel Chenoweth was about a mile and a half beyond Whitesburg (at the mouth of Sandlick) with about seventy five men, but the lack of forage and tired horsed prevented him from traveling to Whitesburg. He reported that these two forces of seventy-five and forty-five men were all the Rebel forces he heard of in these mountains.[249]

On May 31st, 1864, General John Hunt Morgan was in Russell Court-House (Castle Wood) when he wrote a letter to Adj. Gen. S. Cooper, outlining his plans for the invasion of Kentucky. He had just received information that General Hobson had left Mount Sterling for Louisa with 3,000 men; in addition, there were already 2,050 Federal cavalry in Louisa. This information had determined Morgan to move at once into Kentucky, and divert the plans of the enemy. Morgan had about 2,200 men with which he planned to move through Pound Gap, detach a portion of his command to move on Louisa, while he, with the main force, struck for Lexington and Frankfort. He planned to destroy as much of the Covington and Lexington as would not retard a rapid movement, and immediately push towards the Louisville and Frankfort and Louisville and Nashville (rail) roads.[250]

On June 4th, 1864,General Morgan entered Kentucky through Pound Gap, driving from the Gap the Federal Forty-fifth Kentucky, under command of Colonel John Mason Brown, that had been sent there by Major General S.G. Burbridge, the District of Kentucky commander. Brown's regiment skirmished with Morgan's men until they nearly had him flanked; causing him (Brown) to withdraw.

---

[249] ibid, 1, 39, pt.1 pg. 14.
[250] ibid, 64, 65.

236

Burbridge himself started to the Gap but one of Brown's couriers met him on the road there and reported that Morgan's men were already streaming through the Gap, causing Burbridge to detach Gen. Hobson's command to back-track and prepare to receive Morgan should he succeed in eluding Burbridge's forces. With the rest of the command, he continued on towards Pound Gap, arriving to within 20 miles of that place the night of the 5th of June.

Learning that Morgan had encamped June 3rd at Rockhouse Creek, in Letcher County, Burbridge sent Colonel Grider, Fifty-second Kentucky, with part of his regiment and a detachment of the Thirty-ninth Kentucky toward Pound Gap with instructions to obstruct the Gap and roads so that he could hold Morgan there until Burbridge came up if Morgan tried to return to Virginia. With the remainder of the command, Burbridge marched to Beaver, (Martin Ky.) where he selected all the fit men and horses for a rapid movement.

Colonel Brown's command followed Morgan from Letcher County to Mount Sterling, where he next came up with General Burbridge and reported to him. Burbridge later commended Brown for the way he handled his men at Pound Gap and in the interior of Kentucky.[251]

Morgan next advanced to Mount Sterling, Ky., on June 8th, where he surprised a force of Federals in the town, capturing all their camp equipage, transportation etc., various

---

[251] ibid, pgs. 22-26.

supplies, and about 380 prisoners. He remained there one day, then advanced to Lexington, attacked the city about 2 p.m. and captured that place. He burned the Government stables, depot, etc., and moved via Georgetown, to Cynthiana, where he encountered a force under Colonel Berry.

After a brisk engagement, the Yankees took shelter in the houses and "I was forced to burn a large portion of the town," Morgan reported. Colonel Berry was killed in the fight and 400 Federals were captured. At 2 o'clock Colonel Hobson with 600 men attacked a brigade (800) of Morgan's force at Keller's Bridge, and drove them from the bridge.

Morgan reported surrounding Hobson's whole brigade and after a short skirmish, capturing General Hobson and staff, 3 railroad trains, with baggage and horses, and his whole brigade, numbering 2,000 men.

On June 12th, General Burbridge caught up with Morgan's command at Cynthiana, attacking him and capturing nearly 600 Rebels, and reporting killing 300 others. He gave his own loss at 150 killed and wounded. After the battle, Morgan retreated through Flemingsburg and West Liberty, reaching Abingdon, Va., on the 20th of June.

Morgan reported his losses in the raid into Kentucky as 80 killed, 125 wounded, and 150 captured and missing. (This number was doubtless understated.) Burbridge's final report of the battle listed 53 killed, 156 wounded, and 205 missing.[252]

---

[252] ibid, pgs. 19-84.

The following memorandum of Sept. 15th, 1864, will give the reader an idea of the losses of Morgan's command on the Kentucky raid:

Richmond, September 15, 1864.
Hon. A.J. Seddon,
Secretary of War:
Sir: The memorandum I promised to make out for you is as follows: Giltner went to Kentucky with 1,640 men. His returns two days ago show (aggregate) 316 men. General Morgan started to Kentucky with (of his own command) about 800. Its present force is 292. It is reported that 50 recruits came from Kentucky three days ago...........
Very respectfully,
Wm. Henry Norris
Colonel.[253]

Two months after returning from the botched Kentucky raid, the 2,500 men with Morgan had dwindled to 608; a difference of almost 1,900 men. This is a far cry from the 355 total casualties Morgan gave in his report to Adj. Gen. Cooper on July 20th, 1864 from Abingdon, Virginia. Of course, there's also the possibility that some of the missing men were on detached duty somewhere.

The mountain Rebels from Letcher and surrounding counties had accompanied Morgan's raiders as members of Major Chenoweth's 10th Kentucky Mounted Rifles, Col. Benjamin E. Caudill's old regiment. They had been given the job of destroying the

---

[253] ibid, pg. 84.

railroad from Lexington to Boyd's station, on the Kentucky Central Railroad.[254] They also participated in the battle with General Burbridge's forces at Cynthiana, Ky., on Sunday, June 12th , 1864 but the 10th Ky. total losses for the battle and raid are unknown

A couple of unfortunate incidents that occurred during the raid was the alleged robbery of two banks, one in Lexington, Ky., and one in Mount Sterling, Ky., by members of the Confederate Army. In Lexington, Private Humphrey Castleman of the First Kentucky Cavalry, was accused, of, combining and confederating with one Capt. E.P. Byrne and others to rob out of said bank $10,000, and failing to account for the same to the Confederate States, fraudulently applied to be used for the use of himself."

Surgeon R.R. Goode, Provisional Army, Confederate States, was accused of taking about $72,000 from the Farmer's bank of Kentucky in Mount sterling, and failing to account for the money, and applying said money for his own use. One of the witnesses against was Major John T. Chenoweth, tenth Kentucky mounted rifles.

No one was ever tried or convicted of the robberies and the guilt or innocence of the accused was never officially determined, as the war ended before a trial was held. [255]

---

[254] ibid, pg. 66.
[255] ibid, 84.

Chapter Twenty

The Burbridge Raid

The success of General Breckinridge, of the Confederate Army, in driving Brig. Gilliam's brigade from Bull's Gap, in East Tennessee, back to Knoxville, prompted Maj. Gen. Stoneman, commanding at Knoxville, to assemble a force to keep Breckinridge from using his forces to extend his success by advancing into Middle Tennessee or Western Kentucky. He hurriedly assembled the forces of Brig. General Burbridge (4,200) and Brig. Gilliam's brigade (1,500) at Bean's Station in Northeastern Tennessee and left there on Dec. 12th, and reached Kingsport, Tennessee, opposite the North Fork of the Holston River, on the 13th.

Here, General Gilliam's command was in the van, and encountered the forces of Gen. Basil C. Duke's command, under the command of Col. Richard Morgan, as General Duke was then on leave. After a short contest, Gilliam's men succeeded in crossing the river, and killing, capturing, or dispersing Morgan's whole command, including himself and his whole wagon train.

During the afternoon and night of the 13th, Burbridge's 4,200 men pushed on to Bristol, which they reached early in the day of the 14th. Only picket firing broke out in Bristol, and it being blanketed in fog and fearing that Gen. Vaughn of the Rebel army might use the fog to cover his re-enforcement of Gen. Brechinridge's forces, General Stoneman started Burbridge's command for Abingdon with instructions to strike the railroad between Saltville and Wytheville.

At Bristol, all the railroad depots, five railroad trains filled with supplies, about 1,000 stand of small arms, a large amount of fixed ammunition, wagons, ambulances, etc., were destroyed, and 17 commissioned officers and 260 enlisted men captured and sent to Knoxville. At Glade Springs Va., Maj. Harrison of the Twelfth Kentucky (U.S.) destroyed all the bridges from that point to Marion, the large iron-works near Marion, and captured several hundred fine horses. The lead-works in Wytheville were captured and completely destroyed by Colonel Buckley's brigade. Also destroyed there were large quantities of ammunition, both for artillery and small- arms, plus several large buildings filled with subsistence and medical stores, and General Breckinridge's headquarters.

Gilliam had struck Vaughn's Rebel force at Marion, capturing all his artillery, eight pieces, and 198 prisoners of war. Abingdon was captured by Burbridge on Dec, 14th. He captured here one piece of artillery, a large amount of stores, and an engine with some rolling-stock.

During the evening of December 20th, General Burbridge and General Gilliam drove in the pickets in front of the salt-works at Saltville, Virginia. The entrance to the salt-works was defended by a redoubt and some rifle pits on a high rugged hill to the right of the road immediately over-looking the salt-works. The artillery of the Federals opened on the redoubt from an eminence on the right road, and the rebels immediately replied to the Federal artillery with their own from the redoubt. A battalion from the Eighth Tennessee Cavalry (U.S.) was dismounted and ordered forward to drive the Rebels from a ravine from which they had been annoying the artillery. After driving the Confederates from the ravine, they were ordered forward, along with a battalion of the Thirteenth Tennessee Cavalry, to take possession of a higher hill to the right of the redoubt.

The sun set before the attack could be made and the attack was called off until 9 p.m., when Lieutenant Stacy informed General that the redoubt with one piece of artillery had been successfully attacked and taken. Gen. Gillem immediately ordered Stacy to set fire to the salt-works and to storm the fort in Burbridge's front which his troops had failed to take. By 12 midnight, the fort in front of General Burbridge had been taken, with 3 pieces of artillery.

A total of five pieces of artillery was taken in the Rebel works, 3 pieces were found in a blockhouse in the outskirts of Saltville, and 1 piece at the depot, making a total of 9 pieces of artillery captured in and around the salt-works, with a full supply of ammunition.

Shortly after daylight on the 21st, Gen. Burbridge's command entered the salt-works, and in accordance with orders from Major General Stoneman, proceeded to destroy the salt kettles at the lower works, while Gillam's brigade was similarly engaged at the upper works.

All the buildings connected in any way to the salt-works were burned; and the engines and pumps at the wells were destroyed. There were but two wells at the upper works, around 160 feet deep. The diameter of the copper tubes in these wells were found to be the same as that of a 12 pounder gun, and as the most effectual way of destroying them they were filled with 12-pounder shells and railroad iron. Large working parties were employed day and night with sledge hammers breaking the kettles. These kettles were about an inch thick in the edge, and from two to three inches thick in the bottom, and were exceedingly difficult to destroy.

On the morning of Dec. 22nd, the troops evacuated Saltville, Gilliam's troops going by Moccasin Gap, thence by Carter Valley road to Knoxville, where it arrived on the 29th of December. Their march had totaled 461 miles, over "roads of the worst description."

General Burbridge retreated from Saltville after the destruction of the salt-wells, by the road through Pound Gap, and then proceeded to Mount Sterling. While retreating through the Gap, Burbridge paused there long enough to write this after-action report to the United States Secretary of War, E.M. Stanton:

Pound Gap, December 27, 1864.

I have the honor to report that my mounted force, 4,000 strong, in conjunction with General Gilliam's brigade, the whole under command of Maj. Gen. George Stoneman, marched from Bean's Station on 12th of December at daylight. On the morning of the 13th they found Duke's brigade at Kingsport, under Col. Dick Morgan, drawn up to oppose the crossing of the Holston. General Stoneman sent two regiments of my command to support General Gillem, who crossed two regiments at a ford two miles above, flanked the enemy, routing him, killing 15, capturing 85, and a train of 13 wagons, I pursued the rebels to Bristol, which place I captured on the morning of the 14th at 3 o'clock, taking 250 prisoners, 2 trains of cars, 5 engines, and immense stores. I learned that Vaughn was at Zollicoffer, twelve miles below. I marched to attack him, but he slipped away in a dense fog and made off for the salt-works, intending to join Breckinridge. I discovered his flight in time to head him off at Abingdon, which place I captured on December 15, taking one gun, a large amount of stores, and an engine with twelve cars. General Gillem continued the pursuit of Vaughn, coming up with him at Marion, where he was posted in a strong position, from which General Gillem drove him, capturing fifty prisoners. By direction of General Stoneman, I sent Colonel Brown's brigade to support General Gillem, who again came upon the enemy at Mount Airy. General Gillem charged him, driving him in confusion, and capturing seven pieces of artillery, taking a wagon train and some prisoners. Colonel Brown later in the day charged into Wytheville, routing the home guards and capturing four pieces of artillery and eight caissons. Major Harrison, of the Twelfth Kentucky, who had been detached by order of General Stoneman, with 300 picked men and horses, struck the Virginia railroad on the 15th at Glade Springs, captured two trains of cars, got in Vaughn's front, and followed up the line of the road, destroying all the bridges and depots as far as Wytheville, burning a large amount of rolling-stock and the great iron-works near Marion. Col. Brown destroyed the bridges for ten miles above Wytheville, then the expedition started on its return, "the men and horses being thoroughly worn out, and a force of cavalry having made its appearance in our rear. I drove the cavalry force following us, which was Breckinridge's advance, coming on Breckinridge's near Marion, where he was posted on the hills 2,200 strong." An engagement of thirty- six hours ensued, at the close of which Breckinridge retreated toward Saltville; but Colonel Buckley, with a brigade, having got in his rear at Seven-Mile Ford, forced him in confusion toward North Carolina. Colonel Buckley effectually destroyed the lead mines near Wytheville on night of (the) 20th, capturing 100 prisoners. "Our united forces captured the salt-works after some resistance on the 21st of December, taking eight pieces of artillery and some prisoners. The expedition has been entirely successful and will be more felt by the enemy than the loss of Richmond. The salt-works and lead mines are in ruins and cannot be repaired during the war. My forces are now at this place and safe."[256]

Hon. E.M. Stanton, *Secretary of War.*

S.G. Burbridge,
Brevet Major-General

The report of Major General Breckinridge, commanding the Department of Western Virginia and East Tennessee saw things in a different light than Gen. Burbridge:

Wytheville, Va., January 2, 1865.

I have just seen General Burbridge's report of December 28, from Catlettsburg, Ky., (actually from Pound Gap), and although it is scarcely necessary to notice it, I will add, that his statement of the stores, cars, and engines taken is greatly exaggerated; that I have no report yet from Vaughn and Duke of the prisoners from their command, but I know that most of the prisoners taken by the enemy were citizens, afterward turned loose, and for the rest, not more than twenty prisoners were taken, most of them at the capture of Saltville; that the home guard at Wytheville charged by Colonel Brown's brigade consisted of my assistant adjutant-general, three other officers, a clerk in the assistant adjutant general's office, and one drunken soldier, and the artillery

---

[256] O.R., 1, 45, pt. 1, pgs. 806-824.

captured (and left), of several old pieces which had been tested and condemned some weeks before; that the force was not met by me while returning, but was overtaken while marching up the valley; and, finally, that the whole force of the enemy was present in the engagements near Marion, under the command of General Stoneman.[257]

Respectfully,

John C. Breckinridge,
Major General

The losses of the Confederates in the raid are hard to ascertain, although General Stoneman reported capturing 34 Rebel officers, 845 enlisted men, and two newspaper editors. General Burbridge reporting killing and wounding 15 rebels at Kingsport, along with 85 captures. But a fair estimate of Rebel losses in killed, wounded, and captured would total between 500-1,000 total losses.

The Federal losses were reported by General Stoneman as "small," mentioning only one casualty by name, that of Colonel Boyle, of the Eleventh Kentucky Cavalry (U.S.) who was killed. Federal total losses were likely not as great as their adversaries, but were likely between 100-200 total.

Doubtless the raid into Western Virginia and East Tennessee was a major blow to the rebel interests in that area, especially the loss of the salt-making capability at Saltville. The capture of 1,000 rebel soldiers came at a time when the fortunes of the Confederacy were already in decline, due to the lack of ability to

---

[257] ibid, pg. 827.

replenish their ranks after nearly four years of war. This raid helped to hasten the end of the war, which was by now only little more than three months away.

General John Hunt Morgan was spending the night at a house in Greenville, Tn., on Sept. 4th, 1864, when he was roused out of bed by some Tennessee Federal cavalry and shot by a Federal cavalryman when he was discovered hiding in the yard behind a clump of bushes. A soldier wearing a brown jacket rode up to a fence near the bushes and Morgan stepped out of his hiding place, thinking the man was a rebel because of his brown jacket. The horseman demanded Morgan's surrender, much to the surprise of Morgan and one of his captains, J.T. Rogers, who had been hiding with him. At that moment, some more soldiers and their Captain, Wilcox of the Federal army, rode up, and Capt. Rogers and another man, Mr. Johnson, walked toward the Federal Captain Wilcox, while hearing several shouts of "Kill him, kill him!" Rogers looked at General Morgan to see him throw up his hands while exclaiming, "Oh God!" The next time Rogers saw his commander, he was brought into the street, dead. Rogers thought they had been fired on from many directions after surrendering, but he said that because of the distance, he thought the firing had been done innocently. He wasn't sure if Gen. Morgan had been killed after surrendering though.[258]

One of the Confederate regiments that was posted on one of the roads leading into

---

[258] ibid, 1, 39, pt. 1, pg. 492.

Greenville that morning was none other than the 10th Kentucky Mounted Rifles, of Colonel Caudill's "Army," which was commanded by Major Thomas Chenoweth on that fateful morning.

Captain Jim Rogers, of the 10th Kentucky Mounted rifles, who had been captured with General Morgan when he was killed, managed to escape by jumping from the cars as the train went through Nashville, and reported back to his brigade in Lee County, Virginia, in February, 1865.[259]

The month of February also brought word of the killing of John Marshall, General Humphrey Marshall's son, in Castle Woods, Russell County, by one of Clarence Prentice's men of the 7th Battalion Confederate Cavalry, a Capt. Roberts, due to some kind of difficulty between the two men. [260]

---

[259] Guerrant, diary entry Feb.5th, 1865.
[260] ibid, Feb. 14th.

Chapter Twenty One

Mountain Rebels Surrender

At the end of February, 1865, Colonel Giltner's brigade had their headquarters in Stickleyville, Lee County, Virginia. The 4th Ky. Cavalry was on extended leave at this time, in Kentucky. The 10th Kentucky Mounted Rifles were in Turkey Cove, where Col. Caudill was said to be engaged "in a very interesting protracted meeting." [261]

Organization of Col. Giltner's Brigade, March, 1965:

7th Confederate Battalion, Lieut. Col. Clarence J. Prentice.
4th Kentucky, Capt. John G. Scott.
10th Kentucky M. R., Col. Benjamin E. Caudill.
10th Kentucky Cavalry, Lieut. Col. George R. Diamond.

---

[261] Guerrant, diary entry, Feb. 10th, 1865.

Independent Kentucky Company, Capt. Barton W. Jenkins.

64th Virginia, Col. Auburn L. Pridemore.[262]

Desertions continued to be a major problem, even at this late date in the war when peace commissioners and peace delegations were busily trying to bring peace to a divided nation where everyone was tired of war and wanted to see it end. Col. Caudill was still trying to recruit his regiment in Kentucky. On Wednesday, March 22nd, Caudill arrived at Jonesville, Va. with 50 men he brought out of Kentucky. The crime of desertion caused two men to be sentenced to death in Giltner's Brigade. In Feb., Private Harrison Thomas was sentenced to death for desertion and for robbing and bushwhacking in East Tennessee. He was a member of Col. John C. Scott's 4th Ky. Cavalry. In March, Private Henry Bishop of the 64th Virginia Volunteers was sentenced to death for desertion, with sentence to be carried in presence of his whole regiment on March 24th 1865,[263]just two weeks before the war ended.

From Stickleyville Lee County, Va., Col. Giltner reported to Dept. Headquarters in Wytheville that everything was quiet in his front, no movement of the enemy reported of anticipated. He was having no trouble getting corn, but long forage was somewhat scarce. The weather had brought exceedingly unfavorable weather, with a continuous of rain and mud, and has produced an unusual amount of

---

[262] O.R. 1, 49, pt.1, pg.1022.
[263] Guerrant, Feb. 19, Mar. 21, 1865.

disease among the horses, such as foot-evil, scratches, etc., but a few weeks of sunny, dry weather would work a great change for better.

He had extended the furlough of the Tenth Kentucky Cavalry to March 20th, as it seemed to be unavoidable under the circumstances.[264]

On February 25th, Lieutenant General Jubal A. Early wrote Brig. Gen. Echols that General Lee had notified him that Southwest Virginia and East Tennessee had been added to his department. On the same day, in a report to General Echols, Colonel H.L. Giltner noted that he "had Harrison Thomas, Company B, Fourth Kentucky, executed yesterday in the presence of his regiment. He was charged with repeated desertion and robbing and bushwhacking. It was an assumption of authority, but, I believe justified under the circumstances. Nothing but the most severe measures will redeem our army from the great curse of absence without leave and desertion; and the slow process and uncertainty of trial by the military court almost grant an immunity to such offenders." Giltner said that Captain Thompson, of the Twenty-fifth Virginia, and Captain Tyler, of Sixty-fourth Virginia, both recently deserted to the enemy at the Gap. Giltner had tried to arrest Tyler but he had too many friends, and escaped.[265]

Things were now beginning to happen fast, both for the men of Giltner's brigade and for the Southern Confederacy. Gen. Echols was fearful of a move by the Federals fro East

---

[264] O.R. 1, 49, pt.1, 996, 997.
[265] ibid, pgs. 1016, 1017.

Tennessee into his Western Virginia District, causing him to order Giltner's brigade to move within a six hours march of Abingdon or Bristol, Virginia.

On March 22nd, Giltner ordered his brigade to move out from their Stickleyville encampment. By the 24th, they had reached the mouth of Stony Fork in their march. The next day found them encamped around Nickelsville, in Scott County, Virginia. The next morning, their march took them to Hanson's, where they received orders to continue on to Abingdon, which they reached on the 27th.

April 1st found the brigade in Seven Mile Ford, then in Marion on the 3rd of April. When advancing into the town of Wytheville on the 4th of April, the 4th Kentucky met a party of Yankees coming from the town. They first pushed the 4th back but were soon pushed in turn by the whole brigade, including the newly named 13th Kentucky, which held the center of the line. The Federals withdrew and headed up a mountain where some dismounted as if to put up a fight, but were soon driven off by the 64th Virginia. The 4th Ky. lost one man killed in the skirmish and five or six horses. Giltner claimed 15 or 20 Federals killed, wounded or captured.[266]

The mountain Rebels didn't yet know that this would be their last major action of the war for them. April 6th found the brigade in Dublin, Va., and by April 8th they had encamped around New Bern, Va., where their effort to have a country of their own ended.

---

[266] Guerrant, diary entry, April 4th, 1865.

Hearing of the surrender of General Lee's army on April 9th, at Christiansburg, where the brigade had advanced to see if the news of the surrender was true, Giltner's, Cosby's and Duke's brigades made their way to Kentucky via Pound Gap, Giltner heading for Salyersville, where he stopped, and on April 23rd he sent a note to Mount Sterling, asking terms for his brigade's surrender.

The following communications took place between Giltner and Federal officials:

Louisville, Ky., *April 26,1865*
Hon. E.M. Stanton:
A force of 1,000 to 1,500 who are near Mount sterling propose terms of surrender. From my weakness they are arrogant; others are excited. I hope orders taking troops from this department will be suspended.
J.M. Palmer, *Maj. Gen. Commanding*.

Lexington, Ky., *April 26, 1865.*
Major-General Palmer
        Louisville, Ky.:
There are 1,000 or 1,500 rebels here with "flag of truce" and want honorable terms of surrender.
        E.H. Hobson,
            Brigadier-General

Louisville, April 26, 1865.
Brigadier-General Hobson:
Order all posts to be on the alert. Tender them this proposition: "A surrender of men to be paroled, all public property including horses

and arms of soldiers to be given up." Inform me at once of answer.

    P(almer)

    Lexington, Ky., *April 28,1865.*

    Major General Palmer,
    Louisville, Ky.:
    I think they will accept your proposition and terms. Would it be required to have duplicate rolls of all men and officers? Will officers be permitted to retain side-arms? If necessary, I will send an officer to consummate the arrangements, if they accept.

    E.H. Hobson,
      Brigadier-General

    Mount Sterling, April 26, 1865.
    Capt. J.S. Butler, <u>Assistant Adjutant-</u>*General*:
    Outlines of conditions asked for: To be received and treated as prisoners of war; to retain all private property, horses, side-arms, etc.; to be paroled until exchanged; to take no oath of allegiance to the United States Government, or to take up arms in its defense or against any foreign; to imprison officers of any grade or otherwise subject them to insult or violence; to guarantee our safety of life and property while in Federal limits, and give us a safe conduct beyond them to any neutral power wherever desired. We propose to be subject to all civil laws and military regulations established for the government of prisoners of war. Whenever the Confederate Government shall no longer claim an existence, we propose

to return to our allegiance to the United States Government or remove to some other country, to which we claim a safe transit.

    H,N, Benjamin *Maj. Commanding.*

    Mount Sterling, Ky., *April 26, 1865*

    Capt. J.S. Butler, *Assistant Adjutant-General*:

    Flag will not accept your proposition, unless they are allowed to retain their horses.

    H.N. Benjamin,
        Major Commanding.

    Mount Sterling, *April, 26, 1865.*

    Capt. J.S. Butler

Assistant Adjutant-General:

    The flag will accept the following terms: Surrender of officers and men to be paroled; all public property to be turned over to Government ; officers and men to retain their horses and the officers their side-arms. The flag claims their horses to be private property.

    H.N. Benjamin
    Major, Commanding.

    Lexington, Ky., *April 26, 1865.*

    Col. D.A. Mims,

    Louisa, Ky.,

    There are about 1,500 rebels near Mount Sterling negotiating for surrender and from their exorbitant terms it does not promise success. Move Thirty-ninth Kentucky (mounted men) between West Liberty and Mount Sterling at once, and if they do not surrender we will whip them into terms.

257

By order of Brigadier-General Hobson.
J.S. Butler
Assistant Adjutant-General

Mount Sterling, *April 27, 1865*.
Capt. J.S. Butler,
Assistant Adjutant-General;
They will accept the terms, if the officers will be allowed their horses.
H.N. Benjamin

Lexington, Ky.: *April 27, 1865*
Major Benjamin,
Mount Sterling, Ky.:
The terms sent this morning are an ultimatum. After surrender the officers may be treated liberally, and probably will, as regards horses. Several officers of the command have taken the amnesty oath here today, and the two with the flag can do the same. Cannot be paroled, these are considered very liberal terms, and may not be extended hereafter.
By order of Brigadier-General Hobson:
J.S. Butler
Assistant Adjutant-General.

Mount Sterling, Ky., *April, 27, 1865*
Capt. J.S. Butler,
Assistant Adjutant-General:
The major commanding the flag (of truce) says he cannot accept the terms, but will take a copy of the terms and submit it to Colonel Giltner, commanding division, C. S. Army. Shall I send an officer and escort

through with them? They wish to start in the morning. Please give me instructions.

H.N. Benjamin
Major, Commanding.

Lexington, *April 27, 1865.*
Major H.N. Benjamin,
Mount Sterling, Ky.:
Send a flag of truce and twenty-five men under good officer to escort rebel flag not farther than West Liberty or Hazel Green, if the rebels should be that far. Let the officer be intelligent and prudent enough to learn near the force they have. In the meantime more troops are being sent you.

By order of Brigadier-General Hobson:
J.S. Butler,
Assistant Adjutant-General.

Mount Sterling, April 27,1865
Capt. J. S. Butler
Assistant Adjutant-General
The rebels are said to be about eighteen miles from here, in force, I am informed.

H.N. Benjamin,
Major, Commanding.

Hdqrs. First Division, Department of Kentucky,
Lexington, Ky., *April, 27, 1865.*
Maj. H. N. Benjamin:

I am directed to inform you in a private manner of the aspect in view in connection with the flag of truce and the surrender of Giltner's command.

First. They were delayed as long as possible without exciting suspicion at Mount Sterling to enable the Thirty-ninth Kentucky Infantry, part mounted and part infantry, and part of Fourteenth Kentucky, to move from Paintsville, and from Sandy Valley on to West Liberty road and get behind the main body, so as to prevent their retreat if the negotiation did not succeed.

Second. In the meantime every hour they remained still sent us deserters, who are not paroled.

Third. They tried to extort broad terms because of our weak force at Mount Sterling, and we delayed them to get more troops there.

Fourth. By the time they reject the terms proposed there will be enough troops to alter the whole thing, and we will get many deserters before they can get away, with or without a fight.

Fifth. We have given them very liberal terms, and they will be bound to accept them or lose half their men.

Very truly,
J.S. Butler,
Assistant Adjutant-General.

Mount Sterling, *April 27, 1865.*
Capt. J.S. Butler,
Assistant Adjutant-General:

Intelligent deserters, coming in to take the oath, say Giltner had his command about 2,000 strong, and it was estimated there that he would have about 5,000 gathered together to move to this place for the purpose of surrendering.

H.N. Benjamin,
Major, Commanding

Louisa, Ky., *April 27, 1865.*
Capt. J.S. Butler:
The Tenth Kentucky (rebel) of Colonel Giltner's command, has surrendered to me at this place. Terms, release upon the amnesty oath.

D.A. Mims,
Colonel, Commanding.

(This regiment was the 10th Kentucky Mounted Rifles, Colonel Benjamin E. Caudill's regiment recruited in Whitesburg in 1862. Even though the regiment had been re-designated the 13th Ky. Cavalry in March, 1865, the change likely hadn't took hold with the men yet.)

Lexington, Ky., *April 30,1865.*
Capt. J.S. Butler,
Assistant Adjutant-General, Mount Sterling, Ky.:
Will answer tomorrow from Louisville as to paroled officers. Did rebels accept terms? Have they arrived, and how many? Answer.

E. H. Hobson,

Brigadier-General.
Mount Sterling, *April 30, 1865.*
Brig. Gen. E.H. Hobson:

They accepted terms and would have given more if it had been requested. I have papers signed and am now busy paroling officers: seventy-three done. About 105 officers and 800 to 1,000 men, Giltner in command. I cropped his wings first one. Where shall I send True? He and Major Benjamin are at loggerheads and would like to leave. You dispatch where to order him tomorrow.

J.S. Butler
Assistant Adjutant-General.

McCormack's, *April 30, 1865.*
Capt. J.S. Butler,
Assistant Adjutant-General:

Sir: I have the honor to report that I arrived here at 12 o'clock today. Learned the rebels had come to terms and gone on to Mount Sterling. I will return to Louisa by way of West Liberty. Will be at Gill's Mills tonight.

Very respectfully, your obedient servant,
D.A. Mims,
Colonel Thirty-ninth Ky. Volunteers.[267]

With the surrender of Colonel Giltner's brigade, the war ended for the mountain men of Eastern Kentucky and Western Virginia, except for a few scattered small units, who eventually accepted their paroles and went back to their mountain homes, forever changed.

---

[267] O.R. 1, 49, pt.2, pgs. 476-530.

Epilogue

A Union cavalryman described the inhabitants of Southeast Kentucky and East Tennessee in this manner in the fall of 1863: "The few inhabitants seen about our camp were seemingly of the poorest class. The fringed hunting shirt and the coon-skin cap, with tail hanging down behind, both relics of the days of Daniel Boone, had not entirely departed from this region that were an isolated people, and had but little communication with the stirring, busy progressive world around them."[268]

This Union soldier, like many modern day critics, mistook poverty for a lack of initiative and drive, which mountain people have always had plenty of. Their ancestors, who were few years removed by the time of the Civil War, had chosen to live in the mountains and to raise their families there, no matter how difficult they found life to be where there was little level and arable land to be found. These people were strong willed and had strong opinions which they expressed openly, as shown by their prompt rallying to the flag of their choice when the War Between the States was in its infancy.

In Letcher County, Kentucky, in 1860, the population was just 3, 904 souls, and from these few people a whole regiment, except for one company, was raised for the Confederacy. Many other regiments and battalions included men from Letcher County and surrounding counties. They didn't wait to be drafted, but

---

[268] John K. Ward, <u>Blood on the Mountain, Bullets in the Wind, The Civil War in Kentucky.</u>

263

went enthusiastically to the enlistment points to do their part in the war. It has been that way in every war fought by the United States since. Their patriotism extended to the south was from the heart, and after being defeated they transferred that patriotism back to the flag their forefathers had fought for during the first war for independence.

Of course some men from the area stayed with the old flag in the beginning and were also driven by fervent patriotism. The sad part of such men being so strong in their convictions led to many feuds and isolated killings. Some men made the decision to live peaceably around their former enemies, while others couldn't let go the animosity generated by the war. Today, we would call that feeling of being unable to cope with the changes that war has brought, P.T.S.D. After the Civil War it was just called unabated hating, as there were no provisions to help those that had been traumatized by a war where brother fought against brother in the most literal sense of the word.

A few of those mountain men who put on the blue and gray (and brown) during the Civil War made names for themselves in their after war years. A few of those are listed below:

Martin Van Buren Bates was born at Kona, Letcher County Kentucky, on Nov. 9th, 1819. On Nov. 1st, 1861 he joined the 5th Ky. Infantry of Col. John s. Williams Regiment in Prestonsburg, Floyd County, Kentucky. He later transferred to the 7th Battalion Confederate Cavalry, where he served as a 1st

Lieutenant, then as a Captain. He was a giant of a soldier, and was likely the tallest soldier who served either side during the war. His height was reported to be seven foot eleven inches and his weight was over 400 lbs.[269] He resigned his commission in July, 1864, and came home to Letcher County, but later joined a circus and traveled the world. He met and married Anna Swan, who was even taller than Bates, and who was listed in the circus as eight foot three inches tall. After retiring from the circus, bates and his wife moved to Seville, Ohio, where he died in 1919.

Robert Bates was an older brother of Martin Van Buren Bates, and was an average sized man. He was born August 24th, 1825, and died in 1922. He was known as "The Father of Knott County" (Kentucky) for his efforts to create the new county in 1884. He was a Captain in the 7th Confederate Cavalry Battalion, along with his brother Martin. He and Martin were the sons of John and Sarah Waltrip Bates.

Benjamin E. Caudill was born on Sandlick Creek, Letcher County, Kentucky, on January 11th, 1830, the son of John A. Caudill and Rachel Cornett Caudill. He was a Regular Baptist preacher when the Civil War began, but decided to take sabbatical leave to help with the recruitment and organizing of the Fifth Ky. Inf. Regiment, which was sworn into service on November 1st, 1861. Caudill then became

---

[269] The Guinness Book of Records lists Bates as 7' 2½" in height, and his wife as 7'5½"

Captain of Company F of that regiment until he organized the Tenth Kentucky Mounted Inf. in Whitesburg, Ky., in Sept. and Oct., 1862. He then became Colonel of that regiment. Caudill was captured at Gladesville, Virginia (Wise) on July 7th, 1863, and spent over a year in various Federal prison camps. He became one of the "immortal 600" in 1864, when he was sent from Fort Delaware prison to Charleston Harbor, South Carolina , to become a hostage for the Federals in order to stop the rebel artillery firing on them. He was soon thereafter exchanged and finished the war out as colonel of the 10th Kentucky, surrendering in Louisa, Ky., on April 30th, 1865. He died Feb. 11th, 1889.

Thomas Talton "Bad Talt" Hall was a Letcher County native, born in 1850 on Rockhouse Creek, who some say served in the 13th Kentucky Cavalry late in the war, and who was accused of killing several men after the war, but was convicted of only one, Deputy Enoch Hylton, of Wise County, Virginia. He was hung for the murder of Hylton on September 2nd, 1893 in Wise, Wise County, Virginia. (The town of Wise was known during the Civil War as Gladesville.)

Logan Henry Salyers was a Virginia native, born on Copper Creek, in Scott County on May 31st, 1835. He served in the 50th Va. Infantry Regiment as first the Lieut. Col. of the regiment, then after the regiment's Colonel, A.S. Vandeventer, was captured at the battle of the Wilderness on May 12, 1864, Salyers became the commander of the regiment. After the war, Salyers moved from Virginia to Hazard, Perry County, Kentucky, then decided to settle in Whitesburg, where he became a prominent businessman. He died on May 3rd, 1916, and is buried in Whitesburg's Westwood cemetery, beside other Confederate soldiers who died in the rebel hospital located in Whitesburg during the Civil War.

"Bad" John Wright, (also known as "Devil" John Wright,") was born in 1845, in Letcher County, Kentucky. He served first in the 5th Kentucky Infantry Regiment, also as a member of Clarence Prentice's 7th Confederate Cavalry Battalion. He was also thought to have served in the 13th Kentucky Cavalry for awhile. After the war, he was well known as a bounty hunter, one who "always got his man." Despite his nicknames, he was known as an honest and fair man. He died on January 30th,1931.

Marshall Benton "Doc" Taylor was born in 1836 and died October 27, 1893, (by execution.) He was a member of the 21st Va. "special service" Battalion and was thought to have been with the Battalion during the Battle of Pound Gap on March 16th, 1862. Ironically, he was convicted of murdering 5 members of the Mullins family by ambushing them just a few hundred feet from Pound Gap, at the "killing rock" on the old road, and was hung for the crime in Wise, Wise County, Virginia. The character "The Red Fox, in the John Fox Jr. book, The Trail of the Lonesome Pine, was modeled after Marshall "Doc" Taylor.

267

Appendix A

	NAME	RANK	WHEN ENLISTED	WHERE ENLISTED
1	H. H. Stamper	Captain	Nov. 1, 1861	Whitesburg, Ky.
2	J. W. Collier	1st Lieutenant	Feb. 18, 1861	Whitesburg, Ky.
3	Wilburn Amburgery	1st Lieutenant	Sept. 10, 1861	Whitesburg, Ky.
4	Campbell Pigmon	2nd Lieutenant	Nov. 1, 1861	Whitesburg, Ky.
5	Wilburn Amburgery	2nd Lieutenant	Sept. 10, 1861	Whitesburg, Ky.
6	William D. Madden	1st Sergeant	Nov. 1, 1861	Whitesburg, Ky.
7	A. C. Hagans	1st Sergeant	June .., 1861	Whitesburg, Ky.
8	H. H. Sexton	1st Sergeant	Nov. 1, 1861	Whitesburg, Ky.
9	Daniel Bowling	2nd Sergeant	Sept. 9, 1862	Whitesburg, Ky.
10	S. C. Calhoren	3rd Sergeant	Nov. 1, 1862	Whitesburg, Ky.
11	H. H. Sexton	3rd Sergeant	Nov. 1, 1862	Whitesburg, Ky.
12	J. S. Coburn (or J. L.)	4th Sergeant	Nov. 1, 1862	Whitesburg, Ky.
13	O. G. Holcomb	4th Sergeant	Nov. 1, 1862	Whitesburg, Ky.
14	O. G. Holcomb	5th Sergeant	Nov. 1, 1862	Whitesburg, Ky.
15	John Sparkman	5th Sergeant	Nov. 1, 1862	Whitesburg, Ky.
16	J. S. Hampton	1st Corporal	Nov. 1, 1862	Whitesburg, Ky.
17	Joseph Sexton	2nd Corporal	Nov. 1, 1862	Whitesburg, Ky.
18	John Bowling	3rd Corporal	Nov. 2, 1862	Whitesburg, Ky.
19	S. J. Francis	4th Corporal	Nov. 2, 1862	Whitesburg, Ky.
20	Amburgey, Thomas	Private	Sept. 2, 1862	Whitesburg, Ky.
21	Amburgey, William	Private	Nov. 1, 1862	Whitesburg, Ky.
22	Amburgey, Walker	Private	Nov. 1, 1862	Whitesburg, Ky.
23	Amburgey, Alfred	Private	Nov. 1, 1862	Whitesburg, Ky.
24	Amburgey, Wilburn	Private	Sept. 11, 1862	Whitesburg, Ky.
25	Amburgey, Humphrey	Private	Sept. 29, 1862	Whitesburg, Ky.
26	Adams, Moses	Private	Sept. 22, 1862	Whitesburg, Ky.
27	Adams, Gilbert	Private	Sept. 29, 1862	Whitesburg, Ky.
28	Adams, R. D.	Private	Nov. 1, 1862	Whitesburg, Ky.
29	Amburgey, Anderson	Private	Nov. 1, 1862	Whitesburg, Ky.
30	Adams, Drewery	Private	Dec. 23, 1861	Whitesburg, Ky.
31	Black, Lewis	Private	Nov. 1, 1861	Whitesburg, Ky.
32	Back, D. J.	Private	Nov. 1, 1861	Whitesburg, Ky.
33	Back, Henry	Private	Nov. 1, 1862	Whitesburg, Ky.
34	Back, Isaac	Private	Nov. 1, 1862	Scott Co., Va.
35	Baker, Ira	Private	Nov. 1, 1861	Whitesburg, Ky.
36	Berry, A. S.	Private	Mar. 24, 1862	Whitesburg, Ky.
37	Bowling, John	Private	Nov. 1, 1861	Whitesburg, Ky.
38	Bowling, Caleb	Private	Nov. 1, 1861	Whitesburg, Ky.
39	Bowling, Daniel	Private	Sept. 9, 1862	Whitesburg, Ky.
40	Brashears, W. T. B.	Private	Sept. 21, 1862	Whitesburg, Ky.
41	Bond, Stephen P.	Private	Nov. 1, 1861	Whitesburg, Ky.
42	Bond, William E.	Private	Nov. 1, 1861	Whitesburg, Ky.
43	Christian, William	Private	Nov. 3, 1862	Whitesburg, Ky.
44	Childers, A.	Private	Nov. 1, 1861	Whitesburg, Ky.
45	Candill, S. C.	Private	Nov. 1, 1861	Whitesburg, Ky.
46	Croft, J. H.	Private	Nov. 1, 1861	Whitesburg, Ky.
47	Candill, Jesse	Private	Nov. 1, 1861	Whitesburg, Ky.
48	Cornett, W. C.	Private	Nov. 1, 1861	Whitesburg, Ky.
49	Calhoun, S. C.	Private	Nov. 1, 1862	Whitesburg, Ky.
50	Cornett, J. C.	Private	Nov. 1, 1861	Whitesburg, Ky.
51	Calhoun, Thomas	Private	Nov. 1, 1861	Whitesburg, Ky.
52	Coburn, J. T.	Private	Nov. 1, 1861	Whitesburg, Ky.
53	Collier, J. B.	Private	Sept. 25, 1862	Whitesburg, Ky.
54	Candill, William A.	Private	Oct. 3, 1862	Whitesburg, Ky.
55	Cornett, Joseph E.	Private	Nov. 1, 1861	Whitesburg, Ky.
56	Candill, James W.	Private	Nov. 1, 1861	Whitesburg, Ky.
57	Collier, John	Private	Nov. 1, 1861	Whitesburg, Ky.
58	Candill, John M.	Private	Nov. 1, 1861	Whitesburg, Ky.
59	Chatham, D. C.	Private	Nov. 1, 1861	Whitesburg, Ky.
60	Candill, Caleb	Private	Nov. 1, 1861	Whitesburg, Ky.
61	Coburn, O. L.	Private	Nov. 1, 1861	Whitesburg, Ky.
62	Candill, A.	Private	Nov. 1, 1861	Whitesburg, Ky.
63	Combs, Granville	Private	Aug. 21, 1862	Whitesburg, Ky.
64	Dotson, Thomas	Private	Oct. 3, 1862	Whitesburg, Ky.
65	Day, William	Private	Nov. 1, 1861	Whitesburg, Ky.
66	Duff, Shradrack	Private	Nov. 1, 1861	Whitesburg, Ky.
67	Eldridge, John	Private	Nov. 1, 1861	Whitesburg, Ky.
68	Francis, Simon	Private	Nov. 1, 1861	Whitesburg, Ky.
69	Francis, S. J.	Private	Nov. 1, 1861	Whitesburg, Ky.
70	Franklin, Kelly	Private	Nov. 1, 1861	Whitesburg, Ky.
71	Francis, J. W.	Private	Sept. 29, 1861	Whitesburg, Ky.
72	Francis, John	Private	Sept. 29, 1861	Whitesburg, Ky.
73	Gibson, Miles	Private	Nov. 1, 1861	Whitesburg, Ky.

	NAME	RANK	WHEN ENLISTED	WHERE ENLISTED	
74	Gray, Oliver	Private	Dec. 1, 1863	Whitesburg, Ky	
75	Gibson, Joel	Private	Dec. 10, 1861	Whitesburg, Ky	
76	Haney, William T	Private	June 1, 1862	Whitesburg, Ky	
77	Hart, James	Private	Nov. 1, 1861	Whitesburg, Ky	
78	Hicks, Elijah	Private	Nov. 1, 1861	Whitesburg, Ky	
79	Hughes, Henry	Private	Nov. 1, 1861	Whitesburg, Ky	
80	Hughes, G.	Private	Nov. 1, 1861	Whitesburg, Ky	
81	Hitton, Elisha	Private	Nov. 1, 1861	Whitesburg, Ky	
82	Hampton, J. S.	Private	Nov. 1, 1861	Whitesburg, Ky	
83	Holcombe, O. G.	Private	Nov. 1, 1861	Whitesburg, Ky	
84	Holcombe, Oliver	Private	Nov. 1, 1861	Whitesburg, Ky	
85	Hattin, H.	Private	Nov. 1, 1861	Scott Co., Va	
86	Ingram, Clark	Private	Nov. 1, 1861	Whitesburg, Ky	
87	Jones, Granville	Private	Nov. 1, 1861	Whitesburg, Ky	
88	Johnson, Nathaniel	Private	Mar. 30, 1862	Whitesburg, Ky	
89	Lipps, James D.	Private	Nov. 1, 1861	Whitesburg, Ky	
90	Madden, A. J.	Private	Nov. 5, 1861	Whitesburg, Ky	
91	Madden, G. W.	Private	Nov. 1, 1861	Whitesburg, Ky	
92	Mullins, J. A.	Private	Nov. 1, 1861	Whitesburg, Ky	
93	Madden, John	Private	Aug. 31, 1863	Whitesburg, Ky	
94	Madden, William D.	Private	Nov. 1, 1861	Whitesburg, Ky	
95	Pratt, William	Private	Nov. 1, 1861	Whitesburg, Ky	
96	Pratt, Stephen S.	Private	Sept. 12, 1863	Whitesburg, Ky	
97	Pigmon, William	Private	Nov. 1, 1862	Whitesburg, Ky	
98	Reynolds, John	Private	Nov. 1, 1861	Whitesburg, Ky	
99	Sexton, Stephen	Private	Nov. 1, 1861	Whitesburg, Ky	
100	Smith, A. B.	Private	Nov. 1, 1861	Whitesburg, Ky	
101	Smith, E. B.	Private	Nov. 1, 1861	Whitesburg, Ky	
102	Sparkman, John	Private	Nov. 1, 1861	Whitesburg, Ky	
103	Sparkman, Simpson	Private	Nov. 1, 1861	Whitesburg, Ky	
104	Smith, William B.	Private	Nov. 1, 1861	Whitesburg, Ky	
105	Sexton, Joseph	Private	Nov. 1, 1861	Whitesburg, Ky	
106	Slove, Isham	Private	Nov. 1, 1861	Whitesburg, Ky	
107	Slove, James	Private	Nov. 1, 1861	Whitesburg, Ky	
108	Sexton, H. H.	Private	Nov. 1, 1861	Whitesburg, Ky	
109	Sturdivant, Thomas	Private	Sept. 14, 1861	Whitesburg, Ky	
110	Tucker, Reuben	Private	Nov. 1, 1861	Whitesburg, Ky	
111	Wright, William	Private	Nov. 1, 1861	Whitesburg, Ky	
112	Wright, Andrew Sr.	Private	Nov. 1, 1861	Whitesburg, Ky	
113	Wright, Andrew Jr.	Private	Nov. 1, 1861	Whitesburg, Ky	
114	Watts, John	Private	Nov. 1, 1861	Whitesburg, Ky	

ROLL OF COMPANY B, 13th RE(

1	D. J. Candill	Captain	May 22, 1861	Rose Hill, Va	
2	George Hogg	Captain	Nov. 6, 1861	Whitesburg, Ky	
3	George Hogg	1st Lieutenant	Nov. 6, 1861	Whitesburg, Ky	
4	P. M. Duke	1st Lieutenant	Aug. 21, 1862	Whitesburg, Ky	
5	William E. Cornett	1st Lieutenant	Oct. 10, 1862	Whitesburg, Ky	
6	P. M. Duke	2nd Lieutenant	Aug. 21, 1862	Whitesburg, Ky	
7	Hiram G. Pratt	2nd Lieutenant	Aug. 29, 1862	Whitesburg, Ky	
8	William E. Cornett	2nd Lieutenant	Oct. 10, 1862	Whitesburg, Ky	
9	Samuel B. Smith	2nd Lieutenant	Aug. 29, 1862	Whitesburg, Ky	
10	John D. Candill	1st Sergeant	Aug. 29, 1862	Whitesburg, Ky	
11	S. B. Smith	2nd Sergeant	Aug. 29, 1862	Whitesburg, Ky	
12	Ephriam Candill	3rd Sergeant	Sept. 12, 1862	Whitesburg, Ky	
13	R. A. Branson (or R. S.)	4th Sergeant	Aug. 29, 1862	Whitesburg, Ky	
14	W. J. Candill	4th Sergeant	Aug. 29, 1862	Whitesburg, Ky	
15	W. J. Candill	5th Sergeant	Aug. 29, 1862	Whitesburg, Ky	
16	Jesse Candill	5th Sergeant	Sept. 9, 1863	Whitesburg, Ky	
17	William Brashears	1st Corporal	Sept. 4, 1862	Whitesburg, Ky	
18	Berry Sexton	2nd Corporal	Sept. 9, 1863	Whitesburg, Ky	
19	William Candill	2nd Corporal	Sept. 8, 1862	Whitesburg, Ky	
20	William Candill	3rd Corporal	Sept. 8, 1862	Whitesburg, Ky	
21	S. M. Hampton	3rd Corporal	Sept. 9, 1863	Whitesburg, Ky	
22	S. M. Hampton	4th Corporal	Sept. 9, 1863	Whitesburg, Ky	
23	S. A. Brashears	4th Corporal	Sept. 9, 1863	Whitesburg, Ky	

	NAME	RANK	WHEN ENLISTED	WHERE ENLISTED
24	Ashley, Franklin M.........	Private	Sept. 8, 1862......	Whitesburg, Ky...
25	Amburgey, John J..........	Private	Sept. 15, 1862....	Whitesburg, Ky...
26	Ashley, H. J...............	Private	Sept. 15, 1862....	Whitesburg, Ky...
27	Ashley, L. S...............	Private	Sept. 15, 1862....	Whitesburg, Ky...
28	Ashley, H. S...............	Private	Nov. 18, 1862....	Whitesburg, Ky...
29	Banks, Zachariah..........	Private	Aug. 29, 1862....	Whitesburg, Ky...
30	Brashears, Isaac...........	Private	Aug. 25, 1862....	Whitesburg, Ky...
31	Back, Henry J.............	Private	Aug. 29, 1862....	Whitesburg, Ky...
32	Barnes, William...........	Private	Sept. 12, 1862....	Whitesburg, Ky...
33	Brashears, James H.......	Private	Sept. 12, 1862....	Whitesburg, Ky...
34	Brashears, Ezekiel........	Private	Sept. 12, 1862....	Whitesburg, Ky...
35	Banks, Alfred.............	Private	Sept. 15, 1862....	Whitesburg, Ky...
36	Bock, James..............	Private	Oct. 12, 1862....	Whitesburg, Ky...
37	Brashears, Sampson Jr....	Private	Oct. 12, 1862....	Whitesburg, Ky...
38	Brashears, Sampson.......	Private	Aug. 21, 1862....	Whitesburg, Ky...
39	Caudill, Jackson..........	Private	Aug. 21, 1862....	Whitesburg, Ky...
40	Caudill, Stephen J........	Private	Aug. 29, 1862....	Whitesburg, Ky...
41	Caudill, James A..........	Private	Aug. 29, 1862....	Whitesburg, Ky...
42	Caudill, Henry H..........	Private	Aug. 25, 1862....	Whitesburg, Ky...
43	Caudill, Isham H..........	Private	Aug. 29, 1862....	Whitesburg, Ky...
44	Caudill, Henry C..........	Private	Aug. 29, 1862....	Whitesburg, Ky...
45	Caudill, John.............	Private	Oct. 10, 1862....	Whitesburg, Ky...
46	Caudill, Samuel...........	Private	Oct. 10, 1862....	Whitesburg, Ky...
47	Caudill, Jesse............	Private	Sept. 9, 1862....	Whitesburg, Ky...
48	Caudill, William..........	Private	Sept. 9, 1862....	Whitesburg, Ky...
49	Caudill, Isham...........	Private	Sept. 9, 1862....	Whitesburg, Ky...
50	Calhoun, John............	Private	Aug. 29, 1862....	Whitesburg, Ky...
51	Campbell John............	Private	Aug. 29, 1862....	Whitesburg, Ky...
52	Combs, Granville..........	Private	Sept. 23, 1862....	Whitesburg, Ky...
53	Combs, Jesse..............	Private	Sept. 6, 1862....	Whitesburg, Ky...
54	Combs, Elijah.............	Private	Sept. 6, 1862....	Whitesburg, Ky...
55	Cornett, John.............	Private	Sept. 6, 1862....	Whitesburg, Ky...
56	Cornett, Russell..........	Private	Sept. 6, 1862....	Whitesburg, Ky...
57	Cornett, William E........	Private	Oct. 10, 1862....	Whitesburg, Ky...
58	Cox, Sampson D...........	Private	Aug. 29, 1862....	Whitesburg, Ky...
59	Cox, William.............	Private	Sept. 9, 1862....	Whitesburg, Ky...
60	Cornett, Charles L........	Private	Aug. 11, 1863....	Gladesville, Va...
61	Caudill, H. M.............	Private	Sept. 8, 1862....	Whitesburg, Ky...
62	Caudill, Harvey...........	Private	Aug. 21, 1862....	Whitesburg, Ky...
63	Caudill, Abner............	Private	Sept. 12, 1862....	Middlesburg, —...
64	Caudill, Preston..........	Private	Aug. 21, 1862....	Whitesburg, Ky...
65	Caudill, Isaac............	Private	Aug. 21, 1862....	Whitesburg, Ky...
66	Duke, James..............	Private	Aug. 21, 1862....	Whitesburg, Ky...
67	Day, David...............	Private	Aug. 21, 1862....	Whitesburg, Ky...
68	Donnold, William..........	Private	Sept. 9, 1862....	Whitesburg, Ky...
69	Everidge, William.........	Private	Sept. 9, 1862....	Whitesburg, Ky...
70	Everidge, Thomas.........	Private	Sept. 3, 1862....	Whitesburg, Ky...
71	Edwards, James...........	Private	Sept. 29, 1862....	Whitesburg, Ky...
72	Fuller, A.................	Private	Sept. 6, 1862....	Whitesburg, Ky...
73	Fuller, Elijah.............	Private	Sept. 6, 1862....	Whitesburg, Ky...
74	Greer, Madison...........	Private	Sept. 9, 1862....	Whitesburg, Ky...
75	Gibson, Isham............	Private	Sept. 9, 1862....	Whitesburg, Ky...
76	Gibson, Winsome..........	Private	Sept. 11, 1862....	Whitesburg, Ky...
77	Godsey, D. S.............	Private	Sept. 3, 1862....	Whitesburg, Ky...
78	Hogg, Stephen............	Private	Sept. 9, 1862....	Whitesburg, Ky...
79	Huff, James A............	Private	Sept. 9, 1862....	Whitesburg, Ky...
80	Hughes, William..........	Private	Sept. 9, 1862....	Whitesburg, Ky...
81	Hughes, Mathias..........	Private	Sept. 7, 1862....	Whitesburg, Ky...
82	Hall, Riley...............	Private	Sept. 12, 1862....	Whitesburg, Ky...
83	Jacobs, Leonard..........	Private	Sept. 9, 1862....	Whitesburg, Ky...
84	Jones, Joel...............	Private	Sept. 15, 1862....	Whitesburg, Ky...
85	Johnson, Leslie...........	Private	Aug. 21, 1862....	Whitesburg, Ky...
86	Little, William............	Private	Sept. 9, 1862....	Whitesburg, Ky...
87	Miller, James............	Private	Sept. 9, 1862....	Whitesburg, Ky...
88	Moseley, Samuel..........	Private	Sept. 9, 1862....	Whitesburg, Ky...
89	Magard, John.............	Private	Aug. 31, 1862....	Whitesburg, Ky...
90	Noble, Loss..............	Private	Sept. 17, 1862....	Whitesburg, Ky...
91	Owens, Vine..............	Private		Whitesburg, Ky...
92	Pratt, John M............	Private	Sept. 9, 1862....	Whitesburg, Ky...
93	Pigmon, Madison..........	Private	Sept. 7, 1862....	Whitesburg, Ky...
94	Pigmon, William..........	Private	Sept. 7, 1862....	Whitesburg, Ky...
95	Richie, Joshua............	Private	Sept. 7, 1862....	Whitesburg, Ky...
96	Roberts, Riley............	Private	Sept. 9, 1862....	Whitesburg, Ky...

	NAME	RANK	WHEN ENLISTED	WHERE ENLISTED
97	Runion, J.................	Private	Sept. 13, 1862.....	Whitesburg, Ky...
98	Ross, James P............	Private	Aug. 21, 1862.....	Whitesburg, Ky...
99	Summens, James..........	Private	Sept. 4, 1862.....	Whitesburg, Ky...
100	Summer, Wesley..........	Private	Sept. 9, 1862.....	Whitesburg, Ky...
101	Smith, William B.........	Private	Sept. 15, 1862.....	Whitesburg, Ky...
102	Sparkman, Thomas........	Private	Sept. 9, 1862.....	Whitesburg, Ky...
103	Sparkman, Richard........	Private	Sept. 9, 1862.....	Whitesburg, Ky...
104	Sloan, John.............	Private	Sept. 9, 1862.....	Whitesburg, Ky...
105	Sloan, George W..........	Private	Sept. 9, 1862.....	Whitesburg, Ky...
106	Sloan, Nathaniel.........	Private	Sept. 9, 1862.....	Whitesburg, Ky...
107	Sexton, Berry...........	Private	Sept. 9, 1862.....	Whitesburg, Ky...
108	Shepherd, Martin........	Private	Sept. 13, 1862.....	Middle Creek, Ky.
109	Summer, John W..........	Private	Sept. 9, 1862.....	Whitesburg, Ky...
110	Stephens, George........	Private	Oct. 9, 1862.....	Brashearsv'l, Ky...
111	Stephens, William........	Private		
112	Smith, Elias............	Private	Sept. 6, 1862.....	Whitesburg, Ky...
113	Tacket, George..........	Private	Aug. 21, 1862.....	Whitesburg, Ky...
114	Tacket, Abner...........	Private	Sept. 11, 1862.....	Middle Cr'k, Ky...
115	Thornsbury, John.........	Private	Sept. 14, 1862.....	Whitesburg, Ky...
116	Wright, Solomon..........	Private	Aug. 29, 1862.....	Whitesburg, Ky...
117	Whitaker, Stephen A......	Private	Aug. 29, 1862.....	Whitesburg, Ky...
118	Whitaker, Isaac J.........	Private	Aug. 29, 1862.....	Whitesburg, Ky...
119	Whitaker, John W........	Private	Aug. 29, 1862.....	Whitesburg, Ky...
120	Whitaker, M. E...........	Private	Aug. 29, 1862.....	Whitesburg, Ky...
121	Wright, Benjamin.........	Private	Sept. 2, 1862.....	Whitesburg, Ky...
122	Watts, George W.........	Private	Sept. 2, 1862.....	Whitesburg, Ky...
123	Watts, John C............	Private	Sept. 2, 1862.....	Whitesburg, Ky...

ROLL OF COMPANY C, 13th R

1	Anderson, Hayse..........	Captain	Oct. 1, 1862.....	Whitesburg, Ky...
2	Lewis Grigsby............	1st Lieutenant...	Oct. 1, 1862.....	Whitesburg, Ky...
3	John E. Craft............	1st Lieutenant...	Oct. 1, 1862.....	Whitesburg, Ky...
4	Austin Richie............	2nd Lieutenant...	Oct. 1, 1862.....	Whitesburg, Ky...
5	Edward Grigsby..........	2nd Lieutenant...	Oct. 1, 1862.....	Whitesburg, Ky...
6	Wesley Combs............	1st Sergeant.....	Oct. 1, 1862.....	Whitesburg, Ky...
7	John Grigsby.............	1st Sergeant.....	Oct. 1, 1862.....	Whitesburg, Ky...
8	William Grigsby..........	2nd Sergeant.....	Oct. 1, 1862.....	Whitesburg, Ky...
9	Wesley Combs............	2nd Sergeant.....	Oct. 1, 1862.....	Whitesburg, Ky...
10	Joseph Gearhart.........	3rd Sergeant.....	Oct. 1, 1862.....	Whitesburg, Ky...
11	William Grigsby..........	3rd Sergeant.....	Oct. 1, 1862.....	Whitesburg, Ky...
12	David Grigsby............	3rd Sergeant.....	Oct. 1, 1862.....	Whitesburg, Ky...
13	Elijah Messer............	4th Sergeant.....	Oct. 1, 1862.....	Whitesburg, Ky...
14	Joseph Gearhart.........	4th Sergeant.....	Oct. 1, 1862.....	Whitesburg, Ky...
15	Benjamin Grigsby.........	5th Sergeant.....	Oct. 1, 1862.....	Whitesburg, Ky...
16	Elijah Messer............	5th Sergeant.....	Oct. 1, 1862.....	Whitesburg, Ky...
17	Daniel Fugett............	1st Corporal.....	Oct. 1, 1862.....	Whitesburg, Ky...
18	Powell Wright...........	1st Corporal.....	Oct. 1, 1862.....	Whitesburg, Ky...
19	Jackson Gearhart.........	2nd Corporal.....	Oct. 1, 1862.....	Whitesburg, Ky...
20	Daniel Fugett............	2nd Corporal.....	Oct. 1, 1862.....	Whitesburg, Ky...
21	Caleb Roberts............	3rd Corporal.....	Oct. 1, 1862.....	Whitesburg, Ky...
22	Morgan Pugett............	4th Corporal.....	Oct. 1, 1862.....	Whitesburg, Ky...
23	Allen Watson............	Private	Oct. 1, 1862.....	Whitesburg, Ky...
24	Adkins, Samuel...........	Private	Oct. 1, 1862.....	Whitesburg, Ky...
25	Brashears, William T. B...	Private	Oct. 1, 1862.....	Whitesburg, Ky...
26	Bradley, George..........	Private	Oct. 1, 1862.....	Whitesburg, Ky...
27	Bailey, Samuel...........	Private	Oct. 1, 1862.....	Whitesburg, Ky...
28	Bailey, James............	Private	Oct. 1, 1862.....	Whitesburg, Ky...
29	Bailey, Henry............	Private	Oct. 1, 1862.....	Whitesburg, Ky...
30	Combs, Francis...........	Private	Oct. 1, 1862.....	Whitesburg, Ky...
31	Combs, Isaac............	Private	Oct. 1, 1862.....	Whitesburg, Ky...
32	Combs, Nicholas..........	Private	Oct. 1, 1862.....	Whitesburg, Ky...
33	Combs, Mathew...........	Private	Oct. 1, 1862.....	Whitesburg, Ky...
34	Combs, Fielding..........	Private	Oct. 1, 1862.....	Whitesburg, Ky...
35	Combs, Hiram............	Private	Oct. 1, 1862.....	Whitesburg, Ky...
36	Combs, James............	Private	Oct. 1, 1862.....	Whitesburg, Ky...
37	Combs, Felix............	Private	Oct. 1, 1862.....	Whitesburg, Ky...
38	Combs, James Sr.........	Private	Oct. 1, 1862.....	Whitesburg, Ky...

	NAME	RANK	WHEN ENLISTED	WHERE ENLISTED
39	Combs, Elijah............	Private	Oct. 1, 1862.....	Whitesburg, Ky...
40	Combs, Simpson........	Private	Oct. 1, 1862.....	Whitesburg, Ky...
41	Clemens, Francis........	Private	Oct. 1, 1862.....	Whitesburg, Ky...
42	Campbell, William........	Private	Oct. 1, 1862.....	Whitesburg, Ky...
43	Campbell, John............	Private	June 10, 1862....	Whitesburg, Ky...
44	Campbell, Caleb........	Private	Oct. 1, 1862.....	Whitesburg, Ky...
45	Carpenter, John..........	Private	Oct. 1, 1862.....	Whitesburg, Ky...
46	Combs, Jeremiah..........	Private	Oct. 1, 1862.....	Whitesburg, Ky...
47	Chaffin, Nelson............	Private	Oct. 1, 1862.....	Whitesburg, Ky...
48	Combs, Kindrale........	Private	Oct. 1, 1862.....	Whitesburg, Ky...
49	Collins, Hiram............	Private	Oct. 1, 1862.....	Whitesburg, Ky...
50	Combs, Henry G...........	Private	Oct. 1, 1862.....	Whitesburg, Ky...
51	Combs, Martin............	Private	Oct. 1, 1862.....	Whitesburg, Ky...
52	Clements, Francis........	Private	Oct. 1, 1862.....	Whitesburg, Ky...
53	Dobson, John..........	Private	Oct. 1, 1862.....	Whitesburg, Ky...
54	Dobson, William..........	Private	Mar. 1, 1862.....	Whitesburg, Ky...
55	Everidge, Thomas........	Private	Oct. 1, 1862.....	Whitesburg, Ky...
56	Fugate, William...........	Private	Oct. 1, 1862.....	Whitesburg, Ky...
57	Fugate, Alfred........	Private	Oct. 1, 1862.....	Whitesburg, Ky...
58	Fuller, Archibald........	Private	Oct. 1, 1862.....	Whitesburg, Ky...
59	Fuller, Elijah............	Private	Oct. 1, 1862.....	Whitesburg, Ky...
60	Frances, Jesse........	Private	Oct. 1, 1862.....	Whitesburg, Ky...
61	Frances, William........	Private	Oct. 1, 1862.....	Whitesburg, Ky...
62	Fugate, Martin........	Private	Oct. 1, 1862.....	Whitesburg, Ky...
63	Fugate, John..........	Private	Oct. 1, 1862.....	Whitesburg, Ky...
64	Fugate, Levi............	Private	Oct. 1, 1862.....	Whitesburg, Ky...
65	Fugate, Zachariah........	Private	Oct. 1, 1862.....	Whitesburg, Ky...
66	Fuller, Levitacus........	Private	Oct. 1, 1862.....	Whitesburg, Ky...
67	Fugate, Daniel............	Private	Oct. 1, 1862.....	Whitesburg, Ky...
68	Frances, Wesley........	Private	Oct. 1, 1862.....	Whitesburg, Ky...
69	Grigsby, William........	Private	Oct. 1, 1862.....	Whitesburg, Ky...
70	Gearhart, Joseph...........	Private	Oct. 1, 1862.....	Whitesburg, Ky...
71	Gearhart, Martin........	Private	Oct. 1, 1862.....	Whitesburg, Ky...
72	Gearhart, Riley........	Private	Oct. 1, 1862.....	Whitesburg, Ky...
73	Grigsby, Benjamin........	Private	Oct. 1, 1862.....	Whitesburg, Ky...
74	Grigsby, Gabriel...........	Private	Oct. 1, 1862.....	Whitesburg, Ky...
75	Grigsby, John........	Private	Oct. 1, 1862.....	Whitesburg, Ky...
76	Gnoble, Lossan	Private	Oct. 1, 1862.....	Whitesburg, Ky...
77	Gnoble, Elias........	Private	Oct. 1, 1862.....	Whitesburg, Ky...
78	Grigsby, David...........	Private	Oct. 1, 1862.....	Whitesburg, Ky...
79	Griffith, James........	Private	Oct. 1, 1862.....	Whitesburg, Ky...
80	Gnoble, William..........	Private	Oct. 1, 1862.....	Whitesburg, Ky...
81	Gearhart, John........	Private	Oct. 1, 1862.....	Whitesburg, Ky...
82	Gearhart, Henderson........	Private	Oct. 1, 1862.....	Whitesburg, Ky...
83	Hayes, Sylvester........	Private	Oct. 1, 1862.....	Whitesburg, Ky...
84	Hayes, James........	Private	Oct. 1, 1862.....	Whitesburg, Ky...
85	Howard, James............	Private	Oct. 1, 1862.....	Whitesburg, Ky...
86	Howard, Daniel............	Private	Oct. 1, 1862.....	Whitesburg, Ky...
87	Hix, Charles..........	Private	Oct. 1, 1862.....	Whitesburg, Ky...
88	Hicks, John............	Private	Oct. 1, 1862.....	Whitesburg, Ky...
89	Hicks, Elijah............	Private	Oct. 1, 1862.....	Whitesburg, Ky...
90	Ingle, William (C)........	Private	Oct. 1, 1862.....	Whitesburg, Ky...
91	Ingle, Henry S............	Private	Oct. 1, 1862.....	Whitesburg, Ky...
92	Ingle, Sampson............	Private	Oct. 1, 1862.....	Whitesburg, Ky...
93	Ingle, Henry Jr............	Private	Oct. 1, 1862.....	Whitesburg, Ky...
94	Ingle, Henry Sr............	Private	Oct. 1, 1862.....	Whitesburg, Ky...
95	Jones, Andrew...........	Private	Oct. 1, 1862.....	Whitesburg, Ky...
96	Johnston, Preston........	Private	Oct. 1, 1862.....	Whitesburg, Ky...
97	Mullins, Elijah............	Private	Mar. 28, 1862.....	Whitesburg, Ky...
98	Mullins, James........	Private	Mar. 28, 1862.....	Whitesburg, Ky...
99	Moseley, Nelson........	Private	Mar. 28, 1862.....	Whitesburg, Ky...
100	Messer, Alexander........	Private	Oct. 1, 1862.....	Whitesburg, Ky...
101	Mullins, Buckner........	Private	Oct. 1, 1862.....	Whitesburg, Ky...
102	Miller, Samuel............	Private	Oct. 1, 1862.....	Whitesburg, Ky...
103	Miller, William...........	Private	Oct. 1, 1862.....	Whitesburg, Ky...
104	McDaniel, Wiley........	Private	Oct. 1, 1862.....	Whitesburg, Ky...
105	Morgan, Howard........	Private	Oct. 1, 1862.....	Whitesburg, Ky...
106	Mullins, Bowen........	Private	Oct. 1, 1862.....	Whitesburg, Ky...
107	Marshall, Morgan........	Private	Oct. 1, 1862.....	Whitesburg, Ky...
108	Messer, Elijah........	Private	Oct. 1, 1862.....	Whitesburg, Ky...
109	Napier, M................	Private	Apr. 5, 1863.....	Whitesburg, Ky...
110	Noble, George............	Private	Mar. 25, 1863.....	Whitesburg, Ky...
111	Noble, Lawson............	Private	Oct. 1, 1862.....	Whitesburg, Ky...

272

	NAME	RANK	WHERE ENLISTED	WHERE ENLISTED
112	Noble, William............	Private	Oct. 1, 1862.....	Whitesburg, Ky...
113	Owens, William...........	Private	Oct. 1, 1862.....	Whitesburg, Ky...
114	Patrick, James...........	Private	Oct. 1, 1862.....	Whitesburg, Ky...
115	Richie, Benjamin.........	Private	Oct. 1, 1862.....	Whitesburg, Ky...
116	Richie, Samuel...........	Private	Oct. 1, 1862.....	Whitesburg, Ky...
117	Richie, Andrew...........	Private	Oct. 1, 1862.....	Whitesburg, Ky...
118	Richie, Crockett.........	Private	Oct. 1, 1862.....	Whitesburg, Ky...
119	Richie, Nicholas.........	Private	Oct. 1, 1862.....	Whitesburg, Ky...
120	Richie, Martin...........	Private	Oct. 1, 1862.....	Whitesburg, Ky...
121	Richie, Gabriel..........	Private	Oct. 1, 1862.....	Whitesburg, Ky...
122	Smith, William...........	Private	Oct. 1, 1862.....	Whitesburg, Ky...
123	Stacey, Joseph...........	Private	Oct. 1, 1862.....	Whitesburg, Ky...
124	Shepherd, William........	Private	Oct. 1, 1862.....	Whitesburg, Ky...
125	Stacey, James...........	Private	Oct. 1, 1862.....	Whitesburg, Ky...
126	Stacey, Ellsberry........	Private	Oct. 1, 1862.....	Whitesburg, Ky...
127	Teary, William..........	Private	Oct. 1, 1862.....	Whitesburg, Ky...
128	Teary, Daniel............	Private	Oct. 1, 1862.....	Whitesburg, Ky...
129	Workman, Nathaniel.......	Private	Oct. 1, 1862.....	Whitesburg, Ky...
130	Williams, Andrew.........	Private	Oct. 1, 1862.....	Whitesburg, Ky...
131	Wallen, Handford.........	Private	Oct. 1, 1862.....	Whitesburg, Ky...
132	Woodson, Allen...........	Private	Oct. 1, 1862.....	Whitesburg, Ky...

ROLL OF COMPANY D, 13th R

1	Enoch A. Webb...........	Captain	Oct. 4, 1862.....	Whitesburg, Ky...
2	J. T. Rogers.............	Captain	Apr. 1, 1864.....	Whitesburg, Ky...
3	Solomon Wright...........	1st Lieutenant....	Apr. 1, 1864.....	Whitesburg, Ky...
4	Samuel Thompson.........	1st Lieutenant....	Apr. 1, 1864.....	Whitesburg, Ky...
5	B. B. Adams.............	2nd Lieutenant...	Apr. 1, 1864.....	Whitesburg, Ky...
6	J. L. Craft.............	2nd Lieutenant...	Apr. 1, 1864.....	Whitesburg, Ky...
7	John T. Crutchfield........	2nd Lieutenant...	Apr. 1, 1864.....	Whitesburg, Ky...
8	F. G. Cruch..............	1st Sergeant.....	Apr. 1, 1864.....	Whitesburg, Ky...
9	M. R. Croft.............	1st Sergeant.....	Apr. 1, 1864.....	Whitesburg, Ky...
10	U. R. Croft.............	2nd Sergeant.....	Apr. 1, 1864.....	Whitesburg, Ky...
11	Alexander Gearhart.......	2nd Sergeant.....	Apr. 1, 1864.....	Whitesburg, Ky...
12	J. G. Sturgill...........	3rd Sergeant.....	Apr. 1, 1864.....	Whitesburg, Ky...
13	David Keiser............	3rd Sergeant.....	Apr. 1, 1864.....	Whitesburg, Ky...
14	L. A. Webb..............	3rd Sergeant.....	Apr. 1, 1864.....	Whitesburg, Ky...
15	A. J. Austin............	4th Sergeant.....	Apr. 1, 1864.....	Whitesburg, Ky...
16	John Mullins............	4th Sergeant.....	Apr. 1, 1864.....	Whitesburg, Ky...
17	Benjamin Hall...........	4th Sergeant.....	Apr. 1, 1864.....	Whitesburg, Ky...
18	Benjamin Hall...........	5th Sergeant.....	Apr. 1, 1864.....	Whitesburg, Ky...
19	John Mullins............	5th Sergeant.....	Apr. 1, 1864.....	Whitesburg, Ky...
20	C. W. Stidham...........	1st Corporal.....	Apr. 1, 1864.....	Whitesburg, Ky...
21	Riley Webb..............	1st Corporal.....	Apr. 1, 1864.....	Whitesburg, Ky...
22	J. A. Sturgill..........	2nd Corporal....	Apr. 1, 1864.....	Whitesburg, Ky...
23	Joel Wright.............	2nd Corporal....	Apr. 1, 1864.....	Whitesburg, Ky...
24	Andrew Wright...........	2nd Corporal....	Apr. 1, 1864.....	Whitesburg, Ky...
25	Joel Wright.............	3rd Corporal....	Apr. 1, 1864.....	Whitesburg, Ky...
26	S. N. Reynolds..........	3rd Corporal....	Apr. 1, 1864.....	Whitesburg, Ky...
27	Calvin Stidham..........	4th Corporal....	Apr. 1, 1864.....	Whitesburg, Ky...
28	James Wright............	4th Corporal....	Apr. 1, 1864...	Whitesburg, Ky...
29	Adams, Benjamin.........	Private	Oct. 4, 1862.....	Whitesburg, Ky...
30	Adams, George..........	Private	Oct. 4, 1862.....	Whitesburg, Ky...
31	Adams, J. B............	Private	Oct. 4, 1862.....	Whitesburg, Ky...
32	Adams, Jesse B..........	Private	Oct. 4, 1862.....	Whitesburg, Ky...
33	Anderson, John..........	Private	Oct. 4, 1862.....	Whitesburg, Ky...
34	Anderson, William.......	Private	Oct. 4, 1862.....	Whitenburg, Ky...
35	Anderson, Aaron.........	Private	Oct. 4, 1862.....	Whitesburg, Ky...
36	Adams, William.........	Private	Oct. 4, 1862.....	Whitesburg, Ky...
37	Austin, A. J...........	Private	Oct. 4, 1862.....	Whitesburg, Ky...
38	Bentley, J. T...........	Private	Oct. 4, 1862.....	Whitesburg, Ky...
39	Bryant, James..........	Private	Oct. 4, 1862.....	Whitesburg, Ky...
40	Bentley, Hiram..........	Private	Oct. 4, 1862.....	Whitesburg, Ky...
41	Bentley, Layfayette........	Private	Oct. 4, 1862.....	Whitesburg, Ky...
42	Bentley, John...........	Private	Oct. 4, 1862.....	Whitesburg, Ky...
43	Bates, Henry C..........	Private	Oct. 4, 1862.....	Whitesburg, Ky...
44	Blankenship, John........	Private	Oct. 4, 1862.....	Whitesburg, Ky...
45	Banks, James...........	Private	Oct. 4, 1862.....	Whitesburg, Ky...

273

	NAME	RANK	WHEN ENLISTED	WHERE ENLISTED
46	Bentley, Solomon...........	Private	Oct. 4, 1862.....	
47	Bentley, Mug..............	Private	Oct. 4, 1862.....	
48	Boggs, Levi...............	Private	Oct. 4, 1862.....	Whitesburg, Ky...
49	Boggs, Elijah..............	Private	Oct. 4, 1862.....	Whitesburg, Ky...
50	Boggs, Henry..............	Private	Oct. 4, 1862.....	Whitesburg, Ky...
51	Brooks, Francis...........	Private	Oct. 4, 1862.....	Whitesburg, Ky...
52	Case, James..............	Private	Oct. 4, 1862.....	Whitesburg, Ky...
53	Craft, Nehemiah...........	Private	Oct. 4, 1862.....	Whitesburg, Ky...
54	Craft, John...............	Private	Oct. 4, 1862.....	Whitesburg, Ky...
55	Craft, E. D...............	Private	Oct. 4, 1862.....	Whitesburg, Ky...
56	Craft, Nelson R...........	Private	Oct. 4, 1862.....	Whitesburg, Ky...
57	Collier, Samuel...........	Private	Oct. 4, 1862.....	Whitesburg, Ky...
58	Craft, David..............	Private	Oct. 4, 1862.....	Whitesburg, Ky...
59	Franklin, Brandley........	Private	Oct. 4, 1862.....	Whitesburg, Ky...
60	Gines, John...............	Private	Oct. 4, 1862.....	Whitesburg, Ky...
61	Gibson, Miles.............	Private	Oct. 4, 1862.....	Whitesburg, Ky...
62	Gibson, J. J..............	Private	Oct. 4, 1862.....	Whitesburg, Ky...
63	Gibson, Hiram.............	Private	Oct. 4, 1862.....	Whitesburg, Ky...
64	Gibson, John P...........	Private	Oct. 4, 1862.....	Whitesburg, Ky...
65	Gray, George..............	Private	Oct. 4, 1862.....	Whitesburg, Ky...
66	Hall, Preston.............	Private	Oct. 4, 1862.....	Whitesburg, Ky...
67	Hall, Greenway...........	Private	Oct. 4, 1862.....	Whitesburg, Ky...
68	Holbrook, Randolph........	Private	Oct. 4, 1862.....	Whitesburg, Ky...
69	Holbrook, Jesse...........	Private	Oct. 4, 1862.....	Whitesburg, Ky...
70	Holbrook, R. T...........	Private	Oct. 4, 1862.....	Whitesburg, Ky...
71	Hampton, Abel............	Private	Oct. 4, 1862.....	Whitesburg, Ky...
72	Hampton, Nelson..........	Private	Oct. 4, 1862.....	Whitesburg, Ky...
73	Hall, Thomas.............	Private	Oct. 4, 1862.....	Whitesburg, Ky...
74	Hall, Benjamin...........	Private	Oct. 4, 1862.....	Whitesburg, Ky...
75	Houndshell, M. V.........	Private	Oct. 4, 1862.....	Whitesburg, Ky...
76	Hammonds, Ephriam.......	Private	Oct. 4, 1862.....	Whitesburg, Ky...
77	Henson, William..........	Private	Oct. 4, 1862.....	Whitesburg, Ky...
78	Huse, Gabe...............	Private	Oct. 4, 1862.....	Whitesburg, Ky...
79	Hays, John...............	Private	Aug. 1, 1862.....	Whitesburg, Ky...
80	Hall, Hiram..............	Private	Dec. 1, 1862.....	Whitesburg, Ky...
81	Henson, Paul.............	Private	Oct. 4, 1862.....	Whitesburg, Ky...
82	Kinser, David............	Private	Oct. 4, 1862.....	Whitesburg, Ky...
83	Mead, Riley..............	Private	Oct. 4, 1862.....	Whitesburg, Ky...
84	McRoe, Benjamin..........	Private	Oct. 4, 1862.....	Whitesburg, Ky...
85	Mullins, William..........	Private	Oct. 4, 1862.....	Whitesburg, Ky...
86	Morgan, James...........	Private	Oct. 4, 1862.....	Whitesburg, Ky...
87	Mullins, Solomon..........	Private	Oct. 4, 1862.....	Whitesburg, Ky...
88	Newson, George...........	Private	Oct. 4, 1862.....	Whitesburg, Ky...
89	Potter, Reuben...........	Private	Oct. 4, 1862.....	Whitesburg, Ky...
90	Quillan, Malon...........	Private	Oct. 4, 1862.....	Whitesburg, Ky...
91	Quillan, Drewry...........	Private	Oct. 4, 1862.....	Whitesburg, Ky...
92	Quillan, Richard..........	Private	Oct. 4, 1862.....	Whitesburg, Ky...
93	Reynolds, Henry...........	Private	Oct. 4, 1862.....	Whitesburg, Ky...
94	Rogers, Hugh Wm.........	Private	June 8, 1864.....	Lexington, Ky...
95	Shone, Henry F...........	Private	Oct. 4, 1862.....	Whitesburg, Ky...
96	Sturgill, John G..........	Private	Oct. 4, 1862.....	Whitesburg, Ky...
97	Sturgill, Isaac...........	Private	Oct. 4, 1862.....	Whitesburg, Ky...
98	Singleton, Joshua.........	Private	Oct. 4, 1862.....	Whitesburg, Ky...
99	Sallay, Beriah...........	Private	Oct. 4, 1862.....	Whitesburg, Ky...
100	Tucker, O. P.............	Private	Oct. 4, 1862.....	Whitesburg, Ky...
101	Webb, Lewis A...........	Private	Oct. 4, 1862.....	Whitesburg, Ky...
102	Webb, Riley..............	Private	Oct. 4, 1862.....	Whitesburg, Ky...
103	Webb, Archibald..........	Private	Oct. 4, 1862.....	Whitesburg, Ky...
104	Williams, Henry..........	Private	Oct. 4, 1862.....	Whitesburg, Ky...
105	Wright, Andrew...........	Private	Nov. 1, 1861.....	Whitesburg, Ky...
106	Wright, Hiram............	Private	Aug. 1, 1863.....	Whitesburg, Ky...
107	Wright, William..........	Private	Oct. 4, 1862.....	Whitesburg, Ky...
108	Wright, Benjamin.........	Private	Oct. 4, 1862.....	Whitesburg, Ky...
109	Wright, John.............	Private	Oct. 4, 1862.....	Whitesburg, Ky...
110	Woric, J. F..............	Private	Oct. 4, 1862.....	Whitesburg, Ky...
111	Younts, Charles..........	Private	Oct. 4, 1862.....	Whitesburg, Ky...
112	Younts, Solomon..........	Private	Oct. 4, 1862.....	
113	Younts, Elijah...........	Private	Oct. 4, 1862.....	

	NAME	RANK	WHEN ENLISTED	WHERE ENLISTED
1	Archelaus Hammons	Captain	Oct. 5, 1862	Whitesburg, Ky...
2	William I. Hall	Captain	Apr. 23, 1863	Whitesburg, Ky...
3	Elliott G. Mullins	1st Lieutenant	Oct. 5, 1862	Whitesburg, Ky...
4	James B. Fitzpatrick	1st Lieutenant		Whitesburg, Ky...
5	Alexander Mullins	1st Lieutenant	Nov. 2, 1862	Whitesburg, Ky...
6	Abner Caudill	2nd Lieutenant	Oct. 6, 1862	Whitesburg, Ky...
7	Henry Caudill	2nd Lieutenant	Oct. 5, 1862	Whitesburg, Ky...
8	Henry B. Anderson	2nd Lieutenant	Oct. 21, 1861	Whitesburg, Ky...
9	Miles Hall	2nd Lieutenant		Whitesburg, Ky...
10	Gilbert Johnson	2nd Lieutenant		Whitesburg, Ky...
11	Henry Caudill	2nd Lieutenant	Oct. 5, 1862	Whitesburg, Ky...
12	Preston Caudill	1st Sergeant	Oct. 5, 1862	Whitesburg, Ky...
13	John Harris	1st Sergeant	Oct. 25, 1862	Whitesburg, Ky...
14	Lee Hall	2nd Sergeant	Oct. 5, 1862	Whitesburg, Ky...
15	Johnathan Estep	2nd Sergeant	Oct. 14, 1862	Whitesburg, Ky...
16	E. G. Mullins	2nd Sergeant	July 1, 1863	Whitesburg, Ky...
17	William Hall	2nd Sergeant	Oct. 23, 1862	Whitesburg, Ky...
18	Hiram Mullins	3rd Sergeant	Oct. 5, 1862	Whitesburg, Ky...
19	Lee Hall	3rd Sergeant	Oct. 5, 1862	Whitesburg, Ky...
20	Rhodes Mead	4th Sergeant	Oct. 5, 1862	Whitesburg, Ky...
21	Monroe Sloan	4th Sergeant	Oct. 5, 1862	Whitesburg, Ky...
22	Caleb Johnson	5th Sergeant	Oct. 5, 1862	Whitesburg, Ky...
23	Rhodes Mead	5th Sergeant	Oct. 5, 1862	Whitesburg, Ky...
24	Reuben Hall	1st Corporal	Oct. 5, 1862	Whitesburg, Ky...
25	Isaac Caudill	2nd Corporal	Oct. 5, 1862	Whitesburg, Ky...
26	Alfred Hall	2nd Corporal	Oct. 5, 1862	Whitesburg, Ky...
27	Gilbert Johnson	3rd Corporal	Oct. 5, 1862	Whitesburg, Ky...
28	Isham Sloan	3rd Corporal	Oct. 5, 1862	Whitesburg, Ky...
29	David Hall	3rd Corporal	Oct. 5, 1862	Whitesburg, Ky...
30	Reuben Mead	4th Corporal	Oct. 5, 1862	Whitesburg, Ky...
31	John L. Hall	4th Corporal	Oct. 5, 1862	Whitesburg, Ky...
32	Andrew Fouch	4th Corporal	Oct. 5, 1862	Whitesburg, Ky...
33	Adams, John W	Private	Oct. 5, 1862	Whitesburg, Ky...
34	Bryant, Jacob	Private	Oct. 5, 1862	Whitesburg, Ky...
35	Burks, J Johnathan	Private	Oct. 5, 1862	Whitesburg, Ky...
36	William Caudill	Private	June 1, 1862	Whitesburg, Ky...
37	Caudill, Harvey	Private	June 1, 1862	Whitesburg, Ky...
38	Caudill, Abner	Private	June 1, 1862	Whitesburg, Ky...
39	Caudill, Isaac	Private	June 1, 1862	Whitesburg, Ky...
40	Caudill, Preston	Private	Oct. 5, 1862	Whitesburg, Ky...
41	Estep, Joseph	Private	Oct. 5, 1862	Whitesburg, Ky...
42	Fouch, Andrew	Private	Oct. 5, 1862	Whitesburg, Ky...
43	Gray, George M	Private	Oct. 5, 1862	Whitesburg, Ky...
44	Gibson, William	Private	Oct. 5, 1862	Whitesburg, Ky...
45	Hall, Henry	Private	Oct. 5, 1862	Whitesburg, Ky...
46	Harris, John	Private	Oct. 5, 1862	Whitesburg, Ky...
47	Hall, John C	Private	Oct. 5, 1862	Whitesburg, Ky...
48	Hall, Riley	Private	Oct. 5, 1862	Whitesburg, Ky...
49	Hall, Alfred	Private	Oct. 5, 1862	Whitesburg, Ky...
50	Hall, Miles	Private	Oct. 5, 1862	Whitesburg, Ky...
51	Hall, Fielding	Private	Oct. 5, 1862	Whitesburg, Ky...
52	Hall, Anthony	Private	Oct. 5, 1862	Whitesburg, Ky...
53	Hall, David	Private	Oct. 5, 1862	Whitesburg, Ky...
54	Hall, Allen	Private	Oct. 5, 1863	Whitesburg, Ky...
55	Hall, Lee	Private	Oct. 5, 1862	Whitesburg, Ky...
56	Hall, Alvin	Private	Oct. 5, 1862	Whitesburg, Ky...
57	Hall, Marshall	Private	Oct. 5, 1862	Whitesburg, Ky...
58	Hall, James P	Private	Oct. 5, 1862	Whitesburg, Ky...
59	Hall, William J	Private	Oct. 5, 1862	Whitesburg, Ky...
60	Hall, John	Private	Oct. 5, 1862	Whitesburg, Ky...
61	Hagans, Allen	Private	Oct. 5, 1862	Whitesburg, Ky...
62	Higgins, Thomas	Private	Oct. 5, 1862	Whitesburg, Ky...
63	Hall, John L	Private	Oct. 5, 1862	Whitesburg, Ky...
64	Harris, Squire	Private	Oct. 5, 1862	Whitesburg, Ky...
65	Isaacs, T	Private	Oct. 5, 1862	Whitesburg, Ky...
66	Isaacs, J	Private	Oct. 5, 1862	Whitesburg, Ky...
67	Isaacs, George	Private	July 20, 1862	Piketon, Ky...
68	Johnson, Eli	Private	Oct. 5, 1862	Whitesburg, Ky...
69	Johnson, Elisha	Private	Oct. 5, 1862	Whitesburg, Ky...
70	Johnson, Abisha Sr	Private	Oct. 5, 1862	Whitesburg, Ky...
71	Johnson, Abisha Jr	Private	Oct. 5, 1862	Whitesburg, Ky...
72	Johnson, Andrew	Private	Oct. 5, 1862	Whitesburg, Ky...
73	Johnson, Joab	Private	Oct. 5, 1862	Whitesburg, Ky...

275

NAME	RANK	WHEN ENLISTED	WHERE ENLISTED
74	Johnson, John	Private	Oct. 5, 1862	Whitesburg, Ky
75	Johnson, Caleb	Private	Oct. 5, 1862	Whitesburg, Ky
76	Jones, William	Private	Oct. 5, 1862	Whitesburg, Ky
77	Justice, Riley	Private	Oct. 5, 1862	Whitesburg, Ky
78	Johnson, Harvey	Private	Oct. 5, 1862	Whitesburg, Ky
79	Johnson, Gilbert	Private	Oct. 5, 1862	Whitesburg, Ky
80	King, Tandy	Private	Oct. 5, 1862	Whitesburg, Ky
81	King, James	Private	Oct. 5, 1862	Whitesburg, Ky
82	Moore, Henderson	Private	Oct. 5, 1862	Whitesburg, Ky
83	Moore, Jeremiah	Private	Oct. 5, 1862	Whitesburg, Ky
84	Moore, Joel	Private	Oct. 5, 1862	Whitesburg, Ky
85	Moore, Edward	Private	Oct. 5, 1862	Whitesburg, Ky
86	Moore, Calvin G	Private	Oct. 5, 1862	Whitesburg, Ky
87	Moore, Tandy	Private	Oct. 5, 1862	Whitesburg, Ky
88	Mullins, Elisha	Private	Oct. 5, 1862	Whitesburg, Ky
89	Mead, James M	Private	Oct. 5, 1862	Whitesburg, Ky
90	Mullins, Hiram	Private	Oct. 5, 1862	Whitesburg, Ky
91	Quillan, Malon	Private	Oct. 5, 1862	Whitesburg, Ky
92	Reynolds, William	Private	Oct. 5, 1862	Whitesburg, Ky
93	Sloan, Monroe	Private	Oct. 5, 1862	Whitesburg, Ky
94	Sloan, Hardin	Private	Oct. 5, 1862	Whitesburg, Ky
95	Sloan, Shadrack	Private	Oct. 5, 1862	Whitesburg, Ky
96	Sloan, Jacob	Private	Oct. 5, 1862	Whitesburg, Ky
97	Sloan, Pleasant	Private	Oct. 5, 1862	Whitesburg, Ky
98	Sloan, John P	Private	Oct. 5, 1862	Whitesburg, Ky
99	Sloan, Trumbell	Private	Oct. 5, 1863	Whitesburg, Ky
100	Smith, George	Private	Oct. 5, 1862	Whitesburg, Ky
101	Shuler, Franklin	Private	Oct. 5, 1862	Whitesburg, Ky
102	Shuler, Stephen	Private	Oct. 5, 1862	Whitesburg, Ky
103	Sloan, Henry F	Private	Oct. 5, 1862	Whitesburg, Ky
104	Sloan, John	Private	Oct. 5, 1862	Whitesburg, Ky
105	Tucket, Matthew	Private	Oct. 5, 1862	Whitesburg, Ky
106	Thornsberry, Enoch	Private	Oct. 5, 1862	Whitesburg, Ky
107	Thornsberry, Martin V	Private	Oct. 5, 1862	Whitesburg, Ky

ROLL OF COMPANY F, 13th RE

1	Adam Martin	Captain	Sept. 21, 1862	Letcher Co., Ky
2	James C. Walker	Captain	Oct. 10, 1862	Floyd Co., Ky
3	A. Gearbart	1st Lieutenant	Oct. 10, 1862	Floyd Co., Ky
4	Wiley W. Jones	1st Lieutenant	Oct. 14, 1862	Whitesburg, Ky
5	William W. Jones	1st Lieutenant	Oct. 24, 1862	Prestonburg, Ky
6	James C. Walker	2nd Lieutenant	Oct. 14, 1862	Whitesburg, Ky
7	John M. Allen	2nd Lieutenant	Oct. 10, 1862	Floyd Co., Ky
8	Reuben Allen	1st Sergeant	Oct. 10, 1862	Floyd Co., Ky
9	Joseph Martin	1st Sergeant	Oct. 14, 1862	Whitesburg, Ky
10	R. M. Allen	1st Sergeant	Oct. 10, 1862	Floyd Co., Ky
11	Joseph Allen	2nd Sergeant	Oct. 14, 1862	Prestonburg, Ky
12	Benjamin Smith	2nd Sergeant	Oct. 14, 1862	Whitesburg, Ky
13	William M. Riggs	3rd Sergeant	Oct. 14, 1862	Floyd Co., Ky
14	Benjamin Smith	3rd Sergeant	Oct. 14, 1862	Floyd Co., Ky
15	William Riggs	3rd Sergeant	Oct. 14, 1862	Whitesburg, Ky
16	David Allen	4th Sergeant	Oct. 14, 1862	Floyd Co., Ky
17	Allen Martin	4th Sergeant	Oct. 14, 1862	Floyd Co., Ky
18	John Oney	4th Sergeant	Oct. 14, 1862	Floyd Co., Ky
19	Joseph Allen	4th Sergeant	Oct. 14, 1862	Floyd Co., Ky
20	Allen Martin	5th Sergeant	Oct. 14, 1862	Floyd Co., Ky
21	David Allen	5th Sergeant	Oct. 14, 1862	Floyd Co., Ky
22	B. Shepherd	5th Sergeant	Oct. 14, 1862	Floyd Co., Ky
23	Jackson Morgan	1st Corporal	Oct. 14, 1862	Floyd Co., Ky
24	William Triplett	1st Corporal	Oct. 14, 1862	Floyd Co., Ky
25	Douglas Oney	2nd Corporal	Oct. 14, 1862	Floyd Co., Ky
26	Tandy Sloan	2nd Corporal	Oct. 14, 1862	Floyd Co., Ky
27	John Oney	2nd Corporal	Oct. 14, 1862	Floyd Co., Ky
28	Esekrit Morris	3rd Corporal	Oct. 14, 1862	Floyd Co., Ky
29	Isaac Collins	3rd Corporal	Oct. 14, 1862	Floyd Co., Ky
30	Brison Shepherd	3rd Corporal	Oct. 14, 1862	Floyd Co., Ky
31	Wyatt Martin	4th Corporal	Oct. 14, 1862	Floyd Co., Ky
32	Isaac Collins	4th Corporal	Oct. 14, 1862	Floyd Co., Ky

276

	NAME	RANK	WHEN ENLISTED	WHERE ENLISTED
33	Allen, Joel Jr...............	Private	Oct. 14, 1862......	Floyd Co., Ky.....
34	Allen, Joel Sr...............	Private	Oct. 14, 1862......	Floyd Co., Ky.....
35	Allen, John.................	Private	Oct. 14, 1862......	Floyd Co., Ky.....
36	Allen, Hezekiah.............	Private	Oct. 14, 1862......	Floyd Co., Ky.....
37	Allen, Joseph Sr............	Private	Oct. 14, 1862......	Floyd Co., Ky.....
38	Allen, William Jr..........	Private	Oct. 14, 1862......	Floyd Co., Ky.....
39	Allen, William Sr..........	Private	Oct. 14, 1862......	Floyd Co., Ky.....
40	Allen, Reuben...............	Private	Oct. 14, 1862......	Floyd Co., Ky.....
41	Allen, Joseph...............	Private	Oct. 14, 1862......	Floyd Co., Ky.....
42	Adams, Chambers...........	Private	Oct. 14, 1862......	Floyd Co., Ky.....
43	Bradley, Jacob..............	Private	May 15, 1863......	Whitesburg, Ky...
44	Bailey, John................	Private	Oct. 14, 1862......	Floyd Co., Ky.....
45	Brown, David...............	Private	Oct. 14, 1862......	Floyd Co., Ky.....
46	Briggs, Willy...............	Private	Oct. 14, 1862......	Floyd Co., Ky.....
47	Bailey, Andrew.............	Private	Oct. 14, 1862......	Floyd Co., Ky.....
48	Bailey, Henry..............	Private	Oct. 14, 1862......	Whitesburg, Ky...
49	Bailey, Samuel..............	Private	May 15, 1862......	Whitesburg, Ky...
50	Collins, Isaac..............	Private	Aug. 24, 1863......	Floyd Co., Ky.....
51	Conley, Ashford............	Private	Oct. 14, 1862......	Floyd Co., Ky.....
52	Conley, Thomas.............	Private	Oct. 14, 1862......	Floyd Co., Ky.....
53	Coburn, James..............	Private	Oct. 14, 1862......	Floyd Co., Ky.....
54	Coburn, Jeremiah	Private	Oct. 14, 1862......	Floyd Co., Ky.....
55	Crager, James	Private	Oct. 14, 1862......	Floyd Co., Ky.....
56	Collins, Marshall...........	Private	Oct. 14, 1862......	Floyd Co., Ky.....
57	Collins, William............	Private	Oct. 14, 1862......	Floyd Co., Ky.....
58	Couch, H. E................	Private	Oct. 14, 1862......	Floyd Co., Ky.....
59	Conley, Joseph..............	Private	Aug. 24, 1863......	Floyd Co., Ky.....
60	Cassidy, William...........	Private	Oct. 14, 1862......	Whitesburg, Ky...
61	Dingers, Samuel............	Private	June 1, 1863......	Floyd Co., Ky.....
62	Engle, Richard.............	Private	Oct. 14, 1862......	Floyd Co., Ky.....
63	Gearhart, William..........	Private	Oct. 14, 1862......	Floyd Co., Ky.....
64	Gearhart, J. B.............	Private	Oct. 14, 1862......	Floyd Co., Ky.....
65	Howard, Martin.............	Private	Oct. 14, 1862......	Floyd Co., Ky.....
66	Hall, James................	Private	Oct. 14, 1862......	Floyd Co., Ky.....
67	Hughes, Walter.............	Private	Oct. 14, 1862......	Floyd Co., Ky.....
68	Handshew, Andrew..........	Private	Oct. 14, 1862......	Floyd Co., Ky.....
69	Handshew, Adam............	Private	Oct. 14, 1862......	Floyd Co., Ky.....
70	Hays, Epperson.............	Private	Oct. 14, 1862......	Floyd Co., Ky.....
71	Hall, Henry................	Private	Oct. 14, 1862......	Floyd Co., Ky.....
72	Hall, John.................	Private	Oct. 14, 1862......	Floyd Co., Ky.....
73	Hughes, Henry.............	Private	Oct. 14, 1862......	Floyd Co., Ky.....
74	Isaacs, T..................	Private	Oct. 14, 1862......	Floyd Co., Ky.....
75	Jerdin, Robert.............	Private	Oct. 14, 1862......	Floyd Co., Ky.....
76	Jones, William.............	Private	Oct. 14, 1862......	Floyd Co., Ky.....
77	Jones, Joseph..............	Private	Oct. 14, 1862......	Floyd Co., Ky.....
78	Kile, Robert...............	Private	Oct. 14, 1862......	Floyd Co., Ky.....
79	Martin, George.............	Private	Oct. 14, 1862......	Floyd Co., Ky.....
80	Martin, James..............	Private	Oct. 14, 1862......	Floyd Co., Ky.....
81	Martin, Richard............	Private	Oct. 14, 1862......	Floyd Co., Ky.....
82	Martin, Tandy..............	Private	Oct. 14, 1862......	Floyd Co., Ky.....
83	Martin, Joseph.............	Private	Oct. 14, 1862......	Floyd Co., Ky.....
84	Martin, William............	Private	Oct. 14, 1862......	Floyd Co., Ky.....
85	Mullins, Ambrose...........	Private	Oct. 14, 1862......	Floyd Co., Ky.....
86	Manuel, Mac................	Private	Oct. 14, 1862......	Floyd Co., Ky.....
87	Morris, Ezekiel.............	Private	Oct. 14, 1862......	Floyd Co., Ky.....
88	Martin, Wyatt..............	Private	Oct. 14, 1862......	Floyd Co., Ky.....
89	Nolin, Leonard.............	Private	Oct. 14, 1862......	Floyd Co., Ky.....
90	Noble, William.............	Private	Oct. 14, 1862......	Whitesburg, Ky...
91	Neace, Austin..............	Private	Aug. 24, 1863......	Whitesburg, Ky...
92	Osborn, David..............	Private	Aug. 24, 1863......	Floyd Co., Ky.....
93	Osborn, Thomas............	Private	Oct. 14, 1862......	Floyd Co., Ky.....
94	Osborn, R..................	Private	Oct. 14, 1862......	Floyd Co., Ky.....
95	Oney, William..............	Private	Oct. 11, 1862......	Floyd Co., Ky.....
96	Oney, John.................	Private	Oct. 14, 1862......	Floyd Co., Ky.....
97	Oney, Rnuion...............	Private	Oct. 14, 1862......	Floyd Co., Ky.....
98	Oney, David................	Private	Oct. 14, 1862......	Floyd Co., Ky.....
99	Oney, Douglas..............	Private	Oct. 14, 1862......	Floyd Co., Ky.....
100	Oxley, Thomas.............	Private	Oct. 14, 1862......	Whitesburg, Ky...
101	Pennington, James.........	Private	Aug. 18, 1863......	Whitesburg, Ky...
102	Prater, Newman	Private	June 1, 1863......	Floyd Co., Ky.....
103	Prater, Riley	Private	Oct. 14, 1862......	Floyd Co., Ky.....
104	Prater, John	Private	Oct. 14, 1862......	Floyd Co., Ky.....
105	Prater, William	Private	Oct. 14, 1862......	Floyd Co., Ky.....

	NAME	RANK	WHEN ENLISTED	WHERE ENLISTED
106	Patton, John	Private	Oct. 14, 1862	Floyd Co., Ky
107	Patton, Stephen	Private	Oct. 14, 1862	Floyd Co., Ky
108	Right, (Wright) Powell	Private	Oct. 14, 1862	Floyd Co., Ky
109	Riggs, William	Private	Oct. 14, 1862	Floyd Co., Ky
110	Sloan, Jasper	Private	Oct. 10, 1862	Floyd Co., Ky
111	Sloan, Tandy	Private	Oct. 10, 1862	Floyd Co., Ky
112	Sloan, Spencer	Private	Oct. 10, 1862	Floyd Co., Ky
113	Shepherd, B.	Private	Oct. 10, 1862	Floyd Co., Ky
114	Shepherd, David	Private	Oct. 10, 1862	Floyd Co., Ky
115	Shepherd, William	Private	Oct. 10, 1862	Floyd Co., Ky
116	Shepherd, Daniel	Private	Oct. 10, 1862	Floyd Co., Ky
117	Stephens, .G	Private	Oct. 10, 1862	Floyd Co., Ky
118	Stephens, William D	Private	Oct. 10, 1862	Floyd Co., Ky
119	Smith, Benjamin	Private	Oct. 10, 1862	Floyd Co., Ky
120	Slusher, Gardner	Private	Oct. 10, 1862	Floyd Co., Ky
121	Slusher, John	Private	Oct. 10, 1862	Floyd Co., Ky
122	Stinson, James H	Private	Aug. 24, 1863	Floyd Co., Ky
123	Sawyers, William	Private	Aug. 24, 1863	Floyd Co., Ky
124	Sloan, Monroe	Private	June 1, 1863	Whitesburg, Ky
125	Samonds, Thomas	Private	Oct. 14, 1862	Whitesburg, Ky
126	Shuler, Stephens	Private	Oct. 14, 1862	Whitesburg, Ky
127	Shuler, Franklin	Private	Oct. 10, 1862	Whitesburg, Ky
128	Tecters, John	Private	Oct. 10, 1862	Floyd Co, Ky
129	Triplett, William	Private	Oct. 10, 1862	Floyd Co, Ky
130	Turner, Morgan	Private	Oct. 10, 1862	Floyd Co., Ky
131	Terry, Thomas	Private	Mar. 10, 1863	Floyd Co., Ky
132	Thompson, S. W.	Private		
133	Wicker, Robert	Private		
134	Wallace, Richard	Private	Oct. 10, 1862	Floyd Co, Ky
135	Wiseman, Morgan	Private	Oct. 10, 1862	Floyd Co., Ky
136	Workman, Nathaniel	Private	Sept. 1, 1862	Floyd Co., Ky
137	Wallen, Handford	Private	Aug. 24, 1863	Floyd Co., Ky
138	Williams, William	Private	Sept. 1, 1863	Floyd Co., Ky
139	Wells, John	Private	Sept. 1, 1863	Floyd Co., Ky

ROLL OF COMPANY G, 13th R
ALSO KNOWN AS 11th MOUNTED INFANTRY

1	H. M. Combs	Captain	Oct. 14, 1862	Whitesburg, Ky
2	W. S. Landrum	Captain	Oct. 28, 1861	Prestonburg, Ky
3	J. L. Noble	1st Lieutenant	Oct. 14, 1862	Whitesburg, Ky
4	S. H. Combs	1st Lieutenant	Oct. 14, 1862	Whitesburg, Ky
5	S. H. Combs	2nd Lieutenant	Oct. 14, 1862	Whitesburg, Ky
6	William H. Noble	2nd Lieutenant	Oct. 14, 1862	Whitesburg, Ky
7	Samuel C. Candill	2nd Lieutenant	Nov. 1, 1861	Whitesburg, Ky
8	Irvin Allen	1st Sergeant	Sept. 23, 1862	Perry Co., Ky
9	B. Harvey	2nd Sergeant	Oct. 18, 1862	Breathitt Co., Ky
10	John Johnson	2nd Sergeant	Oct. 18, 1862	Breathitt Co., Ky
11	Austin Mace	3rd Sergeant	Oct. 5, 1862	Breathitt Co., Ky
12	Jeremiah Combs	3rd Sergeant	Sept. 23, 1862	Breathitt Co., Ky
13	McCager Nappier	4th Sergeant	Sept. 23, 1862	Perry Co., Ky
14	Austin Mace	4th Sergeant	Sept. 2, 1862	Breathitt Co., Ky
15	William Noble	4th Sergeant	Oct. 1, 1862	Whitesburg, Ky
16	Ira Allen	5th Sergeant	Sept. 26, 1862	Perry Co., Ky
17	Austin Mace	5th Sergeant	Sept. 23, 1862	Breathitt Co., Ky
18	Daniel Fugate	1st Corporal	Sept. 28, 1862	Breathitt Co., Ky
19	Jeremiah Fugate	2nd Corporal	Oct. 1, 1862	Breathitt Co., Ky
19	Samuel Carpenter	2nd Corporal	Sept. 23, 1862	Breathitt Co., Ky
21	Joseph Fugate	2nd Corporal	Sept. 23, 1862	Perry Co., Ky
22	Andrew Carpenter	3rd Corporal	Sept. 22, 1862	Breathitt Co., Ky
23	John Miller	3rd Corporal	Sept. 23, 1862	Breathitt Co., Ky
24	Andrew Allen	4th Corporal	Sept. 26, 1862	Perry Co., Ky
25	Wilson Combs	4th Corporal	Oct. 1, 1861	Whitesburg, Ky
26	Allen, John	Private	Sept. 28, 1862	Perry Co., Ky
27	Allen, Franklin	Private	Sept. 28, 1862	Perry Co., Ky
28	Allen, George	Private	Sept. 23, 1862	Perry Co., Ky
29	Allen, Samuel	Private	Oct. 1, 1861	Whitesburg, Ky
30	Allen, Ira	Private	Oct. 1, 1861	Whitesburg, Ky
31	Allen, Andrew	Private	Sept. 26, 1862	Whitesburg, Ky

	NAME	RANK	WHEN ENLISTED	WHERE ENLISTED
32	Adams, J. W...............	Private	Sept. 26, 1862.....	Perry Co., Ky.....
33	Combs, Ephriam............	Private .....,...	Sept. 23, 1862.....	Perry Co., Ky.....
34	Combs, Alfred.............	Private	Sept. 23, 1862.....	Perry Co., Ky.....
35	Combs, Wilson.............	Private	Sept. 23, 1862.....	Perry Co., Ky.....
36	Combs, Washington.........	Private	Sept. 28, 1862.....	Breathitt Co., Ky.
37	Combs, David..............	Private	Oct. 1, 1862.....	Breathitt Co., Ky.
38	Combs, Jesse..............	Private	Oct. 1, 1862.....	Breathitt Co., Ky.
39	Campbel, Andrew...........	Private	Oct. 1, 1862.....	Breathitt Co., Ky.
40	Campbel, Samuel...........	Private	Sept. 28, 1862...	Perry Co., Ky...
41	Colinsworth, Edward.......	Private	Sept. 28, 1862...	Breathitt Co., Ky.
42	Colinsworth, William......	Private	Oct. 8, 1862	Breathitt Co., Ky.
43	Campbell, J. D............	Private	Sept. 26, 1862...	Perry Co., Ky...
44	Colinsworth, Thomas	Private	Sept. 30, 1862...	Breathitt Co., Ky.
45	Collinsworth, J. W........	Private	Oct. 1, 1862...	Breathitt Co., Ky.
46	Combs, William B..........	Private	Oct. 1, 1862...	Breathitt Co., Ky.
47	Clemens, Franklin.........	Private	Oct. 1, 1862...	Breathitt Co., Ky.
48	Combs, Matthew...........	Private	Mar. 15, —	Perry Co., Ky...
49	Combs, J. P...............	Private	Oct. 1, 1861...	Whitesburg, Ky.
50	Campbell, John............	Private	Oct. 1, 1861...	Whitesburg, Ky...
51	Combs, Hughes.............	Private	Aug. 31, 1863.....	Whitesburg, Ky.
52	Carpenter, Samuel.........	Private	Oct. 11, 1862.....	Whitesburg, Ky.
53	Davis, Wiley O............	Private	Oct. 1, 1862.....	Breathitt Co., Ky.
54	Deaton, William..........	Private	Oct. 1, 1862.....	Breathitt Co., Ky.
55	Deaton, Joseph............	Private	Oct. 1, 1862.....	Breathitt Co., Ky.
56	Duff, Marcus..............	Private	Oct. 1, 1862.....	Breathitt Co., Ky.
57	Davidson, John............	Private	Mar. 24, 1862.....	Perry Co., Ky...
58	Fugate, Nathaniel.........	Private	Sept. 23, 1862.....	Breathitt Co., Ky..
59	Fugate, Lewis.............	Private	Sept. 23, 1862.....	Breathitt Co., Ky..
60	Fugate, William..........	Private	Sept. 23, 1862.....	Breathitt Co., Ky..
61	Fugate, Jeremiah..........	Private	Sept. 23, 1862.....	Breathitt Co., Ky..
62	Fugate, Andrew............	Private	Sept. 23, 1862.....	Breathitt Co., Ky..
63	Fugate, Benjamin..........	Private	Sept. 23, 1862.....	Breathitt Co., Ky..
64	Frances, Lawson...........	Private	Sept. 23, 1862.....	Breathitt Co., Ky..
65	Frances, Preston..........	Private	Oct. 1, 1861.....	Whitesburg, Ky.
66	Frances, Washington.......	Private	Oct. 14, 1861.....	Whitesburg, Ky.
67	Fugate, Zachariah.........	Private	Oct. 23, 1863.....	Whitesburg, Ky.
68	Gwinn, Allen..............	Private	Sept. 23, 1862.....	Breathitt Co., Ky.!
69	Harvey, Samuel............	Private	Sept. 23, 1862.....	Breathitt Co., Ky..
70	Harvey, John..............	Private	Sept. 23, 1862.....	Breathitt Co., Ky..
71	Harvey, Wesley............	Private	Sept. 23, 1862.....	Breathitt Co., Ky..
72	Hughes, Henry.............	Private	Jan. 1, 1862.....	Whitesburg, Ky..
73	Johnson, John.............	Private	Sept. 23, 1862.....	Breathitt Co., Ky..
74	King, Lewis...............	Private	June 14, 1863.....	Gladesville, Va...
75	Landrum, R. S.............	Private	June 20, 1863.....	Gladesville, Va...
76	Landrum, Robert...........	Private	June 20, 1863.....	Gladesville, Va...
77	Landrum, Reuben...........	Private	June 9, 1863.....	Gladesville, Va...
78	Miller, Nathaniel.........	Private	Sept. 23, 1862.....	Breathitt Co., Ky..
79	Miller, Lawson............	Private	Sept. 23, 1862.....	Breathitt Co., Ky..
80	Miller, Wiley.............	Private	Sept. 23, 1862.....	Breathitt Co., Ky..
81	Miller, William..........	Private	Sept. 23, 1862.....	Breathitt Co., Ky..
82	McIntosh, Turner..........	Private	Sept. 23, 1862.....	Breathitt Co., Ky..
83	McIntosh, Verdamon........	Private	Sept. 23, 1862.....	Breathitt Co., Ky..
84	Miller, Andrew............	Private	Sept. 20, 1862.....	Perry Co., Ky....
85	McLemore, Benjamin F....	Private	Sept. 26, 1862.....	Perry Co., Ky....
86	McIntosh, Fugate..........	Private	Oct. 1, 1862.....	Breathitt Co., Ky..
87	Moore, Daniel.............	Private	Oct. 1, 1862.....	Breathitt Co., Ky..
88	Miller, George...........	Private	Oct. 1, 1862.....	Breathitt Co., Ky..
89	Miller, John J............	Private	Sept. 23, 1862.....	Breathitt Co., Ky..
90	Miller, George W..........	Private	Oct. 10, 1862.....	Whitesburg, Ky..
91	Marshall, Jefferson.......	Private	Jan. 8, 1863.....	Gladesville, Va....
92	McQuinn, Wiley............	Private	Feb. 12, 1863.....	Jackson, Ky.......
93	Miller, Granvile..........	Private	Aug. 31, 1862.....	Whitesburg, Ky..
94	McLemore, Josiah..........	Private	Aug. 31, 1862.....	Whitesburg, Ky..
95	May, William B............	Private	Mar. 23, 1863.....	Breathitt Co., Ky..
96	McLemore, Joseph..........	Private	Aug. 31, 1863.....	Whitesburg, Ky..
97	Miller, M.................	Private		
98	Noble, Daniel.............	Private	Sept. 23, 1862.....	Breathitt Co., Ky..
99	Noble, William F..........	Private	Sept. 23, 1862.....	Breathitt Co., Ky..
100	Noble, William D..........	Private	Sept. 23, 1862.....	Breathitt Co., Ky..
101	Noble, Samuel.............	Private	Sept. 23, 1862.....	Breathitt Co., Ky..
102	Noble, John...............	Private	Sept. 23, 1862.....	Breathitt Co., Ky..
103	Noble, Stephen............	Private	Sept. 23, 1862.....	Breathitt Co., Ky..
104	Neace, Austin.............	Private	Sept. 23, 1862.....	Perry Co., Ky....
105	Napper, John..............	Private	Sept. 30, 1863	Breathitt Co., Ky..

279

	NAME	RANK	WHEN ENLISTED	WHERE ENLISTED
106	Noble, Simpson............	Private	Sept. 30, 1863.....	Whitesburg, Ky...
107	Roberts, John.............	Private	Sept. 23, 1862.....	Breathitt Co., Ky..
108	Roberts, John P..........	Private	Sept. 23, 1862.....	Breathitt Co., Ky..
109	Roberts, A. J.............	Private	Dec. 31, 1862.....	Whitesburg, Ky ...
110	Russell, David............	Private	Feb. 12, 1862.....	Breathitt Co., Ky..
111	Roberts, Alison...........	Private	Sept. 23, 1862.....	Whitesburg, Ky..
112	Smith, Richard............	Private	Oct. 14, 1862.....	Perry Co., Ky....
113	Southwood, Sampson......	Private	Oct. 14, 1862.....	Breathitt Co., Ky..
114	Sizemore, Hiram..........	Private	Oct. 14, 1862.....	Breathitt Co., Ky..
115	Sizemore, Jefferson.......	Private	Oct. 14, 1862.....	Breathitt Co., Ky..
116	Sizemore, Ephriam........	Private	Oct. 14, 1862.....	Breathitt Co., Ky..
117	Sizemore, Lewis..........	Private	Oct. 14, 1862.....	Breathitt Co., Ky..
118	Soreech, Henry............	Private	July 14, 1863.....	Gladesville, Va....
119	Watts, Andrew............	Private	Sept. 23, 1862.....	Whitesburg, Ky...
120	Wright, John..............	Private	Sept. 23, 1862.....	Whitesburg, Ky...

ROLL OF COMPANY H, 13th R

	NAME	RANK	WHEN ENLISTED	WHERE ENLISTED
1	S. R. Brashears............	Captain	Oct. 16, 1862.....	Whitesburg, Ky...
2	Stephen A. Whitaker.......	1st Lieutenant....	Oct. 18, 1862.....	Whitesburg, Ky...
3	A. R. Bentley.............	1st Lieutenant....	Oct. 18, 1862.....	Whitesburg, Ky...
4	A. R. Bentley.............	2nd Lieutenant...	Oct. 18, 1862.....	Whitesburg, Ky...
5	H. R. S. Candill..........	2nd Lieutenant...	Oct. 18, 1862.....	Whitesburg, Ky...
6	Elijah Isom...............	1st Sergeant......	Sept. 2, 1862.....	Whitesburg, Ky...
7	John W. Stamper..........	1st Sergeant......		Whitesburg, Ky...
8	Hiram W. Hogg............	2nd Sergeant.....	Sept. 2, 1862.....	Whitesburg, Ky...
9	William Brashears.........	2nd Sergeant.....		Whitesburg, Ky...
10	Elijah Isom...............	3rd Sergeant.....	Sept. 10, 1862.....	Whitesburg, Ky...
11	John T. Kelley............	3rd Sergeant.....	Sept. 10, 1862.....	Whitesburg, Ky...
12	Abraham Childers.........	4th Sergeant.....	Oct. 18, 1862.....	Whitesburg, Ky...
13	Jesse C. Brashears........	4th Sergeant.....	Sept. 21, 1862.....	Whitesburg, Ky...
14	Hiram W. Stamper.........	5th Sergeant.....	Oct. 18, 1862.....	Whitesburg, Ky...
15	John B. Cornett...........	5th Sergeant.....	Sept. 29, 1862.....	Whitesburg, Ky...
16	Nathaniel Sexton..........	1st Corporal.....	Sept. 13, 1862.....	Whitesburg, Ky...
17	James M. Childers........	2nd Corporal.....	Sept. 8, 1862.....	Whitesburg, Ky...
18	Elijah Gibson.............	3rd Corporal.....	Oct. 18, 1862.....	Whitesburg, Ky...
19	William Brashears.........	3rd Corporal.....	Sept. 10, 1862.....	Whitesburg, Ky...
20	Isaac D. Dickson..........	3rd Corporal.....	Oct. 18, 1862.....	Whitesburg, Ky...
21	David Childers............	4th Corporal.....	Oct. 18, 1862.....	Whitesburg, Ky...
22	John W. Stamper..........	4th Corporal.....	Sept. 23, 1862.....	Whitesburg, Ky...
23	Isaac D. Dickson..........	4th Corporal.....	Oct. 13, 1862.....	Whitesburg, Ky...
24	Adams, Benjamin..........	Private	Oct. 18, 1862.....	Whitesburg, Ky...
25	Adams, John..............	Private	Oct. 18, 1862.....	Whitesburg, Ky...
26	Adams, Watson............	Private	Oct. 18, 1862.....	Whitesburg, Ky...
27	Adams, Jesse.............	Private	Oct. 18, 1862.....	Whitesburg, Ky...
28	Brashears, John L........	Private	Oct. 18, 1863.....	Whitesburg, Ky...
29	Brashears, Jesse C........	Private	Oct. 18, 1862.....	Whitesburg, Ky...
30	Brashears, Harvey G......	Private	Oct. 18, 1862.....	Whitesburg, Ky...
31	Brashears, William.......	Private	Oct. 18, 1862.....	Whitesburg, Ky...
32	Bentley, Benjamin	Private	Oct. 18, 1862.....	Whitesburg, Ky...
33	Back, David..............	Private	Oct. 18, 1862.....	Whitesburg, Ky...
34	Buxton, Isaac............	Private	Oct. 18, 1862.....	Whitesburg, Ky...
35	Bowers, William..........	Private	Oct. 18, 1862.....	Whitesburg, Ky...
36	Burton, Isaac.............	Private	Oct. 18, 1862.....	Whitesburg, Ky...
37	Branson, James...........	Private	Nov. 15, 1862.....	Whitesburg, Ky...
28	Bentley, Babbit...........	Private	Apr. 15, 1863.....	Brashearville, Ky.
39	Brashears, H. E...........	Private .:.......	July 17, 1863.....	Gladesville, Va ...
40	Banks, Elijah.............	Private	Oct. 18, 1862.....	Whitesburg, Ky...
41	Cornell, John.............	Private	Oct. 18, 1862.....	Whitesburg, Ky...
42	Cook, Jacob..............	Private	Oct. 18, 1862.....	Whitesburg, Ky...
43	Combs, Shadrach..........	Private	Oct. 18, 1862.....	Whitesburg, Ky...
44	Combs, George...........	Private	Oct. 18, 1862.....	Whitesburg, Ky...
45	Calhoun, Robert..........	Private	Oct. 18, 1862.....	Whitesburg, Ky...
46	Cole, Thompson...........	Private	Oct. 18, 1862.....	Whitesburg, Ky...
47	Collins, Carter............	Private	Oct. 18, 1862.....	Whitesburg, Ky...
48	Cornett, Samuel..........	Private	Sept. 17, 1862.....	Whitesburg, Ky...
49	Childers, David...........	Private	Oct. 18, 1862.....	Whitesburg, Ky...
50	Collier, Stephen..........	Private	Oct. 18, 1862.....	Whitesburg, Ky...
51	Childers, Abraham........	Private		

280

	NAME	RANK	WHEN ENLISTED	WHERE ENLISTED	MUSTER When
52	Dickerson, Isaac	Private	Oct. 18, 1862	Whitesburg, Ky.	
53	Diles, Robert	Private	Oct. 18, 1862	Whitesburg, Ky.	
54	Day, William H	Private	Oct. 18, 1862	Whitesburg, Ky.	
55	Dykes, William	Private	Mar. 1, 1863	Brashearville, Ky.	
56	Englin, Enoch	Private	Oct. 18, 1862	Whitesburg, Ky.	
57	Fields, Daniel	Private	Oct. 18, 1862	Whitesburg, Ky.	
58	Fields, Stephen	Private	Oct. 18, 1862	Whitesburg, Ky.	
59	Fugate, Ira	Private	Oct. 18, 1862	Whitesburg, Ky.	
60	Gibson, Elijah	Private	Oct. 18, 1862	Whitesburg, Ky.	
61	Hampton, Solomon	Private	Oct. 18, 1862	Whitesburg, Ky.	
62	Hilton, R. N	Private	Oct. 18, 1862	Whitesburg, Ky.	
63	Hogg, Hiram H. (or W.)	Private	Oct. 18, 1862	Whitesburg, Ky.	
64	Hull, Wiley	Private	Oct. 18, 1862	Whitesburg, Ky.	
65	Holcomb, William	Private	Oct. 18, 1862	Whitesburg, Ky.	
66	Holcomb, David	Private	Oct. 18, 1862	Whitesburg, Ky.	
67	Isom, Elijah Sr	Private	Oct. 19, 1862	Whitesburg, Ky.	
68	Isom, Elijah Jr	Private	Sept. 12, 1862	Whitesburg, Ky.	
69	Isom, George	Private	Oct. 18, 1862	Whitesburg, Ky.	
70	Isom, Elisha	Private			
71	Jackson, Robert	Private	Oct. 18, 1862	Whitesburg, Ky.	
72	Jackson, Roland	Private	Oct. 18, 1862	Whitesburg, Ky.	
73	Jones, Johnathan	Private	Oct. 18, 1862	Whitesburg, Ky.	
74	Kelly, John Sr	Private	Oct. 18, 1862	Whitesburg, Ky.	
75	Kelly, William E	Private	Oct. 18, 1862	Whitesburg, Ky.	
76	Keath, Riley	Private	Oct. 18, 1862	Whitesburg, Ky.	
77	Kelly, John Jr	Private	Oct. 18, 1862	Whitesburg, Ky.	
78	Kelly, John T	Private	Oct. 18, 1862	Whitesburg, Ky.	
79	Morgan, John	Private	Oct. 18, 1862	Whitesburg, Ky.	
80	Miles, William	Private	Oct. 18, 1862	Whitesburg, Ky.	
81	Mullins, Joseph	Private	Oct. 18, 1862	Whitesburg, Ky.	
82	McIntire, Alexander	Private	Oct. 18, 1862	Whitesburg, Ky.	
83	McDaniel, William	Private	Oct. 18, 1862	Whitesburg, Ky.	
84	Moggad, John	Private	Oct. 18, 1862	Whitesburg, Ky.	
85	Mitchell, Harrison	Private	Sept. 12, 1862	Whitesburg, Ky.	
86	McIntire, William	Private	Oct. 12, 1862	Whitesburg, Ky.	
87	Roberts, Preston	Private	Sept. 22, 1862	Whitesburg, Ky.	
88	Stamper, John	Private	Oct. 18, 1865	Whitesburg, Ky.	
89	Stamper, Hiram W	Private	Oct. 18, 1862	Whitesburg, Ky.	
90	Short, Bucker	Private	Oct. 18, 1862	Whitesburg, Ky.	
91	Sparkmann, William	Private	Oct. 18, 1862	Whitesburg, Ky.	
92	Sexton, William	Private	Oct. 18, 1862	Whitesburg, Ky.	
93	Stamper, William R	Private	Oct. 18, 1862	Whitesburg, Ky.	
94	Summer, John	Private	Oct. 18, 1862	Whitesburg, Ky.	
95	Smith, Jeremiah	Private	Oct. 18, 1862	Whitesburg, Ky.	
96	Steward, Jasper	Private	Oct. 18, 1862	Whitesburg, Ky.	
97	Sexton, William M	Private	Sept. 22, 1862	Whitesburg, Ky.	
98	Short, Wilson	Private		Whitesburg, Ky.	
99	Sembler, John	Private	Oct. 13, 1862	Whitesburg, Ky.	
100	Summer, Stephen	Private	Mar. 16, 1863	Brashearville, Ky.	
101	Tyra, Patterson	Private	Oct. 18, 1862	Brashearville, Ky.	
102	Tyra, John W	Private	Nov. 18, 1862	Brashearville, Ky.	
103	Tyra, Joseph	Private	Oct. 29, 1862	Brashearville, Ky.	
104	Tandy, George	Private	Mar. 27, 1863	Gladesville, Va.	
105	White, William	Private	Oct. 18, 1862	Whitesburg, Ky.	
106	Whittaker, John	Private	Mar. 28, 1863	Brashearville, Ky.	

	NAME	RANK	WHEN ENLISTED	WHERE ENLISTED
1	William Smith	Captain	Oct. 18, 1862	Whitesburg, Ky
2	James Gwin	1st Lieutenant	Oct. 18, 1862	Whitesburg, Ky
3	G. W. Houck	1st Lieutenant	Feb. 11, 1863	Whitesburg, Ky
4	John B. Fitzpatrick	2nd Lieutenant	Oct. 18, 1862	Whitesburg, Ky
5	Isaac Smith	2nd Lieutenant	Oct. 18, 1862	Whitesburg, Ky
6	G. W. Houck	2nd Lieutenant	Feb. 11, 1863	Whitesburg, Ky
7	Joseph H. Brewer	1st Sergeant	Oct. 18, 1862	Whitesburg, Ky
8	Henry Combs	1st Sergeant	Mar. 22, 1864	Hazard, Ky
9	E. Combs	1st Sergeant	Oct. 18, 1863	Whitesburg, Ky
10	David Richardson	2nd Sergeant	Oct. 18, 1862	Whitesburg, Ky
11	Andrew Campbell	2nd Sergeant	Oct. 18, 1862	Whitesburg, Ky
12	Samuel Grigsby	3rd Sergeant	Oct. 18, 1862	Whitesburg, Ky
13	Daniel Napier	3rd Sergeant	Nov. 10, 1862	Whitesburg, Ky
14	Joseph A. Brewer	3rd Sergeant	Oct. 18, 1862	Whitesburg, Ky
15	David Richardson	4th Sergeant	Oct. 18, 1862	Whitesburg, Ky
16	Benjamin Grigsby	4th Sergeant	Oct. 18, 1862	Whitesburg, Ky
17	D. S. Godsey	4th Sergeant	Oct. 18, 1862	Whitesburg, Ky
18	John J. Brewer	5th Sergeant	Oct. 18, 1862	Whitesburg, Ky
19	Elias Smith	5th Sergeant	Oct. 18, 1862	Whitesburg, Ky
20	Jesse Combs	5th Sergeant	Oct. 18, 1862	Whitesburg, Ky
21	Benjamin Grigsby	5th Sergeant	Oct. 18, 1862	Whitesburg, Ky
22	John Godsey	1st Corporal	Oct. 18, 1862	Whitesburg, Ky
23	Philip Williams	2nd Corporal	Oct. 18, 1862	Whitesburg, Ky
24	James M. Combs	2nd Corporal	Nov. 18, 1862	Whitesburg, Ky
25	Benjamin Smith	2nd Corporal	Oct. 18, 1862	Whitesburg, Ky
26	Daniel Smith	3rd Corporal	Oct. 18, 1862	Whitesburg, Ky
27	John Holladay	3rd Corporal	Oct. 18, 1862	Whitesburg, Ky
28	William S. Smith	3rd Corporal	Oct. 1, 1862	Whitesburg, Ky
29	William S. Smith	4th Corporal	Oct. 1, 1862	Whitesburg, Ky
30	William Patton	4th Corporal	Oct. 1, 1862	Whitesburg, Ky
31	D. A. Chaffin	4th Corporal	Oct. 1, 1862	Whitesburg, Ky
32	M. J. Combs	4th Corporal	Oct. 18, 1862	Whitesburg, Ky
33	Allen, James	Private	Oct. 18, 1862	Whitesburg, Ky
34	Allen, Emery	Private	Oct. 18, 1862	Whitesburg, Ky
35	Bigley, Elijah	Private	Oct. 18, 1862	Whitesburg, Ky
36	Booth, A. J.	Private	Oct. 22, 1863	Abington, Va
37	Brewer, John Q.	Private	Oct. 18, 1862	Whitesburg, Ky
38	Brewer, Joseph	Private		
39	Combs, Ira	Private		Whitesburg, Ky
40	Combs, Jesse	Private	Oct. 18, 1862	Whitesburg, Ky
41	Combs, James	Private	Oct. 18, 1862	Whitesburg, Ky
42	Combs, Kendrick	Private	Oct. 18, 1862	Whitesburg, Ky
43	Combs, Milton	Private	Oct. 18, 1862	Whitesburg, Ky
44	Combs, Washington	Private	Oct. 18, 1862	Whitesburg, Ky
45	Combs, Wiley	Private	Oct. 18, 1862	Whitesburg, Ky
46	Combs, Jerimiah C.	Private	Oct. 18, 1862	Whitesburg, Ky
47	Combs, Enoch	Private	Oct. 18, 1862	Whitesburg, Ky
48	Combs, Handell	Private	Oct. 18, 1862	Whitesburg, Ky
49	Combs, Jackson	Private	Oct. 18, 1862	Whitesburg, Ky
50	Combs, Lorenzo	Private	Oct. 18, 1862	Whitesburg, Ky
51	Combs, David	Private	Oct. 18, 1862	Whitesburg, Ky
52	Combs, Austin	Private	Aug. 29, 1863	Whitesburg, Ky
53	Combs, Nicholas	Private	Oct. 18, 1862	Whitesburg, Ky
54	Combs, James M.	Private	Nov. 18, 1862	Whitesburg, Ky
55	Chaffin, D. A.	Private	Oct. 18, 1862	Whitesburg, Ky
56	Davidson, Edward	Private	Oct. 18, 1862	Whitesburg, Ky
57	Davidson, Jeremiah	Private	Oct. 18, 1862	Whitesburg, Ky
58	Eversole, Irvin	Private	Oct. 18, 1862	Whitesburg, Ky
59	Feltner, Lewis	Private	Oct. 18, 1862	Whitesburg, Ky
60	Feltner, John	Private	Oct. 18, 1862	Whitesburg, Ky
61	Fugate, William	Private	Oct. 18, 1862	Whitesburg, Ky
62	Fugate, Gabriel	Private	Oct. 18, 1862	Whitesburg, Ky
63	Farler, Forest	Private	Oct. 18, 1862	Whitesburg, Ky
64	Farler, John	Private	Oct. 18, 1862	Whitesburg, Ky
65	Grigsby, Benjamin	Private	Oct. 18, 1862	Whitesburg, Ky
66	Grigsby, Samuel	Private	Oct. 18, 1862	Whitesburg, Ky
67	Godsey, Clinton	Private	Mar. 2, 1863	Hazard, Ky
68	Guinn, Allen	Private	Oct. 18, 1862	Whitesburg, Ky
69	Hurt, Isaac	Private	Oct. 18, 1862	Whitesburg, Ky
70	Helm, John	Private	Oct. 18, 1862	Whitesburg, Ky
71	Halladay, William	Private	Oct. 18, 1862	Whitesburg, Ky
72	Hicks, Jesse	Private	Oct. 18, 1862	Whitesburg, Ky
73	Hicks, Harrison	Private	Oct. 18, 1862	Whitesburg, Ky

282

	NAME	RANK	WHEN ENLISTED	WHERE ENLISTED
74	Hall, Joseph	Private	June —, 1863	Whitesburg, Ky
75	Jent, William	Private	Oct. 18, 1862	Whitesburg, Ky
76	Jent, Elias	Private	Aug. 1, 1863	Gladesville, Va
77	Lewis, J. B.	Private	Aug. 31, 1863	Whitesburg, Ky
78	Messer, Jesse	Private	Oct. 18, 1862	Whitesburg, Ky
79	McKee, John	Private	Oct. 18, 1862	Whitesburg, Ky
80	McKee, William	Private	Oct. 1, 1862	Whitesburg, Ky
81	Mullins, James	Private	Mar. 16, 1863	Floyd Co., Ky
82	Miller, John	Private	Nov. 2o, 1863	Gladesville, Va
83	Napier, McCrager	Private	Oct. 18, 1862	Whitesburg, Ky
84	Napier, Jerome	Private	Oct. 1, 1862	Whitesburg, Ky
85	Napier, Daniel	Private	Oct. 16, 1862	Whitesburg, Ky
86	Neice, Washington	Private	Feb. 20, 1863	Hazard, Ky
87	Patten, Christopher	Private	Oct. 18, 1862	Whitesburg, Ky
88	Patten, James	Private	Oct. 18, 1862	Whitesburg, Ky
89	Patten, Henry	Private	Oct. 18, 1862	Whitesburg, Ky
90	Patten, William	Private	Oct. 18, 1862	Whitesburg, Ky
91	Richie, Samuel	Private	Oct. 1, 1862	Whitesburg, Ky
92	Richie, Andrew	Private	Oct. 1, 1862	Whitesburg, Ky
93	Richie, Gabriel	Private	Feb. 3, 1863	Hazard, Ky
94	Richie, Henry	Private	Mar. 7, 1863	Hazard, Ky
95	Richie, Joshua	Private	Oct. 18, 1862	Whitesburg, Ky
96	Richic, John	Private	Oct. 18, 1862	Whitesburg, Ky
97	Skeam, Henry	Private	Oct. 18, 1862	Whitesburg, Ky
98	Smith, Elias	Private	Oct. 18, 1862	Whitesburg, Ky
99	Smith, Simeon	Private	Oct. 1, 1862	Whitesburg, Ky
100	Smith, Daniel	Private	Oct. 1, 1862	Whitesburg, Ky
101	Smith, Isaac	Private	Oct. 1, 1862	Whitesburg, Ky
102	Smith, Nicholas	Private	Oct. 18, 1862	Whitesburg, Ky
103	Stacy, John	Private	Oct. 18, 1862	Whitesburg, Ky
104	Smith, Samuel Sr	Private	Aug. 1, 1863	Gladesville, Va
105	Smith, Samuel Jr	Private	Aug. 1, 1863	Gladesville, Va
106	Smith, L. D.	Private	Aug. 29, 1863	Whitesburg, Ky
107	Smith, Shadrack	Private	Aug. 29, 1863	Whitesburg, Ky
108	Smith, John	Private	Oct. 18, 1863	Whitesburg, Ky
109	Thomas, James	Private	Oct. 18, 1862	Whitesburg, Ky
110	Williams, John	Private	Oct. 18, 1862	Whitesburg, Ky
111	Williams, Robert	Private	Oct. 18, 1862	Whitesburg, Ky
112	White, James	Private	Oct. 18, 1862	Whitesburg, Ky
113	Williams, Philip	Private	Oct. 18, 1862	Whitesburg, Ky
114	Walker, Jeremiah	Private	May 10, 1863	Perry Co., Ky
115	Watts, Ambrose	Private	Oct. 18, 1862	Whitesburg, Ky
116	Williams, Elijah	Private	Aug. 29, 1863	Whitesburg, Ky

	NAME	RANK	WHEN ENLISTED	WHERE ENLISTED
1	James Herd	Captain	Dec. 31, 1863	Virginia
2	W. L. Hurst	1st Lieutenant	Dec. 31, 1863	Virginia
3	Champ Hamlin	1st Lieutenant	Dec. 31, 1863	Virginia
4	John Keywood	2nd Lieutenant	Dec. 31, 1863	Virginia
5	George W. McGee	2nd Lieutenant	Dec. 31, 1863	Virginia
6	Elijah Spurlock	2nd Lieutenant		
7	Walter S. Stivers	2nd Lieutenant		
8	A. Crabtree	1st Sergeant	Aug. 18, 1863	Virginia
9	E. Spurlock	2nd Sergeant	Aug. 18, 1863	Virginia
10	E. M. Rose	3rd Sergeant	Aug. 18, 1863	Virginia
11	Simpson Crabtree	4th Sergeant	Aug. 18, 1863	Virginia
12	C. S. Frost	1st Corporal	Aug. 18, 1863	Virginia
13	Thomas Reynolds	2nd Corporal	Aug. 18, 1863	Virginia
14	Isaac Plummer	3rd Corporal	Aug. 18, 1863	Virginia
15	Watt Middleton	4th Corporal	Aug. 18, 1863	Virginia
16	Albert, William	Private	Aug. 18, 1863	Virginia
17	Ayers, William	Private	Aug. 18, 1863	Virginia
18	Ayres, John	Private	Aug. 18, 1863	Virginia
19	Angle, Andrew	Private	Aug. 18, 1863	Virginia
20	Arthur, Edward	Private	Aug. 18, 1863	Virginia
21	Barrett, Harrison	Private	Aug. 18, 1863	Virginia
22	Britton, Chadwell	Private	Aug. 18, 1863	Virginia
23	Bowling, M.	Private	Aug. 18, 1863	Virginia
24	Berry, Evans	Private	Aug. 18, 1863	Virginia
25	Bagley, Elijah	Private	Aug. 18, 1863	Virginia
26	Bowman, George	Private	Aug. 18, 1863	Virginia
27	Crawford, Archibald	Private	Aug. 18, 1863	Virginia
28	Cassaday, William	Private	Aug. 18, 1863	Virginia
29	Combs, James M.	Private	Aug. 18, 1863	Virginia
30	Crawford, Wick	Private	Aug. 18, 1863	Virginia
31	DeBusk, Christopher	Private	Aug. 18, 1863	Virginia
32	Evans, N. W.	Private	Aug. 18, 1863	Virginia
33	Evans, Alfred	Private	Aug. 18, 1863	Virginia
34	Evans, Robert	Private	Aug. 18, 1863	Virginia
35	Green, Daniel	Private	Aug. 18, 1863	Virginia
36	Henderson, Hannibal	Private	Aug. 18, 1863	Virginia
37	Hurst, Henley	Private	Aug. 18, 1863	Virginia
38	Hamlin, George	Private	Aug. 18, 1863	Virginia
39	Hall, John	Private	Aug. 18, 1863	Virginia
40	Hall, Hugh	Private	Aug. 18, 1863	Virginia
41	Jane, Martin	Private	Aug. 18, 1863	Virginia
42	Johnson, Mitchell	Private	Aug. 18, 1863	Virginia
43	Little, B.	Private	Aug. 18, 1863	Virginia
44	McGee, Jacob	Private	Aug. 18, 1863	Virginia
45	McElroy, W. S.	Private	Aug. 18, 1863	Virginia
46	Nowell, James	Private	Aug. 18, 1863	Virginia
57	Nowell, N. W.	Private	Aug. 18, 1863	Virginia
48	Oxley, Thomas	Private	Aug. 18, 1863	Virginia
49	Pennington, James	Private	Aug. 18, 1863	Virginia
50	Pennington, Williams	Private	Aug. 18, 1863	Virginia
51	Parsons, John	Private	Aug. 18, 1863	Virginia
52	Reeves, William	Private	Aug. 18, 1863	Virginia
53	Stivers, Scott	Private	Aug. 18, 1863	Virginia
54	Stephens, Richard	Private	Aug. 18, 1863	Virginia
55	Terry, Thomas	Private	Aug. 18, 1863	Virginia
56	Thompson, S. W.	Private	Aug. 18, 1863	Virginia
57	Terry, Miles	Private	Aug. 18, 1863	Virginia
58	Tuggel, James	Private	Aug. 18, 1863	Virginia
59	Wilson, Frederick	Private	Aug. 18, 1863	Virginia
60	Walters, Calvin	Private	Aug. 18, 1863	Virginia
61	Wilson, Philip	Private	Aug. 18, 1863	Virginia
62	Wells, John	Private	Aug. 18, 1863	Virginia
63	Waller, Green	Private	Aug. 18, 1863	Virginia
64	Yearly, William	Private	Aug. 18, 1863	Virginia

1890 Special Letcher County, Ky. Census

Civil War veterans living in Letcher County in 1890.

Adams, Henry, Private
Adams John S. Private, Co. M, 14th Ky. Cav.
Adams, Solomon, Private, 1861-1865
Adams, Squire, Private, 1861-1865
Adams, Stephen, Private, Co. A, Ky. Inf.
Akeman, Henry, Sgt., Co. D, 19th Ky.
Back, Henry J., Private, Co. B, 10th Ky. Inf.
Back, James, Private, Co. B, 10th Ky. Inf.
Back, Lewis, Private, Co. B, 10th Ky. Inf.
Back, William, Private, Co. B, 10th Ky. Inf.
Back, William C., Private, Co. B, 13th Cav.
Banks, James H., Private, Co. H, Ky. Inf.
Belcher, James, Private, Co. Y, 5th Ky. Inf.
Blair, Samuel H., Private, Co. A., Ky. Inf.
Boatwrite, Granville II., Private & Corp. 25th Va.
Boggs, Elijah, Private, Co. F, Harlan Bn.
Boggs, Letitia, widow of John R. Boggs.
Boggs, Levi, Private, Co. F, Harlan Bn.
Bowen, Jesse
Breeding, John, Private, Co. M, 14th Ky., Cav.
Brown, James w., Private, Co. A Ky. Inf.
Brown, Jesse M. Private, Co. A, Harlan Bn.

Brown, Madison, Private, Co. A, 14th Ky. Cav.
Brown, William, Private, Co. A, Harlan Bn.
Campbell, John C., Co. B, 10th Ky. Inf.
Caudill, David, Private, Co. B, 10th Ky. Inf.
Caudill David D., Private, Co. B, 10th Ky. Inf.
Caudill, Henry H., Private, Co. B, 10th Ky. Inf.
Caudill, Henry M., Private, Co. B, 10th Ky. Inf.
Caudill, Isom H., Private Co. H, 10th Ky. Inf.
Caudill, James, Private, Co. D, Harlan Bn.
Caudill, James W., Private, Co. A, 10th Ky. Inf.
Caudill, John D., Private, Co. H, Va. Inf.
Caudill, John W., Private, Co. B, 10th Ky. Inf.
Caudill, Mary A. widow of Samuel Caudill,
Private, Co. B, 10th Ky. Inf.
Caudill, Samuel A. Private, Co. H, Va. Inf.
Caudill, Stephen J., Private, Va. Inf.
Caudill, William, Private, Co. B, 10th Ky. Inf.
Caudill, William J., Private, Co. B, 10th Ky. Inf.
Clay, Elijah J., Private, Co. A, Harlan Bn.
Collier, David, M., Private, Co. A, Harlan Bn.
Collier, Martin D., Private, Co. F, 3 Forks Bn.
Collier, William D., Corp., Co. C, 45th Ky. Inf.
Collins, Calvin, Private, Co. L, 14th Ky. Cav.
Collins, Dallas, Private, Co. F, 3 Forks Bn.
Collins, Finley, Private, Co. L, 14th Ky. Cav.
Collins, George W., Private, Co. L, 14th Ky. Cav.
Collins, Henry P., Private, Co. L, 14th Ky. Cav.
Collins, James, Corp.,Co. M, 14th Ky. Cav.
Collins, Sanders A., Private, Co. L, 19th Ky. Inf.
Collins, Wilson, Private, 3rd Ky. Bn.
Combs, Shadrach, Corp., Co. M, 14th Ky. Cav.
Cornett, Silas, Private, Co. B.
Cornett, Silas, Private, Co. H, 47th Ky. Inf.
Cornett, William M., Private, Co. H, 47th Ky. Inf.
Craft, Henry, Private, Co. A, 14th Ky. Inf.
Crase, Andrew J., Private, Co. A,10th Va. Cav.
Day, Henry, 1st Lt., Co. F, 3 Forks Bn.
Day, Jacob, Private, Co. C, Harlan Bn.
Day, John B, Private, Harlan Bn.
Day, Joseph, Private, Co. F, 3 Forks Bn.
Day, Randolph A., Private, 3 Forks Bn.
Eldridge, Benjamin, Private, Co. B.
Eldridge, John C., Private, Co. A.
Elkins, Jane, widow of William Elkins.

Everage, Berry.
Eversole, John C., Private, Co. A, Harlan Bn.
Fairchild, Joseph S., Private, Va. Inf.
Fields, David, Private, Co. F, 10th Ky. Inf.
Fields, David S., Private, Co. F, 5th Ky. Inf.
Fields, Mary, widow of John M. Fields Private,
Co. C, Harlan Bn.
Fields, Obediah, Private, Harlan Bn.
Fields, Robert H., Sgt., Co. H, 47th Ky. Inf.
Foutz, Alexander, Private, Co. F, 47th Ky. Inf.
Frazier, James S., Private, Harlan Bn.
Frazier, Soloman, Private, Harlan Bn.
Fry, Andrew J.
Gillis, Elbert, Private Co. H, 47th Ky. Inf.
Halcomb, Henderson C., Private.
Holcomb, James M., Private, Co. H, 47th Ky. Inf.
Halcomb, Jesse, Private, Co. H, 47th Ky. Inf.
Halcomb, Joseph, Private, Co. H, 47th Ky. Inf.
Halcomb, Louisa, widow of Samuel Halcomb,
Private, Co. H, 47th Ky. Inf.
Hale, William R., Private, Ky.
Hall, Benjamin, Private, Co. K, 39th Ky. Inf.
Hall, Ira D., Private & Sgt., Co. H & D., 47th &
4th Ky. Inf.
Hall, John.
Hall, Mary, widow of Elihue Hall, Private, Co. B.
Hall, Richard, Private, Co. A, 39th Ky. Inf.
Hall, Roxanaha, widow of Alfred Hall, Private,
Harlan Bn.
Hall, Samuel, Private, Co. B, 39th Ky. Inf.
Hall, Thomas, Private, Co. K, 39th Ky. Inf.
Hampton, John S., Private, Co. A, 13th Ky. Cav.
Hampton, Margaret, widow of Soloman-
Hampton, Private, Co. B, 10th Ky. Inf.
Haney, William G., Corp., Co. F, 5th Ky. Inf.
Hensley, Nancy, widow of Eli Hensley, Private.
Hill, William, Private, Co. B, Bn.
Hogg, Jamws W., Sgt.,Co. M, 14th Ky. Inf.
Hogg, Stephen, Private, Co. A, 13th Ky Cav.
Huse, Gabriel, Private, Co. K, 39th Ky. Inf.
Ison, Docktan, Private, Co. A, 12th Ky. Inf.
Ison, George, Private, 14th Ky. Inf.
Ison, George H., Private, Co. A, 14th Ky. Inf.
Ison, John, Private, Harlan Bn.

Ison, Margaret, widow of Elijah Ison, Private.
Ison, Moses, Private, Lt., Co. A, Cav. Bn.
Jenkins, William M., Private, Co. A, Ky. Inf.
Jenkins, Archibale, Private, Co. A, 14th Ky. Inf.
Long, William, Private, Va. Inf.
Maggard, David M., Sgt., Co. F, Harlan Bn.
Maggard, William P., Private, Co. F, 3 Forks Bn.
Mead, Albert, Private, Co. C, 25th Ky. Inf.
Mead, James M., Private, Co. C, 45th Ky. Inf.
Mitchel, Hiram, Private, Co. H, 47th Ky. Inf.
Mitchel, Susannah, formerly widow of Hiram W
Stamper, Private, Co. A, 13th Ky.Inf.
Morgan, John, Private, Co. H, 47th Ky. Inf.
Mullins, John, Private, Co. A.
Napper, James, Co. H, 47th Ky. Inf.
Niece, Samuel, Private, Co. K, 10th Ky. Inf.
Polly, Elizie, widow of Edward Polly, Private,
Co. H, 47th Ky. Inf.
Polly, Henry, Private, Co. A, Ky. Inf.
Polly, Isaac, Co. B, 39th Ky. Inf.
Polly, Lettia, widow of Richard Polly,
Private, Co. H, 47th Ky. Inf.
Prichard, Harvy, Private, Co. A, Va. Inf.
Quillen, William, Private, Co. L, Ky. Inf.
Raleigh, William, Private, Co. A, Harlan Bn.
Richardson, Nellie, widow of Richard, Private.
Richmond, Johnathan, Lt., Co. C, 64th Va. Cav.
Roland, John W., Private, Co. E, 13th Tn. Cav.
Sergent, Andrew J., Private, Harlan Bn.
Sergent, David, Private, Harlan, Bn.
Sergent, Stephen, Private, Harlan Bn.
Sergeant, Wilson, Private, Co. A, Ky. Inf.
Sexton, John, Private.
Sexton, William, Corp., 10th Ky. Inf.
Smith, Jacob, Private, Co. B.
Smith, John A., Private, Co. A, 48th Va. Inf.
Smith, Marga, widow of Alexander,Private.
Sparkins, Hanah, widow of Mirah Sparkins,
Private, Co. H., 47th Inf.
Stallard, James W., Private, Co. A, Ky. Inf.
Stamper, Alexander, Sgt., Co. H, 47th Ky. Inf.
Stamper, Ira, Private, Co. B.
Sturgill, Frances, widow of William Sturgill,
Private.

Sturgill, John A.
Taylor, Andrew, Corp., Co. G, 1st Ky. Inf.
Thompson, James A., Private, Va. Inf.
Tucker, Oliver P., Private, Co. G, 1st Ky. Inf.
Tyler, Ambrose, Private, Co. C, 27th Va. Bn.
Vanover, Daniel, Private, Co. B, 39th Ky. Inf.
Vanover, David, Private, Co. B, 39th Ky. Inf.
Vanover, Jane, widow of Henry Vanover,
Private, Co. B, 39th Ky. Inf.
Weaver, Francis.
Wells, William, Private, Co. A, 3 Forks Bn.
Whittaker, Isaac J., Private, Co. B, 10th Ky. Inf.
Whittaker, John W., Private, Co. B, 10th Ky. Inf.
Whittaker, Moses R., Private, Co. B, 10th Ky. Inf.
Whitaker, Stephen A., Lt., Co. H, 10th Ky. Inf.
Wright, John W.,Private, Co. B, 22nd Ohio Inf.
Yonts, Charlie, Private, Ky. Inf.
Yonts, Soloman, Private, 39th Ky. Inf.

BIBLIOGRAPHY

Books

Addington, Luther F, <u>The History of Wise County, Virginia</u>, 1956.

Addington, Robert M., <u>History of Scott County, Virginia</u>, 1932.

Caudill, Harry M., <u>Night Comes to the Cumberlands</u>, Little, Brown and Co., 1963.

Clark, Thomas D., <u>Agrarian Kentucky</u>, The University Press of Kentucky, 1977.

Clark-Kirkpatrict, <u>Exploring Kentucky</u>, 1960.

Cornett, James G., Letcher County <u>Confederate Veterans.</u>

Cornett, Terry, <u>Letcher County History</u>, 1967.

Davis, William C, & Swentor, Meredith l, <u>The Headquarters Diary of Edward O. Guarrent</u>, Louisiana State University Press, 1999.

Ellis, William E., <u>The Kentucky River</u>, the

University Press of Kentucky, 2000.

Fetzer, Dale, & Mowday, Bruce, <u>Unlikely Allies</u>, Fort Delaware's Prison Community in the Civil War.

Johnston, J. Stoddard, <u>First Explorations of Kentucky</u>, Louisville, Kentucky, John P. Morton And Company, printers to the Filson Club, 1898.

Jones, Clabe, Autobiography.

Klotter, James C, & Settlinger, Peter J., <u>Kentucky Profiles</u>, The Kentucky Historical Society, Frankfort, 1982.

<u>Letcher County Veterans</u>, The Letcher County Historical Society.

Mitchell, Robert D., <u>Appalachian Frontiers</u>, The University Press of Kentucky, 1991.

Noe, Kenneth W., <u>Perryville</u>, This Grand Havoc Of Battle, The University Press of Kentucky, 2001.

Preston, John David, <u>The Civil War in the Big Sandy Valley of Kentucky</u>, 1984.

<u>The War of the Rebellion</u>, A Compilation of the Official Records of the Union and Confederate Armies, Government Printing Office, 1884.

Magazines

<u>The Confederate Veteran Magazine</u>, Edited by Cunningham, S.A., Nashville, Tennessee, 1891.

10th Kentucky, 6
21ˢᵗ *Battalion*, 46
29ᵗʰ Va, 47
29ᵗʰ Virginia Regiment, 34
5th Kentucky, 3, 15, 42, 43, 49, 80, 108, 110, 116, 154, 167, 169, 180, 183, 185, 187, 189, 200, 216, 239, 246, 283
A. C. Moore's, 19
Abingdon Va, 14
Ashland, 63
Asst. Adj. Gen. James B. Fry, 95
Big Creek Gap, 216
Big Hill,, 227
Big Sandy, 4, 9, 40
Bowling Green, 18
Bowling Green, Kentucky, 11
Brashearsville, 57
Brig. Gen. William O. Nelson, 21
Camp Lane,, 42
Capt. Andrew Jackson May, 22
Capt. Andrew May, 17
Capt. Gibboney, 15
Capt. Jeffress,, 19
Captain Campbell Slemp, 131

Captain David Caudill, 111
Captain Holliday,, 24
Captain Maness, 134
Captain Shawn, 31
Castlewood, 51
Caudill, Benjamin E., 7
Christopher Gist, 99
Cincinnati, 5
Civil War, 11
Col. A.G.) Jenkins, 74
Col. G.W. Gallup, 210
Col. Jonathan Cranor, 72
Col. William's, 16
Col. Williams, 17
Colonel Ben E. Caudill, 8
Colonel Benjamin Caudill, 183, 205
Colonel Cranor, 59, 129, 132, 157, 174
Colonel De Courcy, 225
Colonel Dils, 7
Colonel Garfield, 72
Colonel John Dils, 179, 183, 192, 205
Colonel Joshua Sill, 22
Colonel Lindsey's regiment, 61
Colonel Metcalf's, 32
Colonel William's, 16
Confederate, 1, 5

Delaware., 7
Dr.Chilton, 66
Eastern Kentucky, 1, 10
Edward O. Guerrant,, 113
Eighth Michigan, 227
Elkhorn Creek, 2
Estillville, 158, 196, 200, 201
Everett's Rangers, 189
Flat Top Mountain, 167
Floyd County, 55
Fort Delaware, 7
Fort Donelson, 12
Fort Henry, 11
Forty- second Ohio,, 80
Fourteenth Reg. Ky. Volunteers, 58
Ge. Felix Kirk Zollicoffer, 12
Gen S. Cooper, 20
Gen. Humphrey Marshall, 18
Gen. Marshall, 19
Gen. W. Preston, 215
Gladesville, 43, 51, 108, 112, 113, 114, 115, 119, 122, 127, 135, 136, 138, 174, 175, 229, 230, 231, 236, 237, 248, 282, 283
Gladesville, Va, 108
Grayson,, 153, 161, 163
Guerrant, 3, 4
Harlan, Kentucky, 110

Hawkins' 5th Kentucky, 200
Hazel Green, 16, 17, 20, 21, 72, 186, 187, 212, 275
Holston River, 197, 198, 222, 257
Humphrey Marshall's, 3
Indian Creek, 113, 153
Ivy Creek, 27
Ivy Mountain, 27
J.P. Benjamin, Acting Sec. of War, 15
Jeffersonville, (Va.),, 20
Jeffress' battery, 62
Jennie's Creek, 73
John H. Trigg's, 19
John N. Clarkson, 192
John's Creek, 24
Johnson County., 76
Jonesville, 42, 138, 196, 199, 208, 268
Joshua Owings, 120
Kentucky, 3
Kentucky River, 3
Lawrence, 7
Lebanon, 51, 122, 123, 127, 150, 151, 152, 154, 160, 164, 166, 167, 200, 249
Lee County, 114
Letcher County, 2, 8
Lieutenant H.H. Duncan, 202

Lieutenants Van Hook, 29
Logan County, Va, 102
Louisa,, xiv, xvii, 3, 13, 63, 127, 175, 210, 211, 212, 214, 227, 250, 251, 273, 277, 282, 304
Major General McClellan, 44
Major Hawes, 15
Major John B.Thompson', 42
Major Joshua V. Robison, 16
Major Pardee, 133
Marshall, xix, 3, 9, 14, 19, 20, 23, 25, 33, 34, 35, 36, 37, 41, 45, 46, 47, 48, 49, 50, 51, 52, 53, 55, 56, 57, 58, 59, 60, 61, 62, 63, 64, 65, 66, 67, 69, 70, 71, 72, 73, 74, 75, 76, 78, 81, 82, 83, 89, 90, 91, 93, 94, 95, 101, 102, 103, 104, 105, 106, 107, 108,떨109, 110, 112, 113, 114, 115, 117, 118, 119, 120, 121, 122, 123, 124, 125, 126, 127, 128, 129, 130, 138, 150, 151, 152, 153, 154, 155, 157, 158, 159, 160, 161, 162, 163, 164, 165, 166, 167, 168, 169, 171, 172, 173, 174, 176, 177, 178, 179, 180, 181, 182, 183, 184, 185, 186, 188, 189, 190, 191, 199, 200, 201, 205, 206, 207, 209, 210, 211, 212, 213, 214, 215, 216, 217, 218, 226, 229, 233, 238, 241, 265, 283
Martin's Mill, 89
Maryland,, 1
Middle Creek, 69, 77, 78, 79, 83, 85, 86, 87, 91, 101, 103, 104, 112, 116, 119, 156, 174, 182, 250
Mill Springs, 12
Mississippi River, 11
Morgan County, 64
Mr. Diltz, 67
Newport Barracks, 75
North Fork, 36
Ohio, 76
Ohio River, 1
Olympian Springs, 49
Owingsville, 45
Paintsville, 3
Pattonsville, 196
Pennsylvania, 1
Pennsylvania XE "Pennsylvania" ,, 1
Perry,, 7

Perryville, Kentucky, 178

Piketon, 2

Piketon,, 2

Pine Mountain, 2

Pound, 2

Pound Gap, xx, 3, 8, 9, 12, 13, 14, 15, 19, 20, 22, 27, 31, 33, 34, 35, 36, 37, 38, 40, 41, 42, 43, 44, 45, 48, 49, 51, 52, 53, 55, 56, 62, 64, 66, 67, 69, 72, 89, 94, 101, 104, 105, 106, 107, 108, 112, 113, 114, 115, 116, 117, 118, 119, 120, 121, 122, 123, 125, 126, 129, 130, 131, 133, 137, 138, 141, 143, 144, 151, 152, 156, 163, 165, 174, 180, 182, 185, 186, 188, 192, 200, 205, 209, 212, 219, 229, 230, 232, 236, 237, 238, 247, 248, 249, 250, 251, 252, 253, 260, 262, 271, 284

Powell's Valley, 114

President Jefferson Davis, 11

President Jefferson Davis XE "President Jefferson Davis" ,, 11

Prestonsburg, 2, 16

Prestonsburg,, xvii, 14, 16, 17, 18, 19, 37, 49, 52, 55, 59, 62, 72, 77, 83, 86, 181, 184, 186, 188, 250, 281

Prestonsburg, Ky, 19

Princeton, 164, 167, 168, 171, 172, 173, 174, 176, 177

Princeton Court House, 168

Private Shawhaw, 119

Quicksand, 113

Rockhouse Creek, 104

Roger's Gap, 223

Russell County, xxi, 122, 153, 158, 162, 164, 165, 200, 265

Saltville, 9, 27, 49, 120, 153, 167, 219, 232, 238, 240, 248, 257, 258, 259, 260, 262, 263, 264

Saltville,, 9

Sam Clay, 29

Scott, 13, 42, 45, 115, 121, 128, 129, 153, 155, 159, 161, 163, 165, 166, 196, 208, 267, 268, 270, 283, 307

Sixteenth Kentucky, 127, 157

Sounding, 2

Southern Confederacy, 1

Stephen Caudill, 10

Tennessee,, 1

Trigg's 54th Virginia, 49

Troublesome, 113

Twelfth Illinois Mounted Infantry, 220

Twenty-second Kentucky, 74

Twenty-second Ky, 81

Virginia, 1, 13

Washington,, 13, 153, 163

West Liberty, 5

Whitesburg, xiv, xvii, 3, 6, 8, 9, 44, 49, 52, 55, 57, 89, 95, 104, 108, 110, 112, 113, 117, 126, 138, 144, 146, 147, 181, 182, 188, 190, 205, 210, 214, 229, 247, 249, 251, 277, 282, 283

William O. Nelson, 17

William's, 15, 16

Wise, xxi, xxii, 6, 7, 8, 10, 13, 42, 45, 113, 123, 127, 129, 131, 133, 137, 138, 152, 153, 159, 161, 163, 166, 174, 175, 208, 230, 232, 233, 249, 282, 284, 307

Wise County, Virginia, 6

Wm. Gribboney, 15

Wolfe,, 7

Wythe County, 162, 163

Wytheville, 9

Zollicoffer, 12

About the Author

Eddie Nickels is a retired coal miner and insurance representative. He is the author of two other books;

Marine Corps Draftee:

A VIETNAM ERA DRAFTEE'S PERSONAL EXPERIENCES OF PARRIS ISLAND AND INFANTRY TRAINING REGIMENT

Six Years to Live:

AN ODYSSEY OF LIFE, DEATH, AND ADVERSITY

He lives in Mayking, Kentucky

www.ingramcontent.com/pod-product-compliance
Lightning Source LLC
LaVergne TN
LVHW051454080426
835509LV00017B/1762